Peace and Conflict Series

Ron Milam, General Editor

CROOKED BAMBOO

A MEMOIR FROM INSIDE THE DIEM REGIME

NGUYEN THAI

EDITED BY JUSTIN SIMUNDSON

FOREWORD BY LARRY BERMAN

TEXAS TECH UNIVERSITY PRESS

This book is typeset in Sabon MT Std. The paper used in this book meets the minimum requirements of ANSI/NISO Z39.48-1992 (R1997). ♾

Cover photograph by Noppanun Phongtang on Unsplash
Unless otherwise noted, photographs courtesy Nguyen Thai.

Library of Congress Cataloging-in-Publication Data

Names: Nguyen, Thai, 1930– author. | Simundson, Justin, editor.

Title: Crooked bamboo : a memoir from inside the Diem regime / Nguyen Thai ; edited by Justin Simundson.

Description: Lubbock, Texas : Texas Tech University Press, [2019] | Series: Peace and conflict series | Includes bibliographical references and index. | Summary: "A memoir with photos from a high-ranking member of South Vietnam President Ngo Diem's staff leading up to, during, and after the Vietnam War"— Provided by publisher.
Identifiers: LCCN 2019031266 | ISBN 9781682830413 (cloth)

Subjects: LCSH: Nguyen, Thai, 1930– | Ngô, Đình Diệm, 1901–1963. | Vietnam War, 1961–1975. | Vietnam (Republic)—Officials and employees—Biography. | Vietnam (Republic)—Politics and government. | Vietnam (Republic)—History.
Classification: LCC DS556.93.N524 A3 2019 | DDC 959.7/7043092 [B]—dc23
LC record available at https://lccn.loc.gov/2019031266.

Printed in the United States of America
19 20 21 22 23 24 25 26 27 / 9 8 7 6 5 4 3 2 1

Texas Tech University Press
Box 41037
Lubbock, Texas 79409-1037 USA
800.832.4042
ttup@ttu.edu
www.ttupress.org

CONTENTS

ILLUSTRATIONS

FOLLOWING PAGE 141

FOREWORD

I heard Nguyen Thai's name for the first time during a conversation with the legendary Vietnamese spy Pham Xuan An. The year was 2003 and I was in the process of writing *Perfect Spy* about An. On this day, An and I were in the midst of one of our many conversations about the nuances in Vietnamese politics and history. We were discussing the November 1963 coup and assassination of Ngo Dinh Diem and his powerful brother, Ngo Dinh Nhu. I asked An for his own thoughts on this major turning point in the war. "You need to speak with the man who understands this history better than anyone. He lives near you in Berkeley. In 1962 he wrote the book *Is South Vietnam Viable*?" I confessed to An that I had not read the book. "Go see Nguyen Thai," urged An. "Thai knew Diem and Nhu better than anyone. Tell him you are writing this new book. He can help you learn more about me."

A few months later I was sitting with Nguyen Thai at his favorite seafood restaurant in the Berkeley marina. Like all of Pham Xuan An's tips, this one would not disappoint. I quickly learned that just as Pham Xuan An had done, Thai had studied in the United States. As President of the Association of Vietnamese Catholic Students in America, Thai met Ngo Dinh Diem at the group's conference in 1952. Diem took an immediate liking to Thai. After this initial meeting, Diem frequently corresponded with Thai about the political situation and unrest in Vietnam. Thai later visited Diem at the Maryknoll Monastery in New Jersey and arranged for Diem to give a visiting lecture at Cornell. When Diem returned to Saigon in 1954, he cabled asking Thai to return to Vietnam and assist him in building an independent south. At this moment, Thai was full of hopes for Vietnam under the leadership of Diem. In May 1957 Diem appointed Thai as Director General of Vietnam Press, where he quickly became a trusted aide and privy to the secrets of the Diem government.

I met with Thai many times after our initial lunch. Our conversations ranged from the process of his own personal disenchantment with the Diem regime to understanding Pham Xuan An, whom Thai had recently visited on one of his trips to Vietnam. In an effort to help me understand the period, Thai provided me with the unedited chapter files of his still untitled memoir. I spent days reading the files and pulling out morsels about Pham Xuan An, the Ngo brothers, and other memorable personalities from the era. The manuscript itself was invaluable to me. That original version was hundreds of pages of free-flowing thoughts and observations, but it was not a book or even a workable memoir as it was. I hoped that the day would come when Thai would find someone to help overhaul the manuscript into a coherent, theme-based memoir for the benefit of a wide audience.

We owe a great debt to Justin Simundson for accomplishing this herculean task. *Crooked Bamboo* offers a fascinating spotlight from an eyewitness to one of the most tumultuous and critical periods for the American war in Vietnam. Those looking for key turning points in history can start with Nguyen Thai's observations on the failures of the Diem regime to build legitimacy, its ultimate demise, and the turmoil that followed. I was fortunate to be a participant at the 2013 conference in Washington, DC, where Thai and Justin first met. I had urged Thai to attend the conference. His comments captivated an audience of scholars and practitioners, giving a hint of how valuable his insights could be. Justin Simundson's prodigious editorial skills have now brought forth those insights in *Crooked Bamboo*, a memoir that casts new light on crucial points in history. Few memoirs accomplish this goal. *Crooked Bamboo* does so in an exemplary way.

LARRY BERMAN
Professor Emeritus, University of California, Davis
Founding Dean, Honors College, Georgia State University

INTRODUCTION

Crooked Bamboo is Nguyen Thai's inside account of South Vietnam's Ngo Dinh Diem regime and the political turmoil that led to South Vietnam's tragedy. Nguyen Thai served President Diem prominently as Director General of Vietnam Press, a semi-autonomous government news agency, and as a close personal aide and translator. Mr. Thai first met Diem while he was studying in the United States and Diem was an exile there. They became close because of their shared background and Mr. Thai's belief in Diem's nationalism and moral leadership. After Diem came to power, Mr. Thai became so trusted by Diem that some in Saigon claimed that Mr. Thai was Diem's "favorite adopted son." During this time working for Diem, Mr. Thai also founded Vietnam's first English-language newspaper, *The Times of Vietnam*. Despite his idealistic faith in Diem, Mr. Thai became disillusioned with the regime and the corrupting role of Diem's family within it. By the time of the first coup attempt against Diem in 1960, Mr. Thai was actively planning to leave the regime. He had to do so in a way, however, that did not even implicitly criticize the government for fear of reprisals.

After leaving the Diem government and going to America for further study, Mr. Thai was convinced by events in Vietnam that he needed to publicly speak out against the regime, whatever the risks. In 1962, he published his analysis of the regime and its problems in *Is South Vietnam Viable?* This detailed examination of the regime predicted its downfall and perhaps contributed to it by providing an authoritative Vietnamese voice against Diem. Following the November 1963 coup that overthrew and killed Diem, Mr. Thai returned to Saigon and took a position in the new government. He quickly realized, however, that little substantial change had taken place and the same political problems remained in South Vietnam. Frustrated, he left government service and went into business. He became the first in Vietnam to import small, inexpensive Honda motorcycles, which rapidly took over Saigon's streets and became a centerpiece of South Vietnamese society.

After losing a leg during a Viet Cong (VC) attack in his hometown of Hue in 1967, Mr. Thai began to realize that the situation in South Vietnam was hopeless. Although he resumed political activity, trying to persuade leaders to come to a peaceful political accommodation, he also moved his family to the United States in anticipation of South Vietnam's collapse. Later, in the 1990s, Mr. Thai was prominent in calling for reconciliation between overseas Vietnamese and the Communist government and was one of the first high-level South Vietnamese officials to return to Vietnam.

Although Mr. Thai had been working for almost two decades on this memoir, it is only very recently that he resolved to actually share it. It was, in its origin, mostly an exercise in self-examination, written to make sense of his own life and the historical events of which he was part. Mr. Thai is, in certain ways, a very proud and confident man, but he is definitely not an ambitious self-promoter. Mr. Thai believed that too many self-serving books had already been published about Vietnam, a problem that he did not want to exacerbate. He is also at heart a journalist and has a tendency towards detachment that led him to minimize his contributions. As a result, Mr. Thai wrote for himself and his own understanding without much intention of making his account public. It would have been unfortunate if that had remained the case, however, because Mr. Thai's story is one of extraordinary historical value.

As a trusted young aide to South Vietnam's first president, Ngo Dinh Diem, Mr. Thai was in a unique position to observe the behind-the-scenes intrigues that led eventually to the Vietnam War. He was a regime insider, yet he did not become personally invested in defending and protecting the regime. His positions as the Editor and Publisher of *The Times of Vietnam* and as Director General of Vietnam Press also gave him a valuable perspective. From those jobs, Mr. Thai was well positioned to observe what happened in South Vietnam and he developed a network of contacts that kept him informed throughout the Vietnam War era. The depth and range of Mr. Thai's connections were notable, particularly because of his friendships with CIA legend Edward Lansdale, Communist super-spy Pham Xuan An, and the politically powerful General Nguyen Chanh Thi. This combination of his closeness to President Diem, his highly regarded journalistic work, and his social associations made him someone who was frequently consulted during critical political episodes. As a result, he was often a central witness to the political machinations of the time without being a direct and interested party.

Fortunately, Mr. Thai came to realize that his voice needed to be heard. The catalyst of that realization was the 2013 Vietnam Center and Archive Conference in Washington, DC, which was also where I met him. The conference was in commemoration of the fifty-year anniversary of Diem's fall, and Mr. Thai presented on a panel of witnesses of the regime. His participation helped him see not only the importance of what he had experienced but also the fact that there is still a dearth of firsthand Vietnamese accounts of that pivotal time. Although historians have vigorously debated and written about the Diem era, the upheavals of South Vietnam's history have meant that relatively few South Vietnamese directly connected to the regime were able to add their vital knowledge to the historical scholarship. Furthermore, the few who were able to share their stories typically did so only in Vietnamese and some had evident personal agendas. Mr. Thai resolved to put out his memoirs not just for his own sake but also to give voice to his many friends and colleagues who never had the opportunity to contribute to the historical narrative of those turbulent days.

That conference was a revelation for both Mr. Thai and myself, one that fortuitously brought us together. When I met him, I was impressed with Mr. Thai's unique experiences and his honesty about them. As a PhD candidate researching the history of journalism and propaganda about South Vietnam prior to the Vietnam War, I saw immediately how valuable his knowledge was not only to my own research but also to historians in general. I peppered him with question after question and continued to do so after the conference by email. Mr. Thai's responses were informative and quite useful, but I also got the sense that he was testing me, trying to gauge my knowledge of South Vietnam's politics. He hinted about the existence of the memoir but would not yet let me see it, not until he was satisfied I had the aptitude to understand it.

When I traveled to the San Francisco Bay area to interview Mr. Thai in March 2014, he finally showed me the memoir manuscript he had been working on for years. He explained to me that he very much wanted to publish it now, but he needed help. His memoir manuscript required extensive editing and rewriting, which he was no longer able to do. Mr. Thai was not in good health and, because his hands shook so much, he could only type a few sentences at a time with laborious effort. Mr. Thai also believed that a historian, who would understand what was valuable in the memoir and be able to explain the memoir's context, should do the editing. Apparently, I had passed his tests and he believed I was familiar enough with the time period that I could be the one to help him finish the memoir. It was a daunting challenge for a young graduate student, but Mr. Thai's confidence and my belief in the significance of his memoir led me to accept his proposition that I edit the book for publication.

Mr. Thai had already written hundreds of pages—more than double this final published book—but it was mostly a rough draft that he had been hastily writing just to get his thoughts down. It had also been written over the course of many years, resulting in discontinuities and repetitions that interfered with the narrative. It took me some time to sort it all out and unravel what exactly this story should include. At first, I considered limiting the memoir only to Mr. Thai's association with the Diem regime. After reading and rereading, consulting trusted mentors, and getting more clarifications from Mr. Thai, however, I decided that the memoir should in fact remain Mr. Thai's full story. While the Diem regime era would be the focus, I thought it was necessary to see that time in its context and to witness the catastrophic aftermath of Diem's failures. Mr. Thai's varied career after the Diem regime also casts an intriguing light on the life and attitudes of South Vietnam's social elite, exposing their dilemmas and weaknesses. On the other hand, I decided that much of the extensive political analysis Mr. Thai had written would have to be put aside. Although incisive, that analysis was mostly superfluous because it was already more poignantly illustrated in the story of Mr. Thai's life itself. Finally, I devoted a great deal of effort into streamlining the story and putting it into a context that would be clear to anyone, expert or not. As part of that effort, the names of some individuals who are peripheral to the story have been omitted.

Throughout the process of editing and rewriting, Mr. Thai has kindly provided me with numerous explanations and amplifications whenever needed. He has also read and approved all of the edits and modifications I made while providing useful suggestions along the way. Besides Mr. Thai himself and his original rough draft manuscript, I have frequently relied on his 1962 book *Is South Vietnam Viable?* for details and elaborations on his thinking. Although Mr. Thai's work on that book is an important point in this memoir, I also draw attention to it because it is an underutilized work by researchers. It was published in the Philippines and in limited numbers, making it difficult to access today, but it is an invaluable guide to the inner workings of the Diem regime. Wherever possible, I have also verified facts and stories in contemporary news articles, archival materials, and other historical documents. This is, however, Mr. Thai's memoir and as such it represents his views and perspectives, some of which cannot be definitively confirmed.

In general, I believe there is good reason to view Mr. Thai as a credible and reliable witness to the events he describes. His training as a journalist and idealistic faith in the values of that profession led him to prioritize seeking the truth above other considerations throughout his life. Even where that truth was inconvenient and contrary to what he desired, Mr. Thai would accept what he believed the facts told him. He also habitually checked and rechecked the facts as he saw them, as well as his own assumptions. Such habits are deeply ingrained in him and are reflected in this memoir, which is both self-aware and self-critical. With a few minor exceptions, Mr. Thai does not display a significant distorting bias or personal agenda. There are no events for which he hopes to claim credit or on which he seeks to deflect blame. Retroactively elevating his own importance is contrary to his self-effacing character. There is, naturally, an element of self-justification, particularly when it comes to the position that Mr. Thai took regarding the need to remove the Diem regime, but that justification is at the same time tempered by Mr. Thai's honesty, sincerity, and extensive self-criticism. Ultimately, Mr. Thai's primary purpose in this memoir is to inform and help teach some lessons from his life.

Of course, Mr. Thai did have a very particular point of view that necessarily limited his perception in some ways. His relatively elite position in society, his anti-Communism (which was not passionately ideological, but still strong), and his American education all set him apart in ways that made it sometimes difficult for him to comprehend his fellow countrymen. This means that the memoir does not shed much light on the actions or thinking of ordinary Vietnamese, while the Communist insurgency in the South Vietnamese countryside is largely in the background. That insulation of the South Vietnamese elite, however, is incredibly revealing in itself and Mr. Thai does much to explain both the causes and consequences of that isolation from the realities of the war and revolution that engulfed the nation.

Mr. Thai is, indeed, well aware of his own limited perspective; one of the chief merits of this memoir is his willingness to expose the weaknesses of his perspective and that of the rest of the South Vietnamese leadership class. Throughout the memoir, Mr. Thai is harshly critical of the Saigon elite and he largely includes himself in that criticism. The one exception to that is in the area of economic success. Mr. Thai is reluctant to admit to having utilized his privileged social position for economic gain, typically instead referring to his success as a result of "luck" or skillful use of his connections. It is hard to imagine, however, a South Vietnamese citizen of a lesser background having the kind of luck or access to powerful people that Mr. Thai enjoyed. It is important, though, to differentiate Mr. Thai's privilege from the corruption of which he is so critical. While he did materially benefit from an elevated position in a strife-torn society, he did not engage in things like bribery, embezzlement, or abuse of his official authority for his own profit. Instead, he largely pursued opportunities that he believed served a greater good while still benefiting his own self-interest.

One weakness of the Saigon elite that emerges quite clearly, and of which Mr. Thai himself is guilty, is how South Vietnam's leaders never formulated truly coherent, practical, or broadly acceptable solutions to the immense problems confronting their country. Consequently, Mr. Thai is sometimes unclear on some rather important issues. Were Vietnamese or Americans ultimately responsible for what happened in South Vietnam? Was democracy of central importance, or was it secondary for South Vietnam? What should have happened and who should have led after the overthrow of Diem? Mr. Thai presents some intriguing ideas and alternatives (some in retrospect, and some that he believed at the time), but even with the benefit of hindsight his views contain some unresolved dilemmas. Many of these ambiguities were a result of the complicated, uncertain circumstances or the limitations imposed by outside forces. It is also important to remember that, despite his significant authority, Mr. Thai was still a relatively young (he was 33 at the time of Diem's overthrow) and inexperienced figure who was usually attempting to exert influence through more powerful patrons. I have done my best along with Mr. Thai to explain why these ambiguities existed and put them in their proper context, but I also believe that the inconsistencies are important because of what they reveal about the dilemmas many South Vietnamese faced and their inability to resolve them.

Mr. Thai also has a very human tendency to forgive or excuse his friends and those he personally liked while portraying those he opposed in a more uniformly negative light. Mr. Thai is willing to criticize people like Diem — who was practically an adopted uncle — or his friend General Nguyen Chanh Thi, but he also can consider their motives and intentions. That is not really true for figures like Mr. and Mrs. Ngo Dinh Nhu, General Nguyen Khanh, or President Nguyen Van Thieu. They all appear much more one-dimensional, even if much of the criticism Mr. Thai directs at them is objective and appropriate. Although Mr. Thai was never really a political partisan who unfailingly or unquestioningly supported a party or faction, he still had notable political inclinations and a tendency to reject those who did not conform to his inclinations. As Mr. Thai wrote in *Is South Vietnam Viable?*, the Diem regime had multiple power centers, in part, to give its supporters an illusion that they were following a government that truly represented their priorities.[1] Mr. Thai, with his American education and as someone who originally came to the regime because of Diem himself, believed in the need for something close to a true democracy, even if there was some need to limit it and develop it slowly. He also opposed the naked factionalism and patronage that drove much of South Vietnamese politics, both during the Diem era and afterwards. Mr. Thai therefore was fairly uniform in his opposition to leaders who represented the power of factionalism and patronage, especially Mr. and Mrs. Nhu and Nguyen Khanh. In this regard, Mr. Thai's political views aligned with those of many Americans who pushed for more (but still quite limited) democracy in South Vietnam. When influential Americans like Michigan State University Group leader Dr. Wesley Fishel cited Mr. Thai as among the "young men...who have the qualities of leadership which Vietnam will need in the years ahead," it is not at all clear whether this reflected Mr. Thai's influence on them or their American influence on him.[2] In all likelihood, it was both.

The most notable subject on which Mr. Thai is less than impartial is that of Mrs. Ngo Dinh Nhu. Like many South Vietnamese nationalists who became opposed to Diem's rule, Mr. Thai viewed Mrs. Nhu as the embodiment of all that was wrong with the regime. There was good reason for that, and it was primarily her actions and abrasive style that won Mrs. Nhu scorn from Mr. Thai and others like him. There was also an element of sexism in the opposition of men like Mr. Thai to this woman, who upset the patriarchal Confucian order in both a personal and political sense. On the other hand, much of the criticism directed at Mrs.

Nhu, including its more sexist manifestations, can be better understood as a form of scapegoating. Many people — Mr. Thai included — had a hard time blaming Diem for their government's many shortcomings. They enthusiastically supported him in the past and had tied their own identity to him, so to indict him was to indict themselves. They did not have that kind of connection with Mrs. Nhu and she was a very visible target, so criticizing her as a substitute for criticizing the regime as a whole or Diem himself was easier and more socially acceptable.

For Mr. Thai, though, this wasn't some theoretical or impersonal debate. Mrs. Nhu personally targeted him for punishment for alleged disloyalty to the regime, and she was someone that he legitimately had reason to fear. As Wesley Fishel noted, Mr. Thai was a prime example of a talented young leader who was "stifled and smothered by the heavy hand" of the government, and it was Mrs. Nhu who was largely responsible for that.[3] She was really his only antagonist within the regime even after he turned against it; he enjoyed at least cordial if not friendly relations with all of the other principle figures of the regime. It is thus fairly understandable that Mr. Thai might have some personal antipathy toward Mrs. Nhu. While he seems to see only the worst of Mrs. Nhu, he is also still quite sincere and has good reason for his criticisms. Many of the accusations Mr. Thai levels against Mrs. Nhu — such as her political corruption, shady business dealings, and underhanded acts like having mobs ransack opposition newspapers or unjustly imprisoning and even "disappearing" political opponents — have been corroborated by historians, although some of the rumors were exaggerated to a degree (particularly those about the Nhus' corrupt businesses and personal enrichment).

The story of the relationship he observed between Mrs. Nhu and her brother-in-law Diem is an even more sensitive subject and one that Mr. Thai and I discussed extensively. It is problematic, from a historian's standpoint, because it cannot really be confirmed, but it is something worth considering nevertheless. Mr. Thai wanted the story told in spite of its salaciousness, not because of it. He adamantly believed he witnessed something strange, which was confirmed to him by his friend Vo Van Hai. Mr. Thai himself was not fully certain if there was in fact something physical or romantic between Mrs. Nhu and Diem, but he did know that their relationship was clearly unusual and that Diem was emotionally affected enough to have it influence his thinking and judgment. It is not a claim that can be unquestionably established, but it would be a mistake to dismiss it. Mr. Thai is clearly telling what he perceived to be the truth, circumstantial evidence makes the claim seem at least plausible, and slander for slander's sake is simply out of his character. Furthermore, as Mr. Thai explains, although the intense interest in the personal behavior of the President and his family members might strike a modern reader as peculiar or petty, it was at that time a matter of serious political concern within Vietnam.

Another area where there might be some doubt about the memoir is regarding Mr. Thai's relationship with the CIA. He was quite close with members of the CIA, and suspicions of his being a CIA agent followed him for years. He did exhibit some characteristics of a good intelligence operative, exerting influence behind the scenes and maintaining a strong network of sources. Mr. Thai, however, is adamant that he never worked for the CIA. He even laments the fact that he did not utilize his CIA connections to more actively shape South Vietnamese policy and politics. Given the positions he held, his connections, his friendships with a wide variety of Americans in Saigon, and how his nationalist politics overlapped with American interests, it is not too surprising that Mr. Thai was well acquainted with members of the CIA. That did not mean that he worked for them, however. Early in his career, the Lansdale connection jumps out as a red flag but it becomes less indicative upon closer inspection. As Rufus Phillips, one of the members of Lansdale's team, explained to me, Lansdale's mission "was not a classical intelligence" one but "mainly a political action" one, so recruiting assets for the CIA was not something they did.[4] Later in Mr. Thai's career, during the Vietnam War, he spent much of his time trying to avoid political entanglements, not seeking them out, which would have been puzzling to do if he were in the intelligence business. It would also be strange for him to now be so open about his many CIA interactions and yet not admit to being an actual agent, if that were the case. Finally, working for the CIA would have been contrary to Mr. Thai's consistent belief in the need for openness and integrity in Vietnam's politics.

That belief in the need for openness is embodied in this memoir, which is ultimately what makes it so valuable. For my part, working on this memoir has been a rewarding and enlightening experience, a feeling I hope is shared by readers. I am grateful to Mr. Thai for the opportunity to present his remarkable story to the world. He has been an ideal subject and as easy to work with as any editor could hope for. I also greatly appreciate Dr. Larry Berman for his kind and insightful foreword to this book as well as all of the advice he has given me. Likewise, Dr. Ron Milam, Dr. Steve Maxner, and Dr. Edward Miller all provided useful guidance and input on the process of editing this memoir. I owe many thanks to my parents and brother for their support and encouragement. Finally, I must express gratitude to my wife Linh, for giving me a deeper understanding of Vietnamese culture and for her patience with the demands of my scholarship.

JUSTIN SIMUNDSON
Texas Tech University

AUTHOR'S ACKNOWLEDGMENTS

I wish to thank the following individuals for their help in making this book happen in what will be my 90th year:

Maria Tabia, Melissa Dickerson, Gerry Guerrero—for your kind help at the nursing home.

Nguyen Thi Mai Khoi—for the great help you gave me during the many months that I was very sick. Without your help, the project could not have been finished.

Binah Senderowicz—for wheelchairing me around Washington, DC, during the 50th anniversary, "Vietnam, 1963" conference.

Daniel Senderowicz—for the help you gave me with all computer-related matters.

Nguyen Huu Dzu—for your hospitality when I visited Kiev. You gave me a very objective picture of the communist regime and the Vietnamese community in the Soviet Union.

Pham Khac Lam (trained in China and Soviet Union, Director General of Hanoi's Television)—for the friendly and frank, unbiased comments that you made when I visited Hanoi.

Larry Berman—for the encouragement and support you gave me when I was about to drop the project.

Justin Simundson—for the excellent editorial job that you have done.

Peer Reviewers—for your constructive critical comments.

Texas Tech University—for your support and enthusiasm for this project.

Honda Motor Company, especially Messrs. **Inayoshi** (General Manager of Asian Honda in Bangkok), and the late **Ted Kumamoto** (of the Head Office in Tokyo).

The Nieman Foundation—for the opportunity to spend time at Harvard to think about the problems of Vietnam.

The late General **Edward Landsdale**—for visiting me at the Grall Hospital in Saigon and for your nice letter of introduction to the INS.

The late General **Do Mau**, Deputy Prime Minister of South Vietnam—for agreeing with me about the corruption of the Ngo family.

The late **Vo Van Hai**, personal secretary to President Diem—for sharing the secrets of the regime.

The late **Pham Xuan An** ("The Perfect Spy")—for sharing the secrets after keeping them so long.

The late **Hoang Thanh** and your father—for your enthusiasm and great hospitality to me and my family.

The late Dr. **Nguyen Duong Quang** (Director of the Vietnam–Germany Friendship Hospital in Hanoi)—for your hospitality when I visited Hanoi in the early 1990s. Your brothers (one belonging to the Socialist Party, another an anti-communist ARVN colonel killed by communists in 1975) and you represent the tragic division of Vietnamese families during the War. However, you yourself are a great example of how in moving beyond the social constructs of political parties, nations, and cultures, and combining the best of what they offer, we can provide healing and achieve good things for all humankind.

CROOKED BAMBOO

Chapter 1

YOUTH

EARLY CHILDHOOD

I was born on the first day (Tet) of the Year of the Horse, January 30, 1930. Although I was the last born of six children, this auspicious timing led my family to believe I would be an exceptional person. There is a Vietnamese saying that such a moment at the start of the new year marks the "beginning of big things" (Tam duong khai *thai*), so I was named *Thai*. Because I was born at the 12th hour, I also had the nickname *Ngo* to evoke this lucky beginning. My father often told me that I was a special kid. According to my mother, however, because I was so "special" I was also very difficult to raise and I suffered from terrible diseases. The many sicknesses I endured as a youngster were quite scary for my parents, but I was lucky that I did not suffer any lasting damage. Because of the illnesses, while I was still quite young my parents tried to hide me from the evil spirits by using the subterfuge of "selling" me to a famous Chinese astrologer. This astrologer also predicted special things for my life in the horoscope he wrote for me, based on the stars derived from my date and hour of birth.

I lived with my parents until I was a teenager, and after that I alternated between living with them and attending boarding school. I had a chance to stay with them in three different provinces of Annam, as the French labeled their protectorate of central Vietnam. First was Phu Yen province, where my father was Deputy Province Chief (the *An Sat*, below the Governor of a smaller province). Phu Yen was a nice, peaceful province in southern Annam. It was sparsely populated and had beautiful beaches lined with coconut trees. Later, we lived in the city of Vinh in Nghe An province, where my father was the number three mandarin below the Governor and the First Deputy Governor. Nghe An was much larger than Phu Yen and much more politically important. There was little fresh water and the soil was poor, so it was an impoverished province. Life in Nghe An had always been difficult and, consequently, the people there had a reputation for being argumentative and rebellious. Not coincidentally, it was the birthplace of many Vietnamese revolutionaries, including Ho Chi Minh. The last place we lived was in Thanh Hoa province where my father was First Deputy Province Governor (*Bo Chanh*). Thanh Hoa, the northernmost part of Annam, was probably the nicest province in that section of Vietnam. It had several rivers and produced all kinds of delicious fruits and other foods, much of it for the royal court in Hue. I was too young then to fully understand the situation, but it seemed to me that the mandarin administration in Annam was merely a façade to show that there was a native (*indigene*) administration in place while real power was exercised by the French. My father tried to follow the example his father had set before him when dealing with the French: be friendly without being subservient.

My favorite place and my happiest days were in Song Cau. There, I had easy access to the beaches and the sea. I could play, fish, catch all kinds of sea creatures, and observe the wonders of nature at work. I especially liked playing with the local fishermen's sons, who were my age and whose dark suntans I admired. To play with them, however, I had to sneak away from my *linh le*. He was a soldier-servant assigned to my high-ranking mandarin father, and my parents had him watch over me. Luckily for me, he liked to take naps during the day. Once, I snuck away in the middle of a hot day while the linh le "watching" me was snoring under a coconut tree. I joined the fishermen's sons on a swim out to a big ship anchored in the bay, very far from shore. Our group of five kids swam several kilometers out but none of us had any fear whatsoever of the sharks or other dangers threatening us. We took more than a few hours to swim out to the ship and get back. Meanwhile, my linh le was frantically searching for me and had to go home to report my disappearance to my parents. He was probably more scared of losing his job than of something happening to me. When I got back, my parents were happy enough to see me return safely that I escaped without any spanking for my escapade!

Eventually, my parents decided that I had to be sent to the same boarding school in Hue where my older brother Dzien was already an upperclassman. I was to go to the Institut de la Providence and be in French Sixième (six years away from the Première class, who take the *Baccalauréat* at the end of their secondary schooling). It was the best Catholic school in the whole of Indochina and it accepted only the sons of French officials, the highest-ranking Vietnamese mandarins, and the richest landowning families. The Catholic priests from the famous Missions Etrangères de Paris founded the school and, except for a few lay teachers in unimportant positions, they ran it. They had the dual purpose of propagating French culture and Catholic religion to the Vietnamese elite like my family. It was almost the same as being sent to a French Catholic *lyceum* in France itself. Prayers were said in the school's chapel, in classes, and in the refectory where meals were served.

Unofficially, French was to be used at all times and Vietnamese was discouraged, if not banned. Looking back, I do not know how I made the transition from life in Song Cau, where I spoke only Vietnamese, to life at Providence where I was supposed to speak only French. I had to adapt quickly, and luckily I did. It wasn't long before I was holding my own in quarrels with French boys who tried to bully me in fights over who had reserved the ping-pong tables or the soccer field first. I had many fights — actual fistfights and not just verbal arguments — with the French boys, who I later learned were sons of big shots in the colonial administration. I really had no notion about French colonial rule and I had no idea that, as an Annamite (as the French used to call us Vietnamese), I was supposed to behave in a submissive manner toward the French colonial masters. At times, I was surprised when a French Catholic priest would take the side of a French boy when I knew I was right. It never crossed my mind at the time that it was because of colonialism or ethnic discrimination, but many of my Vietnamese classmates undoubtedly shared such slights.

On the other hand, I was surprised at the unexpected kindness shown to me by a Vietnamese professor at Providence. His name was Ta Quang Buu, and he had an apartment right next to the infirmary. I had to go to the infirmary to have injuries from the day's activities attended to almost every evening. On many nights, Mr. Buu asked me to come into his apartment after I had my wounds bandaged. He gave me oranges to eat and was very nice to me. I guess he liked me because I was a gutsy Annamite kid who was not afraid to fight against the French boys who were behaving like bullying colonialists. Later, Buu represented the Hanoi government, serving as its non-communist, nationalist face before the international community when he signed the 1954 Geneva Agreement that put an end to the Indochina War.

FAMILY

For several generations my ancestors had been mandarins, government officials serving the kings of Vietnam. In many ways, they occupied a middle ground between the French and the Vietnamese. Culturally and socially, they had a unique identity that mixed traditional, indigenous philosophies — particularly Confucianism — with foreign influences. This set them apart from both the French and the mass of Vietnamese people. Politically, mandarins like my ancestors tried to balance French colonial rule with Vietnamese sovereignty and interests. That meant collaboration with the colonial state, particularly in the late 1800s and early 1900s, but it also occasionally meant resistance and acts of defiance against it.

My great-grandfather became the first mandarin in our family after leaving his home province, Quang Tri, to move to the imperial city Hue and work in the Nguyen dynasty's court. My grandfather followed in his father's footsteps and rose higher in the mandarin ranks, becoming a respected official who was well known in Hue for his integrity and courage. He also built our family house in Hue along the beautiful Perfume River. His time of service was filled with the turbulence that resulted from the establishment of French colonial rule. Working for King Thanh Thai, my grandfather was Chief of Staff for the King's Secret Council, which was an important but dangerous position. In 1889 he was also one of three leaders the king sent to Paris to negotiate with the French in an unsuccessful attempt to stop "colonialist encroachments" on the Court of Annam. My grandfather eventually became the Governor of An Tinh, which combined the politically important provinces of Nghe An (where my father later served) and Ha Tinh. In 1903, my grandfather suddenly resigned his position. He told the king that he needed to go home to take care of his sick mother. In the Confucian tradition, which highly respected filial piety, such a resignation could not be turned down. I suspect that the real reason he resigned, however, was the difficulty caused by the French colonialists' increasing encroachments. At that time the French were becoming increasingly hostile to King Thanh Thai, whom they eventually exiled under the pretext that he was insane.

My grandfather, unfortunately, died a short time later in 1905 at the relatively young age of 49. My father was only seven at the time, but he was still well educated and taken care of because my grandmother had always seen to the family finances. In the true Confucian spirit, my grandfather had taken no interest in money and property and had left such matters to his enterprising wife. She hired tutors for my father and made sure he succeeded in the triennial exams in Chinese characters that were the requirement to become a mandarin. At 17, my father became the youngest ever to pass his exams and graduate as *Cu-nhan* (equivalent to a Master of Arts in the Chinese education system), opening the door to a career as a mandarin. At that young age, my father also married my mother, who was only 16. Their marriage was an arranged one, as tradition required between two mandarin families of equal status. Her father, a prominent mandarin native to the southern Mekong Delta, had taught himself French and had been summoned to the Imperial Court in Hue to serve as King Thanh Thai's official French interpreter.

According to tradition, my mother became a member of my father's family upon her marriage. All her life, she was very afraid of my domineering grandmother, who was the uncontested matriarch after my grandfather passed away. My mother may have been a bit intimidated by my grandmother, but my grandmother was really a remarkable woman. Through hard work, she had amassed a fortune selling dry areca nut, which was chewed with betel in Vietnam. She did not know how to read or write but had wide-ranging contacts with all kinds of people, from the high and mighty to the poorest people in her community. She was friends with the mother of the King and many high-ranking mandarins. She visited with them in the same friendly and tactful way as when she chatted with the poor people of her neighborhood, who often stopped to pay respect to her.

My parents had six children, but only four of us survived to adulthood. Of the four of us who survived, there were two girls, Tran and Loc, and two boys, Dzien and myself. My younger sister, Loc, became a Catholic nun after the tragic death of her fiancé, Le Thieu Huy. He was an exceptionally bright young man from a good family and he had been a top graduate of the prestigious Lyceum Albert Sarraut in Hanoi. Like many bright young men in Vietnam during World War II, he eagerly joined and graduated from the first Vietnamese military academy, the Youth Vanguard Military School, which was created in March 1945 by the pro-Japanese government. It was there that Huy met my older brother Dzien, who was also a student, as well as my sister Loc. After the August Revolution of Ho Chi Minh's Viet Minh, Huy was summoned to Hanoi and given the special mission in Laos. He was supposed to work with the Viet Minh-allied Pathet Lao leader, the "Red Prince" Souphanouvong, and to protect the Red Prince at any cost. While they were trying to cross the Mekong River and find safety in Thailand in 1946, French paratroopers attacked them, killing Huy. My sister Loc remained in Vietnam for a time, but in 1950 she left to study at the University of Montpellier and shortly thereafter joined the Order of St. Augustine as a nun.

My older brother Dzien, like Huy, was sent to Laos for a time after graduating from the Youth Vanguard Military School. He left the Viet Minh military service fairly quickly, however, because he was suspected of being connected to the anti-Communist Dai Viet Party. He later graduated from the National Institute of Administration in Saigon and received training at Michigan State in public administration. In the mid-1950s he was a District Chief under the Diem government, and in the late 1960s he joined South Vietnam's diplomatic service. He served until the collapse of the Saigon government in 1975, when he had to close down the South Vietnamese Embassy in Dakar, Senegal, as the chargé d'affaires there. Afterwards he stayed in France as a refugee for a few years, and then in the mid-'90s he returned to Ho Chi Minh City where he has been living ever since.

HISTORICAL TURNING POINT IN 1945

In 1945, war and revolution were in the air. Big matters were in the making and although I was still too young to really understand, I could sense then that my father was worried about the course of events. Since 1941, Indochina had sat apprehensively on the edge of war. While the French still remained officially in control, their authority in Indochina had been considerably weakened by the German conquest of France itself. When Japan demanded the use of French Indochina as a new base to attack the Allies in Southeast Asia, French officials had little choice but to agree. This uneasy relationship lasted until March 1945 when the Japanese decided to end French authority over their colony. They attacked and disarmed most of the French military forces and then forced King Bao Dai to proclaim Vietnam independent. That independence, however, really only meant there would now be a new pro-Japanese puppet government instead of a French one.

My father had a good sense of what was about to happen, fortunately, and he quit his job as First Deputy Governor of Thanh Hoa province a few months before the Japanese putsch. After my father's resignation, he immediately took my mother, my sister Loc, and me on a car trip south, from Thanh Hoa to Hue. As we drove along the main highway linking Hanoi to Hue and Saigon, I saw many corpses wrapped in straw mats along the roadside. My father explained to me that many people were dying of starvation because of the shortage of rice in the country. The Japanese had requisitioned most of the rice to feed their troops and fuel their trucks, and almost two million Vietnamese died as a result. Occasionally, we saw some people by the road who were still alive, but they were so emaciated they looked more like ghosts.

My father, who usually was quite calm, was nervous throughout this trip, as if danger were lurking close behind us. We drove without incident, though, until we reached a stretch of the national highway running through the province of Quang Tri. In his writings, my friend Bernard Fall later referred to this dreary, deserted road as "The Street without Joy." There, our chauffeur announced to my father that the car had blown out two tires and there was no spare left to continue the trip. My father immediately told us to take whatever belongings we could carry and follow him. He gave some money to the chauffeur to buy food and repair the tires and ordered him to stay with the car until it could be driven to Hue. We walked for many kilometers until we finally reached a village near a river. My father talked to the local people and negotiated for a sampan to take us to Hue. To this day, I still marvel at the resourcefulness and quick thinking of my father on that occasion. We went on rivers, canals, and bays, eventually arriving safely at the wharf right in front of our ancestral home.

By that time I was attending Khai Dinh Lyceum in Hue, so my family's relocation didn't affect me much. I was in school the morning that the Japanese took over, on March 9, 1945. The Vietnamese students like myself didn't know that it would happen, so we were in class as usual. After hearing a few gunshots nearby, we suddenly noticed that none of the French kids had shown up for class that day. We learned afterwards that they were at home with their parents who, as officials of the French colonial administration, had been arrested by the Japanese. There were not that many Japanese troops in Hue really. As a curious schoolboy, though, I watched the street in front of our school all morning and I was impressed with the truckloads of Japanese troops I saw moving back and forth. Later, I understood that the Japanese had made it appear that they had more troops than actually existed in order to intimidate their adversaries. The Japanese decision to seize control must have surprised the French, because there was little resistance. Some French troops in northern Vietnam succeeded in escaping toward southern China, but throughout the country, the French were quickly neutralized without much bloodshed. At Khai Dinh Lyceum, the only differences I observed after the March coup were the absence of my French classmates and the addition of Japanese as another foreign language class.

In my family, however, the Japanese takeover and its aftermath brought major change. The overthrow of the French opened the way for the creation of the first Vietnamese military academy, The School for Vanguard Youth. I was too young to join, but witnessing the experiences of my brother Dzien and my sister Loc's fiancé, Huy, had a deep impact on me. Although it was exciting to see Dzien and Huy in their neat military uniforms while they underwent their training, what happened after they graduated taught me some important lessons and helped redirect my own life.

Sometime around late 1946, while Huy was in Laos with the Pathet Lao Red Prince, Dzien and one of his friends from The School for Vanguard Youth were sent near the Laotian border to fight the French at Khe Sanh. Somehow, I was allowed to go along, even though I was only 16 and did not officially join the Viet Minh. My brother and his friend were assigned to transportation. The trucks they had did not run on gasoline but on "gasogene" generated by burning coal in a bulky tank welded to the truck. In action, they were grossly inadequate because they were extremely slow to start. I recall vaguely that a convoy of these gasogene trucks had to be abandoned at Khe Sanh when an attack by French paratroopers forced a quick retreat. What I remember much more vividly about my Khe Sanh experience, however, was the severe case of malaria I contracted. It took months to bring down the fever, and even after that the malaria was not cured completely. Its unbearable effects plagued me for months. Every day, at precise intervals, I shook violently and alternated between fever and chills. My liver was also badly damaged. At the time, the only medication available to me was "quinobleu," which was a form of quinine injection. It took months of the quinobleu injections before I could even really get by and it was only years later, after I had stayed in the United States for a long time, that I was totally rid of recurrences of my Khe Sanh malaria.

After recovering from that malaria and hearing about Le Thieu Huy's death, I started seriously thinking about my own future. I came to the decision that I had to go back to school and continue my studies. It was foolish to play soldier, as I and many other youngsters did then. I had followed my brother and the Viet Minh army "for fun," without fully realizing what it involved and what the consequences could be. Huy's death made me realize that if a sacrifice had to be made, it needed to be made freely and consciously; otherwise, it could be a total waste. I told myself that unless I learned and grew up more than Huy had done, there would be no point for me to join or sacrifice myself for anything. In hindsight, I believe that was indeed a wise decision to continue my studies instead of joining the Viet Minh and sacrificing myself to a cause that I did not fully understand.

SELF-SUPPORT IN SAIGON

The revolutionary events in 1945 upset the normal social order in Vietnam. My family's previously affluent mandarin status suddenly became a liability. Our existence in that period of upheaval was precarious in many ways, not least because we feared victimization by the up-and-coming proletarians. One of my grandmother's servants, who used to pull her rickshaw, became the chairman of the local Viet Minh administrative committee in Hue. My grandmother had treated him fairly well before, so he left us alone and did not do anything against us even though we were bourgeois. My father still felt it was best to leave Hue as a precaution and seek refuge in the countryside. We took a sampan out of the city to a remote village, staying there for a couple of weeks without incident. One day, though, my father suddenly told us we had to go back home to Hue. That was a wise choice since we learned afterwards that some other city folks who had sought safety like us had been murdered and stripped of their belongings in another nearby village. It was a dangerous time.

With my family's change in fortune, I had to become self-supporting. From 1946 until 1948 I taught Latin at Providence School while preparing myself to take my Baccalauréat exams. After 1945 there had been a change in the leadership of the school. The French priests who were regarded as the "old guard" — those most associated with French colonialism — returned to France. Other French priests whose outlook was more progressive and better adapted to the new political climate in Vietnam replaced them. Father George Lefas, who came from a classy Paris family, took over the direction of the school. He tried to encourage Vietnamese participation in the school and hired more Vietnamese teachers, which helped me get my job as an elementary Latin teacher.

I passed the first parts of my Baccalauréat on the first try in June 1948. In the French educational system, this degree's final exam was the last obstacle before university. All the subjects covered in the past six years of secondary education were reviewed and candidates had to prove that they had a good command of all of them. The subjects ranged from natural sciences and mathematics to history and geography, as well as languages, including the classic languages like Latin and Greek and modern languages like English. Most important of all, I was supposed to have a good knowledge of French, which was the "mother" tongue, regardless of the fact that I was Vietnamese. I was supposed to perform exactly the same as a French student. Ridiculously, I was even supposed to know the geological composition of the regions of France, to be familiar with the behavior of French rivers, and to remember the important dates of French history. It did not matter at all that, as a Vietnamese, I was not given the chance to learn anything about the geography and history of my own country.

I was supposed to take the second part of the Baccalauréat exams in Hue in June 1949, but I got a bad case of smallpox so I had to go to Saigon to take the exam later at the end of July. I passed it, and the next month I applied for a scholarship in America. It was by luck that I came to that decision, which was to steer my future in a new direction. I knew nothing about the US education system and, as was normal for a French-trained Vietnamese student, I was planning to leave for university in France. I was very interested in becoming fluent in English, though, so I often went to the US Information Service (USIS) library to read books in English. One day I happened to run across the Foreign Service officer who was in charge of USIS in Saigon, Francis Cunningham. He suggested that I should apply for a US scholarship. Somehow, I decided it would be a good challenge and perhaps a "pioneering innovation" to go study in the United States instead of France. So I followed Mr. Cunningham's suggestion and applied for an American scholarship. Then I waited a year for the result.

While waiting in Saigon, I supported myself by working part-time at the British Consulate (which also helped me get as much practice in

English as possible) and I stayed at the French Chaplain's office right next to the Saigon Cathedral. Before I accepted the job at the British Consulate, I had also had a job interview with the American Foreign Broadcast Information Service (FBIS). FBIS specialized in the reception and translation of foreign broadcasts all over the world, so the job was translating Vietnamese to English and vice versa. I turned down the job for practical reasons, which was probably good because I was unaware at the time that FBIS was connected with the CIA. In the fall of 1949, I registered as a first-year student concurrently at the Faculté de Droit and the Faculté de Lettres at the Saigon University. I thought that I could handle both subjects, law and literature, because I enjoyed them both. The Saigon University was affiliated with the University of Paris and all the professors there were French. I passed the final exams at the end of the first year in both Law and Letters; I thought that if I did not get the American scholarship I would continue my studies at a university in France instead.

THE UNIVERSITY OF PORTLAND

Luckily, in March 1950, I was offered a scholarship in the United States by Father Jacques Houssa. He represented the Vietnamese Catholic Bishops and was trying to find scholarships at Catholic universities in America for promising Vietnamese Catholic students. I turned him down, however, because Mr. Cunningham of USIS informed me that the Institute of International Education in New York also was offering me a scholarship at the University of Portland in Oregon, which I decided to accept.

I flew to Hue in June to say goodbye to my parents and to receive some cash grants, which were given to me by a representative of the Bao Dai government in Central Vietnam. In August, I left Saigon to fly to Paris, where I stayed a couple of weeks to see friends and relatives. I left Paris and landed in New York City on September 2. I stayed for a few days in New York and met a few Vietnamese who were students at NYU, Yale, and MIT. I then left New York and flew to Portland. While I was waiting for the plane in New York I had difficulty understanding what was said on the loudspeaker in the airport. To me, everything sounded so fast and blurry. My knowledge of English was based mainly on what I had learned in weekly English classes, which were taught by a French teacher whose English was heavily accented. I had also mostly learned to translate from English into French instead of directly listening, which left me struggling to keep up with what was being said. I vaguely understood that the loudspeakers were announcing arrivals and departures, but the details eluded me. As a result, I sat there and did not realize until it was nearly too late that my flight had been announced.

When I first applied for a scholarship in the United States, I knew nothing about the American university system. I figured that it must be similar to the French system, with state-supported schools that followed a common program of study and identical academic standards approved by the state. Of course, I discovered quickly after arriving that American universities were very different from French ones, most importantly in that they had differing academic standards for the same degrees. The University of Portland, run by the Holy Cross Fathers, was selected for me because I was Catholic and had expressed a preference for a school located in an area with a mild climate. Had I known more about the American university system and the schools in the Portland area, however, I would have preferred to study at Reed College, which had a much higher academic standing. I was glad, though, to discover that there were two other Vietnamese students at the University of Portland.

I quickly got adjusted to the way of life of an American student. As soon as I got used to English and had no problem understanding or speaking, I was asked by the Director of Foreign Students at the university to participate with other foreign students in speaking engagements at local civic clubs. Each of us was supposed to give short speeches on our country and to answer questions from the audience. The idea was to promote understanding of those foreign places, which were totally alien to the American public. At times I was asked the most unexpected kinds of questions because most Americans in the early 1950s had no idea where Vietnam was and knew nothing about its culture and history.

I immersed myself in student life and participated in many extracurricular activities. I enjoyed playing tennis and taking dance lessons. Most weekends I was invited to spend time with the families of my American classmates, who were generous and sincerely welcoming. I kept busy year-round with many different activities like basketball games, dance parties, and the public speaking engagements. I had time for it all because I really had no problem getting As in my undergraduate courses. With the American course credit system, I did not have to cram as much for the final exams as I would have at a French university. I was able to complete my bachelor's degree in only two years with a 3.84 grade point average. That was the highest for my class that year, so I was designated the flag-bearer for the graduation procession in the summer of 1952.

The American way of life also involved earning money, so I took a few different part-time jobs while I was a student. I worked at a printing press, a greenhouse, and a fast food restaurant. For me, coming from a Vietnamese mandarin family with servants to help with menial tasks and money to spend, it was a great experience. It was interesting to see what life was like for the American worker. It also taught me the value of labor and the satisfaction that came from earning money through sweat and hard work. Fortunately, I never experienced any sort of discrimination at these jobs, either. Looking back, I am grateful that I was exposed to this kind of lesson outside the classroom. It was something sorely lacking in my traditional Vietnamese training and strict French education.

The experiences I had in public speaking and leadership were similarly valuable lessons that I had not had enough of before coming to the United States. Even in my first year of law school in Vietnam, where we were learning to become lawyers, there had been no opportunity for us to practice debating. I got a good dose of public speaking practice when I was invited to participate in an international student seminar sponsored by the American Friends Service Committee in August 1951. The seminar at Kalamazoo College in Michigan brought together outstanding foreign students from all over the United States. While there, I made good friends with students from Chile, Pakistan, and India. I was quite impressed by the Quaker spirit of the organizers as well. By some strange coincidence the seminar's Director, Professor Allan Cole of the Fletcher School of Law and Diplomacy, was one of the first American professors to do research on Vietnam and Indochina, so it was very interesting to meet him there. I must have learned much in public speaking and debating from that summer seminar at Kalamazoo College, because as soon as I returned to Portland I was selected to direct a public debate organized at Reed College on the occasion of the UN Day that year.

GRADUATE SCHOOL AT CORNELL UNIVERSITY

In April 1952, I decided to accept a graduate scholarship at Cornell University in Ithaca, New York. It was a difficult choice because I was also offered scholarships at Harvard, Fordham, and the Fletcher School of Law and Diplomacy. What tipped the scales in favor of Cornell was their new

Southeast Asia Program, which had a very strong emphasis on Vietnam. They offered me more assistantship money than the other universities as well. Cornell also had the best collection of books and research materials on Vietnam and, to my surprise, I found many books and periodicals that I had not been able to get in Saigon. Another advantage of Cornell was that there were a couple of other Vietnamese students studying there already, which was rare in those days when there were fewer than fifty Vietnamese students in America.

It was tough for me to decide what major to take at Cornell and what career to pursue afterwards. I thought of continuing my law studies to become a lawyer in Vietnam. I decided against it, however, because I reasoned that unless the country had a decent government that followed the rule of law first, lawyers could not properly function or defend justice. The first priority in an underdeveloped country like Vietnam, I thought, should be a good government that serves the interests of the country. Anyone interested in helping improve a developing country had to focus first on improving its government; therefore, I chose public administration as my major, with a minor in Southeast Asian studies.

I was obviously very idealistic in those days, but I was also lucky that my idealism was rewarded by a unique set of political circumstances in the 1950s. The United States was looking for a nationalist, anti-communist Vietnamese leader to fight against the Communist Viet Minh and build up the country as an American ally. The man whom US policymakers decided to support was Ngo Dinh Diem, who was a friend and colleague of my mandarin father. As chance would have it, I was soon to become a close aide to him after he came to power, which gave me an opportunity to apply what I learned about theories of government to real life.

MEETING NGO DINH DIEM

In late August 1952, Father Jacques Houssa organized a convention in Chicago of Vietnamese Catholic students studying in America. Father Jacques invited me to participate in the Chicago convention and told me that Ngo Dinh Diem would be coming to meet me. At the convention, I was elected President of the Association of Vietnamese Catholic Students in America, which numbered about thirty members scattered around various colleges. In addition to this honor, I was lucky enough to meet one of the few Vietnamese girls studying in America, Nguyen Tuyet Mai. She was an attractive student on a scholarship at Mundelein College in Chicago, and our meeting at the convention was the beginning of two years of courtship. We got married in East Lansing, Michigan, on July 3, 1954, which was just a week before I ended up returning to Saigon at the request of the new Prime Minister of South Vietnam, Ngo Dinh Diem.

My first meeting with Diem was just a brief one on August 30. He congratulated me on my election as President of the Association and talked about the organization's importance as a nucleus for training future Catholic leaders for Vietnam. He also talked about the old times when he and my father worked together in Annam for a Catholic Interior Minister named Nguyen Huu Bai. He asked about my aunt as well. Her husband had worked for his brother Ngo Dinh Khoi. I later heard that after my aunt's husband died, Khoi had urged his brother Diem to marry her. That event did not come to pass, however, and Diem remained a lifelong bachelor. In any case, Diem was no stranger to my family and these interconnecting relationships between our two families seemed to lead him to cultivate my support. He asked me to come and see him in Lakewood, New Jersey, where he was staying during his exile, telling me he wanted to discuss several projects related to the situation in Vietnam.

Diem was very nice to me during our first meeting. He struck me positively as a simple and honest man, and I saw him as a respectable elder and a family friend. The personal connections were significant, but I also knew he had a good reputation as an incorruptible Vietnamese nationalist, having heard of how he resigned his position as Interior Minister in 1933 over his disagreement with the colonialist policies of the French authorities. I could also see that he, an exile in the United States, badly needed my help. He spoke no English then and even when he could give speeches in French he was not a great speaker. More important, he was not at all familiar with America and its people. At that time, as a young Vietnamese student, I thought the least I could do was to maintain contact with this man. Little did I know that very soon Ngo Dinh Diem was to assume power and become the "greatest little man in Southeast Asia," supported by the US government as the key leader on the front line of anti-communism in Asia.

As soon as I was settled in Ithaca, I got involved in Vietnamese politics, which took considerable time from my studies. Cornell was not nearly as easy as my undergraduate education had been. The competition was intense, and at times the reading lists for the seminars were overwhelming. I had to study hard to make the required grades (at least Bs), but still

I could not help spending time on Vietnamese politics. At the time, the pro-French Saigon government's Embassy in Washington was trying to put out more propaganda and was recruiting Vietnamese students to publish a monthly magazine with frequent anti-Diem themes. They asked me to contribute articles, but I refused. I did not want to do propaganda work for anyone, much less to denigrate someone for no valid reason.

I was unsure if my refusal to cooperate with the Embassy's propaganda landed me on their black list or if it was just coincidence, but afterwards I received several letters asking me to come to the Embassy "to discuss the problem of my passport renewal." I was reluctant to do so because there was nothing to "discuss." It was a simple and clear-cut matter: I needed an extension of my US student visa and therefore needed my expired passport extended to be valid at least six months beyond the visa. The standard procedure should have been either to extend my passport automatically or to deny an extension with an explanation of the reason. Thankfully, US Immigration apparently understood the situation and I was not threatened with deportation or given any trouble. That situation dragged on for months, all the way until August 1954 when the Embassy received a cable from the new Prime Minister in Saigon, Ngo Dinh Diem, requesting me to return to Vietnam to help him as soon as possible and ordering the Embassy to assist me. So instead of fixing my passport situation so that I could remain in America, the Embassy finally issued me a new passport so that I could leave promptly and without any trouble.

DIEM PESSIMISTIC AND DISCOURAGED

Sometime in the fall of 1952, I drove down from Ithaca to Lakewood to visit with Ngo Dinh Diem. He was a resident guest there of the Maryknoll Fathers, who gave him free room and board while he was living in exile in America. When I saw him, he told me to rent a hotel room in town so that we could talk as long as needed, because the monastery had a curfew that began early in the evening. We ended up talking all night about the political situation of Vietnam and the prospects there for the emergence of a truly nationalist government.

Two small things impressed me during that visit with Diem. The first was his insistence on paying the few dollars for the room we rented. It was not an expensive room, costing no more than ten dollars, and I told Diem I would pay for it. As a graduate assistant I was paid a few hundred dollars a month, so it was no matter for me. Diem adamantly refused to let me take the bill, though, insisting on paying it himself. He obviously did not have much money, because I saw him produce only a five-dollar bill and then pay the rest with pocket change. I really respected that simple gesture. Despite his situation as an exile with hardly any means of supporting himself, he had insisted on paying because it was a question of principle. To me, that was clear proof of honesty and integrity.

The next morning, before saying goodbye, I asked Diem if I could take a picture of him. He said, "Sure!" It was while aiming the camera that I noticed Diem's jacket. It was not yet torn — it was still in one piece — but it was almost worn out and had apparently come from the Salvation Army or some other charity. I told myself, "This picture of Diem, the politician in exile, is going to be precious one day when he becomes an important leader." I was quite impressed by Diem's honest, dignified acceptance of his poverty. I thought to myself then that he definitely deserved to be helped.

Years later, after he became the object of a ridiculous cult of personality, with posters hanging all over Saigon of him in an immaculate white sharkskin suit and black tie, Diem brought up the photo with me. He asked, "Do you remember that picture that you took of me at the Maryknoll Seminary? I would like to have it." I immediately suspected that Diem, who was by then at the height of power and an object of public adulation, wanted to get rid of his old picture. That shabby Salvation Army jacket, once a sign of his sincere and self-sacrificing efforts to lead a nationalist Vietnam, was now an unwanted reminder to him of a time when he was poor and powerless. I still had the photo but I told Diem, "I don't know exactly where I put it, Mr. President!" This was a significant episode that, to me, revealed how Diem had forgotten that it was precisely his selflessness, honesty, and integrity that earned him people's support — including my own — and brought him to power.

During our all-night talk in Lakewood, Diem briefed me on what he planned to do, as well as what his brothers — Ngo Dinh Nhu in Saigon and Ngo Dinh Luyen in Paris — were doing to help him gain power. He did not sound too optimistic about his chances for success, though. He complained that he had not been very successful in convincing American policymakers to listen to his nationalist anti-French, anti-Viet Minh views. The US government badly needed the cooperation of the French in NATO and could not afford to antagonize France over Indochina. To illustrate his point, Diem mentioned the case of a State Department employee who was sympathetic to his nationalist views. He had given Diem a ride in New York City but then asked Diem to make sure to keep it a secret. He said he might lose his job if word got around and his bosses at the State Department knew that he had helped Diem. Diem told me that because of the realities of politics, the United States could not afford to be idealistic and had to close its eyes to whatever France decided to do in Indochina. America did not want to get so directly involved in Vietnam yet, Diem believed.

Another obstacle that Diem faced was that Americans he talked to always asked him how he could be more successful than the French had been in Vietnam. What more could he do to defeat the Communists than the prestigious French generals had done? Could he mobilize more men to fight against the Communists than the thousands of French soldiers in Vietnam? What political backing did he have in Vietnam? To these pointed questions, Diem could only answer that he believed that his anti-colonialist, anti-Communist reputation would rally the Vietnamese people behind him. He could guarantee nothing, however. Diem concluded that unless this skeptical American attitude changed, there was no point in his staying in the United States any longer. He told me that he was considering retiring to a monastery in Belgium to pray and meditate as a devout Catholic for the rest of his life.

Diem was giving up, and he said the future was up to young Vietnamese like myself. We had to convince Americans that they must change their policy and help a genuinely nationalist government replace the pro-French Bao Dai government. He suggested starting a round-robin letter chain with five other Vietnamese students studying in America and Canada. Diem would send me weekly letters analyzing the situation in Vietnam, and then I was supposed to pass them on to the next member of the chain. I told Diem that I was glad to cooperate with this arrangement. Diem typed these letters himself and even took the trouble of putting all the Vietnamese accents in by hand. Unfortunately, later I lost all of those letters he sent me. I had been carefully saving them, but when I hurriedly left America to return to Vietnam in August 1954 I left them behind with some other personal belongings. After I had settled in Saigon I requested the Vietnamese Embassy to have these belongings shipped to me in Vietnam. The Embassy did send everything but, regrettably, I somehow never received any of it. I was too busy helping Diem at the time to do anything but accept the loss as a fait accompli.

I tried to encourage Diem when I visited with him, saying that he should be more optimistic about his prospects for success because he had barely begun to fight for his cause in the United States. I asked him if he would be willing to come to Cornell if the Southeast Asia Program there invited him as a guest speaker for a graduate seminar about Vietnam. He said yes, so when I returned to Ithaca I arranged for Professor George Kahin, who was the Director of the Southeast Asia Program, to invite Diem to Cornell in February 1953. Diem gave his speech in French but unfortunately was not very impressive at all. For many of the Cornell graduate students, who had been studying Vietnamese politics in detail, the speech was too general and simplistic. The only positive impression that Diem really conveyed was that he was a simple, honest man who strongly believed that with God's help justice would prevail in Vietnam. Bernard Fall was present for Diem's speech because he often visited Cornell while working on his PhD at nearby Syracuse University. Fall, a French citizen, was very well informed on Vietnam because of his close contact with the French intelligence services there. He was eager to challenge Diem's generalities. I had to intervene as tactfully as I could to stop Fall from grilling Diem, so I promised Fall that I would discuss his objections at length after Diem departed Cornell. Fall and I became good friends over the years (I was invited to his wedding in New York City), but it was difficult to defend the weak speech Diem gave.

In May 1953, as he had planned, Diem left for France and entered a Benedictine monastery in Bruges, Belgium, because he was so discouraged by how his efforts had led nowhere. The deteriorating situation in Indochina, however, was setting the stage for a remarkable reversal in Diem's fortunes. France's obvious failure and the humiliating battle at Dien Bien Phu finally convinced some Americans that it was time to try the nationalist solution Diem had been advocating. Meanwhile, the overriding determination of the new Paris government, led by Pierre Mendès France, to remove France from the war quieted their objections to this change in policy. Although Diem had been discouraged by his lack of accomplishments in America, a number of influential voices he had met began to speak in his favor, especially Catholics like Massachusetts Senator John F. Kennedy, Montana Senator Mike Mansfield, and Cardinal Francis Spellman. With this combination of desperation and American support, Bao Dai turned to Diem just a month before the start of the pivotal Geneva Conference. Diem's younger brother, Ngo Dinh Luyen, who had been negotiating with Bao Dai and the French government for Diem, asked his brother to leave the Belgian monastery in June 1954 to meet with Bao Dai in Nice and be appointed Prime Minister of the State of Vietnam.

Diem inherited a confused and grave situation upon arriving in Saigon, with a great deal of uncertainty over what the Geneva Conference would bring. Moreover, Diem had very little visible, public support in Saigon. Behind the scenes he had some help preparing the way for him, but it really seemed to me like there was hardly anyone willing to help him. As one of the few Vietnamese in the United States who had already assisted him, I was called upon to return to Vietnam and join Diem. Idealistic and disregarding the dangers, I welcomed the opportunity. I would help implement the nationalist solution for Vietnam I believed in, following a leader I respected. With that decision to heed Diem's call, my life became intimately tied to him and his government.

Chapter 2

WITH NGO DINH DIEM THE EARLY YEARS (1954–1957)

Immediately after his return to Saigon, Ngo Dinh Diem cabled the Vietnamese Embassy in Washington to ask me to return to Vietnam to help him. I was supposed to transmit the same message to the other five Vietnamese students who were part of the round robin he had set up. Because of various logistical and personal delays, our whole group of six could not return to Vietnam until August 16, 1954. On that day we boarded a flight to Paris, where we were greeted by an aide to Ngo Dinh Luyen, Diem's brother and now Roving Ambassador to Europe. Our group met with Ngo Dinh Luyen and then we left for Saigon on August 20. Vo Van Hai, who was an early follower of Diem and his Private Secretary, and the Finance Secretary met us upon our arrival at Tan Son Nhut airport in Saigon on August 24.

Within just the first few days after our arrival, I got a good idea of the disarray of Prime Minister Ngo Dinh Diem's government. At the time he was occupying the smaller Gia Long Palace rather than the Norodom Palace (which was soon renamed Independence Palace) because Norodom Palace was still occupied by the French Commissioner General of Indochina. At first, Vo Van Hai showed our group into a vacant room at Gia Long Palace. Hai said the room had been used before by Emperor Bao Dai on the rare occasions when he happened to visit Saigon. It was unlikely that Bao Dai would return from France, so Hai thought that our group could use it for temporary quarters. But a few days later, we were told that the room "belonging to His Majesty" had to be left vacant and we had to move somewhere else. I said Vo Van Hai should tell Diem that there was no sense in making us move and leaving the room unused just in case Bao Dai came back. This suggestion, unsurprisingly, had no effect, but it was an eye-opening incident for me. Later, Hai told me that "you guys just came back from America and you do not realize how confused the situation is here. You must understand that the *old man* ["*Ong Cu*" in Vietnamese, referring to Diem] does not have the final say on anything."

Diem himself soon confirmed this pessimistic warning about the precarious situation. I went to see him to report some alarming rumors that I had heard, especially about the shaky support of the American Embassy for him. What worried me most was that General Lawton Collins, the personal envoy of President Eisenhower in Saigon, had a very low opinion about Diem. The rumor around town was that Collins was being fed the French line — that Diem was an inept leader — by an attractive French intelligence service agent. When I saw Diem, he was sitting in his big armchair, chain-smoking while looking pensively at the ceiling. After hearing my report, he said in a weary voice, "You guys try to do what you can on your own to help because I am already very tired and cannot do anything more myself." Hearing that from Diem himself, I realized just how desperate his political position was.

In those days, Diem was fighting for political survival in Saigon and there were not many followers visible at his side. When I was at Gia Long Palace I saw only a few of the early supporters of Diem. Colonels Nguyen Ngoc Le and Do Mau were there most of the time. As military officers, they had to report to General Nguyen Van Hinh, the pro-French, anti-Diem Army Chief of Staff. They both had a hard time with General Hinh because of their known anti-French and pro-Diem views. Later on, when Diem succeeded in consolidating his power, he appointed Nguyen Ngoc Le as his first Director General of Police and Do Mau as Director of Military Security. Besides these two military followers, only two of Diem's civilian aides appeared periodically in the palace to consult with him: Tran Chanh Thanh (who was later Minister of Information) and Tran Trung Dung (who was Diem's Assistant Minister of Defense). At the time, they both appeared to be idealistic nationalists who were dedicated to supporting Diem as the symbol of honest Vietnamese patriotism. Unfortunately, they had no political following of their own to bring to Diem's aid and were mostly helpless.

On the other side loomed a powerful coalition of enemies who stood to lose much if Diem succeeded in consolidating his power. First in line was General Hinh, Chief of Staff of the fledgling Vietnamese Army, who owed his important position to French political backing. Next were the French-supported politico-religious sects such as the Cao Dai and Hoa Hao, whose militias had been paid to fight alongside French troops. Last, but not least, was the Binh Xuyen mafia organization, which controlled Saigon's opium smuggling, prostitution, and gambling. With the profits from those lucrative enterprises, the Binh Xuyen had also recently bought control of the National Police Directorate General from Chief of State Bao Dai. These gangsters, who had thrived under the corruption and turmoil of the past, could not survive under an effective and honest nationalist government, so they were the first to move against Diem.

BINH XUYEN CONTROL IN SAIGON–CHOLON

I was so young and idealistic that I was not even aware of the very serious danger I was in because I was a close aide to Diem. After our group had to move out of Gia Long Palace we stayed in a hotel in the Chinese twin cities of Saigon–Cholon, which were controlled by the Binh Xuyen. One night I went out with Tran Trung Dung, the Assistant Minister of Defense. Dung introduced me to a Chinese businessman named Ly Kai, explaining that he was an important banker who had been the financial adviser to Bay Vien, the boss of the Binh Xuyen. Recently, though, Ly Kai had decided to side with Diem. I thought that he really had guts to break away from Bay Vien to join Diem's side because the Binh Xuyen were one of the most dangerous foes of Diem in 1954. They were also known for their brutality against their enemies because they operated without any respect for the law. Bay Vien was not one to forgive someone who dared double cross him. He must have felt Ly Kai had to be punished severely as an example to anyone who might be tempted to betray him. Only a few days after meeting Ly Kai with Dung, I learned that Ly Kai had been killed by the Binh Xuyen. His executioners had eaten his liver as well, according to the stories I heard.

As a young idealist who had just returned from the peace and orderliness of the United States, I was quite shocked by Ly Kai's murder. I already knew vaguely about Bay Vien and his Binh Xuyen mafia, but I was not aware of just how brutal and barbarous they were. All of a sudden, I became very aware of just how dangerous Saigon was, and in a personal way because I had visited with Ly Kai so recently. It was now clear that the law and order I had enjoyed in the United States were sorely lacking here in Vietnam. If Ly Kai had been killed that way by the Binh Xuyen they could also easily target me for working with Diem. For the time being, their forces controlled Saigon and Cholon and Diem was not in a position to protect me or anybody else who dared to help him.

After the Ly Kai incident, I told Vo Van Hai that it was not safe for us to be in Cholon, so close to the Binh Xuyen headquarters. He arranged to move us to another government house on Hai Ba Trung Street in central Saigon. Ly Kai's death scared some of the other members of my group enough to prompt them to request safe jobs at Vietnamese embassies abroad. The first to leave was Du Phuoc Long, who was very nervous about the insecurity in Saigon and eager to get back to America. After his sudden, unannounced departure from Saigon we learned that he had contacted Madame Tran Van Chuong, the Permanent Observer of South Vietnam at the UN in New York. She was in Saigon at the time and arranged to have her husband (the Ambassador to the United States) give him a job at the Vietnamese Embassy in Washington, DC. After Du Phuoc Long's departure from Saigon, two others also managed to get themselves assigned as Consul General in Djakarta, Indonesia, and Consul General in New Delhi, India.

With these departures, our original group of six American-trained students was down to three of us who remained in Saigon to help Diem. Of the three of us, however, I was the only one who continued to work closely with Diem in Gia Long Palace. I was also the only one to refuse to join the secret Can Lao Party of Ngo Dinh Nhu (Diem's brother and primary adviser). The two others, Huynh Van Lang and Bui Kien Thanh, both joined the Can Lao and worked on Nhu's secret projects. Lang was appointed Director General of the Exchange Office, which controlled the issuance of licenses for exchanging Vietnamese piasters into foreign currency at the official rate, which was highly advantageous for those who managed to obtain the licenses. It was an important and sensitive position, which Nhu wanted to control, so Lang was a good choice as he was also the Treasurer of the Can Lao Party. Thanh similarly became a Can Lao Party member and worked for Nhu on covert financial projects for the Can Lao as an executive at the National Bank of Vietnam.

MY INITIAL ASSIGNMENTS

Because of my proficiency in English and French and my interest in journalism, I was initially tapped to serve as Diem's Press Secretary and interpreter for meetings with foreign VIPs. When Diem asked me where I wanted to work, however, I immediately told him I would like to work in the office administering American aid to Vietnam. I thought that foreign aid was one of the most important forces shaping South Vietnam, so it would be an important and fulfilling job for me. In 1954 the office handling Foreign Aid was called the Administration de l'Aide Étrangère (Administration of Foreign Aid, or AAE). A French-trained public works engineer named Dinh Quang Chieu was the Administrator General there. I went to AAE to work as Chieu's assistant a few days after my return to Vietnam. I saw immediately that Chieu had a very limited view of the scope of his office, and I realized that the agency needed a major overhaul to match the enormous importance American aid had for Diem and South Vietnam. Chieu had a "small accounting" approach to his work and wasted all his time adding up the various accounts and detailed items, even though all of it was already appropriated. This was not adequate for the increasingly important role that US aid was supposed to play. I quickly reported to Diem what I had observed and intended to change, but he did not say anything.

I did not know for sure if Chieu lobbied Diem to keep me away from his AAE office to protect his job, but it seemed he must have because the next day I was called to the Palace. Diem told me that I was needed much more with him and that I would serve as his Press Secretary and interpreter after all. I told Diem that if I was to function effectively, an office of the Presidential Press Secretary had to be created and organized with adequate staff and equipment. Diem did not object, so I thought that he agreed with my suggestion. Afterwards, however, nobody took any action whatsoever, despite my repeated reminders to Diem.

Very soon I learned that this kind of situation was all too common in the Palace because Diem was no great organizer or decision maker. He just behaved in modern administration like an old-time mandarin. He was incapable of systematically organizing a plan and then adhering to it for maximum efficiency. Everything he did seemed to be done on a moment's impulse or because of some urgent external pressure. There were no preset goals or plans of action. I found it quite difficult to work with him under these conditions. Adding to my difficulties, my own position was one that was completely improvised and grossly inadequate. I was only "detached" to the President's Office to work as the Presidential Press Secretary. Officially, I was still on the payroll of AAE as an Assistant to the Administrator General. I told Diem that it was difficult for me to function in this makeshift way, but there was no rush to remedy the situation.

As the South Vietnamese government was organized then, the President's Office was patterned on a French model and there was no provision for an American-style Press Secretary with Cabinet rank. There was a Minister of Information, who often acted as the spokesperson for the Government. At the President's Office itself, press relations was one of the many duties handled by the President's Chief of Private Cabinet, Vo Van Hai. With Diem, though, Hai functioned more like a Private Secretary in charge of the confidential matters of the President. Hai did not have any staff of his own to help and he worked impossibly long hours, staying in the Palace at all times without any organized schedule. It seemed that Hai was working in the same unorganized and unsystematic way as Diem was. As a result of all of this, although I had the duties of a Presidential Press Secretary, there was no clear chain of command for me to follow when it came to Diem's press relations. I also lacked the personal authority and the staff that were necessary to carry out my important responsibilities properly.

Although Diem's outdated mandarin way of doing things troubled and frustrated me, I told myself that I had to be patient. I was young and inexperienced, after all. I had just returned from America and I still had much to learn of the ways of an underdeveloped country like Vietnam. Furthermore, I told myself that my job was to help Diem in any way possible and not to change him. Reluctantly, I tried my best to do what Diem wanted me to do. What he wanted most of all was to have me available at all times at the Palace for anything he could think of doing, much like Vo Van Hai. Most of the time, this meant interpreting for Diem. I did not like interpreting much, however, and it became an even more bothersome task later when I was appointed Director General of Vietnam Press in 1957. I hoped to build up Vietnam Press into a national news agency that functioned as independently from the government as possible, so I repeatedly suggested to Diem that he should call someone else from the Foreign Affairs Ministry to interpret for him. Diem insisted, though, that I had to be available at all times to interpret for him.

I later heard reports that Diem would complain that I was "too arrogant" because I "often refused Presidential orders to come to the Palace to interpret." Eventually, I realized that Diem liked me to interpret for him and felt more at ease with that arrangement because he considered me basically as a member of his family. Interpreters from the Foreign Affairs Ministry, on the other hand, were "strangers" to Diem. He didn't have the same confidence and trust in them, no matter how competent they were. With me, he felt comfortable enough to ask for help beyond just basic translation. Often, when he did not know a word or how to formulate an idea, he would whisper to me in our unique Vietnamese accents from Hue, which were not easily understood even by most other Vietnamese. That way I could prompt him the right way without anyone else knowing that I was telling him what to say. On some other rare occasions, when I noticed that Diem said something wrong, I was candid enough to point it out to him in Vietnamese and I would skip the error in my English translation. Those things could not happen with a stranger, because with strangers Diem felt he had to appear as an omniscient and omnipotent leader at all times. He seemed to see it as a big advantage when he had me interpreting for him, because any mistake he made would "stay in the family" and not cause him to lose prestige.

DIEM AND TRINH MINH THE

While Diem was still an underdog Prime Minister, fighting for survival against a host of political enemies in Saigon, he continued to display many of the qualities that had earned him his reputation as a trustworthy leader of integrity. At that time, he still appeared to be a man of honesty and simplicity. Colonel Edward Lansdale, the legendary CIA agent sent to Vietnam after his success in the Philippines, encouraged Diem to imitate the example of Philippine President Ramón Magsaysay. That meant getting close to the people and showing that he cared for them. In those early days, Diem made several field trips to the provinces to do that. Those meetings with people were casual and real, unlike later when they became staged events. I enjoyed being with Diem on those trips. He seemed relaxed, talking directly with the people who came to see him. Sometimes he would turn to me and ask, "What do you think I can say to these people here?" I would scribble some short sentences for him and he improvised on the spot, using simple, direct language to address the people. On those occasions there was genuine communication and contact between the people and their leader, whose reputation they had heard about but whom they had never met.

In 1954, it seemed to be a miracle that Diem survived and succeeded in defeating his many political enemies in Saigon. More than anything, I believe, it was precisely the humble attitude of Diem and his reputation of honesty that rallied many of the good people in Vietnam to his side against his largely crooked enemies. People from all walks of life did not hesitate to do whatever was needed to help him survive because they believed in Ngo Dinh Diem, and Diem lived up to those beliefs at the time. One of the first very important political successes for Diem, as engineered by Lansdale, was the decision of General Trinh Minh The to rally to Diem's side and to start fighting against the Binh Xuyen gangsters.

Trinh Minh The had risen through the ranks of the Cao Dai militia forces, but he broke away from the mainstream of the Cao Dai sect because it was still pro-French. He adopted an anti-French, anti-Communist position and established his headquarters in the Black Lady Mountain near Tay Ninh, where he fought against both Communists and French. With his reputation as a hard fighter and a man of integrity, General The succeeded in rallying many followers and troops to his command. He had become a significant force by the time Diem came to power in Saigon. Because his political stand was identical to Diem's — anti-French and anti-Communist — General The immediately attracted the attention of Diem and Lansdale. In early February 1955, I was sent for a meeting with General The along with a few of Lansdale's aides. The purpose of the meeting was to "compare notes" on the critical situation in South Vietnam and to adopt a plan of action to counter the various threats against Diem. I was immediately impressed with The, who appeared to be a direct and honest man. I was glad that this seasoned guerrilla fighter had rallied to Diem's side.

The joining of forces between Ngo Dinh Diem and Trinh Minh The enhanced not only Diem's military power but also his political strength. Symbolically, it was the coming together of the Confucian mandarin with an unblemished reputation of honesty from Central Vietnam and the tough guerrilla leader with an uncompromising nationalist position from South Vietnam. I thought it was a good foundation to build on for a genuine movement toward union among all nationalists in the country, regardless of religious affiliation, social background, or regional difference. Unfortunately, the union was not to last and the politics of intrigue soon took over. Trinh Minh The himself was killed during the armed confrontation between Diem and the Binh Xuyen. In one of the final skirmishes with the Binh Xuyen, as they were withdrawing from Saigon, The was mysteriously shot in the back.

Although there was a large state funeral for him and the papers reported that General The had been shot by "French colonialists and their Binh Xuyen allies," rumors circulated in Saigon that he was actually killed on Ngo Dinh Nhu's secret order. The reasoning, which I thought was at least somewhat credible, was that Nhu was afraid that The's increasing popularity and close friendship with Lansdale made him a threat to Diem. The's anti-Communist and anti-French credentials, which were proven on South Vietnam's battlefields, were much more impressive than Diem's. Critics of Diem argued that Diem's nationalist reputation was based more on exaggerations spread by his supporters than on reality. Diem's story that he had resigned as Interior Minister in 1933 as a result of his unmet demand for "nationalist reforms," even if true, was a much weaker narrative than The's years of actually fighting against the French and Communists. Furthermore, The was not saddled with a corrupt family, as Diem's was perceived to be by many in Saigon, myself included. The, therefore, could have become a dangerous political rival for Diem. The apparently had trusted Diem, though, and he did not watch his back. That moment — with the Binh Xuyen basically defeated and The's help no longer essential — was an opportune one for Nhu to have The eliminated. He could be shot and his death blamed on the Binh Xuyen and the French. Although there was no smoking gun proof of this story about The's mysterious death, it seemed plausible to me. Saigon's tumultuous politics were filled with other such conspiracies, intrigues, and rumors, so it was hard to dismiss the story as fantasy although it was also difficult to accept it as a certain fact. I also believed that Nhu was definitely ruthless enough to give such an order.

Although I was puzzled by Trinh Minh The's death, I knew that it was unwise to investigate further. I feared that discovering the truth of such a suspicious episode would make me someone who knew too much in the eyes of the Ngo family, a dangerous position indeed. I reasoned with myself that I was not back in Vietnam to investigate the Ngo family, especially Ngo Dinh Nhu, but to serve the country and help Diem. Years later, after I had settled in the United States and Lansdale had retired, I asked him about the incident. In his characteristically enigmatic way, Lansdale related to me what he saw while visiting Diem immediately following The's death. He said that Diem wept as he was holding General The's military hat. Lansdale added that Diem said something to the effect that he was shocked and surprised when Nhu had brought the news. It was typical of Lansdale to relate events blandly like that, avoiding controversial matters, and he told me much the same as what he wrote in his memoir.[1] I strongly suspected that Lansdale knew more of The's death than he told me, though. I interpreted his cryptic remarks on the incident to mean that even if Nhu had ordered the assassination, Diem himself had not known (and probably would not have approved) of any plans to kill The.

Unsatisfied with Lansdale's understated account, on a visit back to Vietnam in the early 1990s I sought out the truth from the famous Communist spy Pham Xuan An. He had a reputation for knowing the deepest secrets of South Vietnamese politics, and we had been close friends. I first met An in 1959, when he had just returned from journalism training in the United States and I hired him at Vietnam Press. An had a good rapport with Dr. Tran Kim Tuyen, the head of Ngo Dinh Nhu's secret service, the innocuously named Presidential Office of Political Research. As a result, I assigned An as Vietnam Press's liaison with Tuyen to cover politically sensitive news coming from the President's Office or from Nhu and Tuyen. Like everyone else in Saigon, I had no idea whatsoever that An was a Communist mole back then. An was simply an extremely likeable guy with a good sense of humor and a sharp mind. He seemed to know everybody in South Vietnam and to know about everything that happened. That made him a perfect journalist, in addition to an intelligence-gathering spy. He collected great information for both of his jobs, and I had never had any reason to distrust or disbelieve him.

An still lived in Saigon in the 1990s, where he served as a living encyclopedia on the secrets of Vietnamese politics for international journalists and authors. Although he suffered from gout and from his lifetime of chain smoking, An was as quick-witted as ever and still remembered everything and everybody in Vietnam. I visited him many times then to talk about the past. One of the things I asked An about was Trinh Minh The's death. An did not hesitate in telling me that it had been exactly as I had suspected: that Trinh Minh The had been assassinated on Ngo Dinh Nhu's order. According to An, Nhu had bought off an officer in The's Cao Dai faction to carry out the secret killing. Additionally, he said, two Cao Dai generals and a Saigon politician with Cao Dai connections had known about the assassination of The. I believed An and thought these details sounded truthful. An was also no longer close with the Communist government (and had never seemed to be involved in spreading disinformation), so I couldn't see any agenda that he might have been pushing when it came to this mysterious, long past event.

Pham Xuan An's version of the assassination of The by Ngo Dinh Nhu was logical and it also explained another mysterious event that I personally witnessed. In February 1957, I was with Diem at a fair in the highland city of Ban Me Thuot when there was an assassination attempt on him. I was standing just a few feet from Diem as he was cutting the ribbon to open the fair. Suddenly, I heard some commotion nearby and I saw Diem's bodyguards subduing a small man with a submachine gun. It was an extremely reliable weapon designed for paratroopers, but luckily the gun jammed after a couple of wild shots and Diem was unharmed. Afterwards, I noticed that there were no newspaper reports or any other accounts of the incident, nor was there any information about the man who tried to kill Diem. I heard a rumor that he was connected with the Cao Dai and that his unsuccessful assassination attempt was retaliation for the murder of Trinh Minh The. Another rumor speculated that the Communists were really behind the plot. The truth was a little bit of both, as the would-be assassin Ha Minh Tri was a Communist agent with ties to the Cao Dai. Tri was arrested by Nhu's secret police and quietly held in jail because Diem and Nhu did not want any more attention paid to the affair. They kept him alive, hoping to extract information on his accomplices, but Tri never divulged the information. In 1965, after the coup that overthrew the Diem regime, Tri was released from jail along with a great number of other political prisoners.

REPEATED MANILA TRIPS

During late 1954, Diem was having heated confrontations with the pro-French Armed Forces Chief of Staff General Hinh. At first, Gen. Hinh had the upper hand because he had the whole Vietnamese Armed Forces under his command, whereas Diem had little except a small bodyguard. Eventually, after Gen. The's troops and a number of military units rallied to Diem's government, the balance of power shifted. The threat of General Hinh was finally ended when Diem refused orders from Bao Dai to go to Paris "for consultations" about the dispute with Gen. Hinh. In all likelihood, Bao Dai would have removed Diem from office, but instead Diem stayed in Saigon and removed Hinh from command. Before the tide turned in Diem's favor, however, Lansdale and his aides resorted to some clever schemes to stall any decisive action by Gen. Hinh against Diem. One way that Lansdale bought time for Diem was by organizing sudden trips to Manila for Vietnamese military officers to meet President Magsaysay. These were officially "study" trips to see how the Philippines had defeated their Communist insurgency. Their main purpose, however, was to temporarily remove Gen. Hinh's key subordinates so that Hinh could not stage a coup. I went as an aide representing Diem, and Lansdale sent one of his team members, Rufus Phillips.

Perhaps because of my repeated trips to the Philippines in the company of Hinh's key aides, Diem got the idea that I was a sort of a "Manila expert" who knew the town well. As a result, I was a member of his delegation when he made a state visit to the Philippines at the invitation of President Magsaysay. Because of the Lansdale connection and the assistance the Philippines was providing Vietnam, relations between South Vietnam and the Philippines were quite friendly. Lansdale encouraged Diem to model his presidential style after that of Magsaysay, who was accessible and friendly with the people he led. In those early days Diem generally listened, although later he became aloof and condescending to the people.

Sometime in 1957, a few months after being appointed Director General of the Vietnam Press news agency, I was summoned to the Palace and Diem told me that I had to go to the Philippines as a member of the South Vietnamese delegation to the Asian Public Administration Conference in Baguio, the mountain resort near Manila. Although I had studied public administration at Cornell and was also teaching on the subject at the National Institute of Administration (NIA) in Saigon, I told Diem that my priority was Vietnam Press and I did not want to go to the conference. I had a lot of work to do at Vietnam Press because I had just started reorganizing it. Diem, however, overruled my objections and said that I had to go to Manila and make sure that everything was secure for the South Vietnamese delegation. It was a very distinguished delegation, including the head of the NIA, Professor Vu Quoc Thong, the Secretary General of the President's Office, and the Mayor of Dalat, who was a protégé of Ngo Dinh Nhu.

The conference in Baguio went smoothly, without incident. When it ended, the delegation left Baguio for Manila. On that last day before flying back to Saigon, we stayed at the Manila Hotel. Because our work was finished, I went to visit a friend in Manila that night and left the other delegates on their own. They wanted to go see the jai alai game that was being played in a building not too far from the hotel. They should have just taken a regular taxi there, but instead they took a convertible car driven by a crook, who apparently had connections with local thieves. The driver offered them a cheap price for the ride to the game as bait to lure the delegates, who were not familiar with Manila. When they accepted the ride, instead of going to the jai alai game the driver drove the delegates into a dark alley where a bunch of guys dressed like women jumped them and stole their wallets.

The next morning, the delegates told me about the incident and said that they wanted to file a police report. They had lost their wallets and some money, so they wanted it all back. I dissuaded them from doing so, explaining that they would probably never get anything back. If they brought attention to the incident, however, they might face uncomfortable questions by local reporters, who could write some unpleasant stories, such as, "What were these VIPs doing in a dark alley in Manila and why were they with those 'transvestites'?" There might also end up being some unpleasant stories back home, I cautioned. The better course of action, I told them, was to keep quiet and fly home to Saigon without filing any official complaint about the incident, which they did.

BANDUNG CONFERENCE IN INDONESIA

South Vietnam was invited to participate in the famous Bandung Conference in April 1955. Whereas most delegations to the conference were led by the country's head of state, it was impossible for Ngo Dinh Diem to leave Saigon at the time when his political survival was still threatened by General Hinh and the Binh Xuyen. Diem instead sent Nguyen Van Thoai as head of the South Vietnamese delegation. Thoai was the Minister of Planning and Reconstruction and was also related to Diem's sister. He was barely known in Vietnam, however, because he had spent most of his life as a research scientist at the famous Collège de France in Paris. Other members of the delegation included myself, Nguyen Huu Chau (who later became Diem's Secretary of State at the Presidency), NIA head Professor Thong, and his brother who was a law professor. Swashbuckling General The, as unlikely a diplomat as could be imagined, was also sent as a delegation member. He was quite memorable, wearing a khaki shirt riddled with bullet holes at an international conference. He proudly refused to change out of it, however, because he said the shirt was proof to all attending that he had really fought to defend his nationalist beliefs against both Communists and colonialists. Regrettably, I did not get much opportunity to talk with The on this trip, which was the last time I saw him before he was killed.

As the only member of the delegation who spoke English, I was very busy throughout the conference. There was no interpreting provided by the conference for the confidential political sessions, so I had to act as the ear and brain for the whole delegation in these important discussions. I had to explain what was being said by the other delegations and at the same time I had to be drafting speeches for our delegation to respond and participate in the discussions. Professor Thong, in his nervous way, always wanted to know immediately what was said in English, sentence by sentence. I told him it was impossible for me to instantaneously interpret like that as I had to listen carefully to the whole speech in order to prepare rebuttal speeches as needed. I had to function as spokesman for the delegation as well as its unofficial interpreter, so it was quite a stressful job.

Because Thoai and I got along well, we took the same suite at the hotel assigned to our delegation and we worked closely together during the whole conference. There was some tension in the air because Communist North Vietnam was there, as was a delegation from Red China led by Chou En Lai. There also seemed to be rivalry among the several political stars vying to command the attention of the conference participants, including President Sukarno of the host country Indonesia, Prime Minister Nehru of India, and the urbane Chinese Foreign Minister Chou En Lai. Considering that the purpose of the Bandung Conference was to promote "pancha sila" (the five principles of peaceful coexistence) among nations of Asia, Thoai and I decided that it was appropriate for our delegation to show that South Vietnam was opposed only to Communist aggression, not to peaceful coexistence. Tactically, we decided to demonstrate that we were not rabidly anti-Communist, bent on attacking the Communist delegations at every opportunity. We intended to display a good sense of restrained civility and make clear our desire to cooperate.

I remember two incidents during the conference that tested our position. First, before the conference even officially opened, our delegation was invited to meet with Prime Minister Nehru of India at the residence of the Indian delegation. We received a simple invitation to tea from Nehru, but the reason for the meeting was not clear to us. Thoai and I decided to accept the invitation anyway, because our intention was to show openness and cooperation with anything reasonable. We suspected that there was some secret ploy in Nehru's mind in inviting us to tea, but we thought that going to find out was much better than not going. We did not want to risk unnecessarily antagonizing such an important country for South Vietnam. Not only was India a key neutralist country that we hoped to win over, but it was also the chair of the International Control Commission (ICC) overseeing the Geneva Accords after the French Indochina War.

At the Indian tea party, only Prime Minister Nehru and his daughter Indira Gandhi (who later became Prime Minister of India herself), serving as official hostess, were present. Immediately upon arrival, we sensed that Nehru was edgy and nervous. After the civilities, Nehru started lecturing us about the merits of India's neutralist policy and the necessity for peaceful coexistence in the world and especially in Asia. The lecture included several critical comments against South Vietnam, which were uncalled for and improper in such a setting. The tone was pedantic and arrogant, far from diplomatic. We were shocked, and I thought to myself, "What is this man trying to do? Why this uncalled-for lecture? Who does he think he is?"

Thoai and I quickly decided to rebut Nehru's lecture. We pointed out that we had come to the conference because we believed in the spirit of true peaceful coexistence, and that was why we decided to accept his unexpected invitation. We hoped that India was interested in friendly relations with South Vietnam as well as all other countries of Asia. We politely explained that the people of South Vietnam, like the people of India, wanted self-determination and refused to have any form of government imposed against their will. Like those in India, people in South Vietnam had not fought Western colonialism in order to be subjected again to another form of oppression. We insisted that we should not be misunderstood as being rabidly anti-Communist for anti-Communism's sake. We too wanted to coexist peacefully with our neighbors, but we were also determined to defend our right to remain *non*-Communist Vietnamese, living peacefully in a free society, without being threatened by armed infiltration from our neighbor.

As he was listening, it seemed that Nehru suddenly realized we were reasonable after all, and we should not have been lectured in the first place. Soon afterwards, when the exchange of speeches ended, Mrs. Indira Gandhi took Thoai and myself aside and said, "Please accept our apologies. My father has been very tired and nervous, coming to this conference." Very charmingly, she explained further in great sincerity that somehow he wrongly felt that he was the "host" instead of President Sukarno and this was "*his*" conference. Therefore, he felt that he had the duty to lecture everyone on India's neutralist policy and "pancha sila." She concluded, "You obviously did not need to be lectured and I see that your non-Communist position is very understandable and we respect it. Please again accept our apologies." We told her that we understood fully and that everything was fine, and then we left on very friendly terms. Thoai and I observed after the tea party incident that Nehru seemed to be very friendly toward the South Vietnam delegation, the way we hoped things would be.

The second difficult incident during the Bandung Conference related to the precarious position of the Diem government. At that moment Saigon was on the verge of hostilities between Diem and the Binh Xuyen. Very late one evening, while Thoai and I stayed up to talk, we thought of going down to the hotel newsstand to get a copy of the latest newspapers. To our great surprise, we saw banner headlines reading, "South Vietnam Delegation Head Resigns!" I was shocked and asked Thoai if it were true and how did it happen. He said that it was not true and that he had been misunderstood. He explained that before leaving for Bandung he had left his aide with a statement to be used in case of armed confrontation with the Binh Xuyen. Thoai said that the statement was drafted to say that he was for national unity among all non-Communist Vietnamese because it was enough to fight against one common Communist enemy, so there was no need to fight among non-Communists as well. He maintained in the statement that further bloodshed and division had to be avoided at all cost. Finally, the statement said that he would resign and give up his ministerial post if that national union policy were not followed.

Thoai thought that apparently there had been a gross misinterpretation of his statement, which evidently had been made available in Saigon and used as an indirect protest against Diem's confrontation with the Binh Xuyen. He speculated that his aide, who was sympathetic to the Binh Xuyen and had French friends, must have leaked it to the press prematurely. I suggested to Thoai that he should immediately make a statement at Bandung to deny the misinterpretation of his leaked statement and to make it clear that he was still the head of the South Vietnamese delegation. He did what was suggested, and as a result the South Vietnamese delegation got additional press coverage and Thoai had the opportunity to clarify his support of Ngo Dinh Diem.

My participation in the Bandung Conference of 1955 was an eye-opener. It was a unique occasion for me to see in action many of the major political figures of the world, from Nehru of India to Nasser of Egypt. I must say that among them all Chou En Lai, whose statesmanlike and urbane behavior impressed the whole conference, emerged as the greatest star. I regretted, though, that there was no communication between the South Vietnamese delegation and the North Vietnamese, who were led by Prime Minister Pham Van Dong. The issue of communication between the two antagonistic governments was extremely sensitive, especially in the context of the intense Cold War atmosphere prevailing in 1955. Despite that, I still felt that it would have been useful to establish at least some minimum degree of communication between the two delegations. From the point of view of South Vietnam it would have been politically wise to initiate communication with North Vietnam, because if they rejected our initiative they would appear intransigent and lose stature. Due to the Cold War climate and the shaky position of the Diem government at the time, however, no thought was given to this issue and nothing was done to take advantage of the opportunity provided by the conference to open up communication between the two Vietnams.

It was perhaps a naive hope on my part to believe in such cooperation amidst the tensions of the Cold War, but it was sincere even if futile. I really thought that Ngo Dinh Diem should have had better political vision. He could have shown the world that he was a real patriot who put the interests of the Vietnamese people — regardless of whether they lived in the North or the South — above the shortsighted necessities of Cold War alignment. The Bandung Conference could have been the starting point for a new political drive to enlist the support of the whole world for the survival of a free, non-Communist South Vietnam. Diem could have become the peacemaker, supported by the West, the entire Vietnamese people, and the non-aligned nations in the world, advocating peaceful coexistence between South and North Vietnam as well as other Communist countries. South Vietnam could have gained a stronger political position as a non-Communist country eager to live in peace with all its neighbors but also resolved to defend its freedom for self-determination as a non-aligned nation.

This political position was too progressive for the mid-1950s when the world was divided in Cold War confrontation, but it could have made a significant contribution toward the reduction of hostility between North and South Vietnam as well as other countries divided by the Cold War.

Diem in 1955, with his credentials as the nationalist leader who had just united South Vietnam against French colonialists and their protégés, could have convinced his powerful American ally to adopt an enlightened Vietnam policy, which would have averted the need for war in Vietnam. Such an enlightened approach would have also benefited the whole Asian continent. The main purpose of the 1955 Bandung Conference, after all, was to promote such policies. In 1955 and 1956, some of the most respected non-aligned Asian leaders, like Nehru and U Nu of Burma, repeatedly came to Saigon to visit Diem and steer him in this direction. I had to interpret for Diem during several of these meetings. I remember well the obvious sympathy Nehru and U Nu had for Diem. At that time, Diem had just consolidated his power as the President and had not yet become involved in the politics of corruption and family dictatorship. I firmly believed that there was a real opportunity then for Diem to have become an enlightened leader who preserved peace and independence for both Vietnams.

Unfortunately, though, despite the friendly overtures made by Nehru and U Nu, Diem failed to adopt a farsighted policy of serving the interests of the entire Vietnamese people, instead embracing armed conflict as dictated by the Cold War. There were, of course, enormous obstacles to adopting a non-dogmatic policy that would overcome the ideological divisions of the time (including on both the Communist and anti-Communist sides), but I still felt that Diem missed the chance to present himself to the people of Vietnam and the whole world as a patriot and peacemaker. Instead, he started to become an unpopular dictator in South Vietnam, pursuing shortsighted Cold War policies and allowing the country to become the victim of his family's corruption. It was a major missed opportunity.

PUBLISHING VIETNAM'S FIRST ENGLISH-LANGUAGE NEWSPAPER

By the end of 1955 Ngo Dinh Diem had greatly strengthened his position, thanks in part to the covert help of Lansdale and his team. Despite heavy odds against him, Prime Minister Diem had succeeded in defeating all his enemies to become the uncontested leader of South Vietnam. Diem made perhaps his first political mistake at this point, though. In a rush, while other urgent problems still had to be addressed, the government organized a referendum to remove Bao Dai as Head of State and make Diem President of a new "Republic of Vietnam." Although it was indeed proper for Diem to try to change the ambiguous "State of Vietnam" into the Republic of Vietnam, the referendum and Bao Dai's removal were carried out in an unwise manner that undermined the new Republic's legitimacy and needlessly humiliated the former Emperor. Just like phony elections in Communist countries, of which Diem was very critical, this nationwide election was so rigged that Diem won with a nearly unanimous 98.2 percent of the vote. This referendum could have been settled differently, fairly and without manipulation, because Bao Dai had already lost much credibility in South Vietnam and Diem had gained considerable respect since he had returned to Saigon. Instead of winning an honest vote and establishing a precedent for democracy in South Vietnam, however, Diem relied on deceit to give his election the illusion of universal approval. This first, fraudulent election was a bad sign of what was to take place under the guise of electoral process in Vietnam.

The decision by Diem to organize this sham election against Bao Dai spoke volumes about Diem's true character, doing considerable political damage to him in the long run. It began the destruction of Diem's reputation for honesty, which was his primary — and almost only — asset as a politician. Bao Dai had appointed Diem Prime Minister before, and Diem himself had sworn allegiance to Bao Dai as Head of State and Emperor (although he did not officially possess that title after his 1945 abdication). For someone like Diem, with his reputation of Confucian integrity and absolute respect for his given word, to reverse course and break his own promises was seriously to compromise his image. Furthermore, on a more practical level, by humiliating Bao Dai, Diem antagonized and lost the support of some important members of the royal family who were still in Vietnam.

After nearly two years working with Ngo Dinh Diem, I was beginning to see the real man behind the legend and I was somewhat disillusioned. Nevertheless, I kept telling myself that I had to stick it through. I had just barely begun the long struggle to adapt and learn how to help Diem build a free, democratic society in South Vietnam. I encouraged myself by reasoning that now was the time for me to discard my idealistic thinking about democracy and government that I had developed at Cornell and to see how a "government of men" in an underdeveloped country really functioned. I was curious to see whether such a government could be transformed eventually into a "government of law" leading toward the idealistic "government of the people, by the people, and for the people." Could it work in South Vietnam under Diem?

I was somewhat puzzled at this time by Ngo Dinh Nhu and his increasing importance in Diem's government. After I met Diem in the United States, the second member of the Ngo family I met was Ngo Dinh Luyen, Diem's Roving Ambassador in Europe. Throughout 1955 and 1956, I met him many more times at the Independence Palace in Saigon. During those days when Diem was still in a shaky position, Luyen seemed to have influence with Diem comparable to that of Nhu and Diem's other brothers. After Diem became more firmly established, however, it was evident that Nhu shoved Luyen aside. Luyen was sent overseas and asked to stay away from Diem, so I didn't get to meet with him anymore. It appeared to me that Nhu had won the battle to establish a monopoly on advice to Diem.

Personally, I had a fairly good relationship with Ngo Dinh Nhu. Instinctively, though, I stayed away from him as much as possible. In the early days, when I was working in Independence Palace handling press relations for the President, I had a revealing experience with Nhu that I remembered a long time afterwards. It was nothing unpleasant, but it showed me the way Nhu operated, and my reaction perhaps showed Nhu that I would not readily accept his devious methods. While I was trying to organize the Presidential Press Bureau, I hired some staff with journalistic backgrounds to assist me. One day at the end of the month, Nhu brought me a big bundle of money wrapped in a newspaper and told me to use it any way I wanted. I told him that I could not take so much cash and that I preferred to pay my employees by check, which would be better for accounting purposes. Nhu just frowned at me with obvious displeasure and then walked away without saying anything. I suspected Nhu thought that I was a weird fellow for refusing to accept all that money!

One practical lesson I began to learn after working close to Diem for a while was that if I wanted to organize my work systematically I had to try to stay away from him as much as possible. I had learned that Diem was not good at organizing or planning. Everything he did or ordered to be done seemed to be prompted by that moment's impulse and there was constant improvisation on the spot. I found it very difficult to work under these conditions. I told myself, however, that Diem was the leader and I was the follower, so I had to adapt myself accordingly. Because of this, I realized that I had to abandon my plans to reorganize the Presidential Press Office.

I saw no way to change the existing press setup into a more efficient and logical one because Diem himself preferred handling press relations according to his whims. If Diem felt that the Minister of Information could handle the press on a particular subject, then the Minister would serve as the spokesman. If, on the other hand, Diem felt that someone other than the Minister of Information should be his spokesman, then that person would be summoned to take care of the matter. There was no regular channel for press relations or single person with the competence and stature to be the permanent spokesman for the President in the way that the US Presidential Press Secretary served. Vo Van Hai, Diem's Private Secretary, was technically supposed to handle press relations for the President. Without any staff of his own, however, he functioned more like a faithful relative helping an elderly, mandarin family member than as a high-level government spokesman. My own Presidential Press Office, which had no definite function nor official status, added to this confusing situation rather than relieving it.

Realizing that I could not hope to improve the chaos of Diem's press relations and disliking the stress of working closely with Diem in his disordered way, I lost interest in continuing as the Presidential Press Secretary. I still wanted to help Diem as the leader of South Vietnam, but I wanted to work as far away from him as possible. While I was thinking of a way to translate that idea into practice, two different suggestions prompted me to make a move. First, an American couple, Gene and Ann Gregory, arrived in Saigon and looked me up. Gene had worked for USIS in Saigon during the 1950s and had taken some courses at Cornell, but he only knew me by reputation from some of my professors. Gene and Ann told me that they were interested in collaborating with me to publish a privately owned English newspaper. A few days later, at one of the cocktail receptions given by the US Ambassador, by coincidence I was talking with the Minister of Information and the Director of US Aid. The latter observed that there were only Vietnamese and French newspapers in Saigon, so English-speaking people had nothing to read and no way of getting South Vietnamese views. Half-jokingly and half-serious, both of them turned to me and said, "You came back from the US. Why don't you, with some of your US-trained Vietnamese friends, start an English newspaper?" In jest, I replied, "Okay, if you will buy and support it, I'll publish it."

The idea of publishing the first English newspaper in Saigon for the benefit of the English-speaking community was a good one in principle, but it was a formidable challenge in practice. The difficulties were overwhelming. In 1956 there was only a handful of Vietnamese who were proficient enough in English to write newspaper articles. At the time there were no computers accessible and the technical job of typesetting in English was almost impossible. The biggest printing plant in Saigon lacked any typesetters who could read English, so the errors were endless. Because they could not read the language, it was very slow for them to set each letter of the unfamiliar English words and they made many mistakes. After the proofreader corrected the errors that were made the first time, there was no certainty that the typesetters would not introduce new errors afterwards. Often, an error on the first word of a sentence would be corrected and retyped by the typesetter, but then a new error would appear on the second word of the sentence and the same process was repeated again and again. Luckily for me, I found the most patient proofreader in Ann Gregory. She put up with an almost endless correction process in the beginning. It took some time, but eventually the typesetters became better acquainted with English words, which made the process at least bearable.

I was aware of these difficulties involved in the publishing of the first English newspaper in Saigon, but I decided to try it because I thought it was worth doing. I could get away from government service and at the same time help some of the American-trained Vietnamese who had returned to Saigon. At the time, there was a kind of discrimination against the American-educated Vietnamese who were looking for government jobs. The French-educated Vietnamese who were working in the Civil Service Personnel Office had no knowledge of the US education system and did not know how to evaluate the American degrees. They did not even know that an American bachelor's degree was supposed to be equivalent to a French *Licence*. They confused American bachelor's degrees with the French Baccalaureat, thus disqualifying US-educated candidates from government jobs requiring university degrees. I hired a few of these jobless returnees to work with me on the new English newspaper.

I resigned from government service and decided at first to publish a weekly paper, patterned on the prestigious British *Manchester Guardian*. It was named *The Times of Vietnam*, and I was its first Publisher and Editor. The weekly paper was an instant success and I got a very good response from readers, both in terms of editorial comments and paid subscriptions. After a number of issues, I decided to make it a daily newspaper. I was very busy once we made *The Times of Vietnam* daily because our staff was limited in terms of both number and talent. I ended up writing most of the important articles and editorials myself. Besides assuming the editorial duties, I was also the business manager for the newspaper and I handled the sensitive task of dealing with the Information Ministry censors.

The censors did not know enough English to comprehend the exact meaning of what was written in the paper. They often decided to block articles that they did not fully understand, just to be on the safe side. My patience was sorely tested with these censors at times. Fortunately, they knew that I was a close friend of their boss, Minister of Information Tran Chanh Thanh. I played tennis with him regularly and we were on very good terms. As a result, whenever I intervened, the censors released the articles that at first they had decided to stop. Minister Thanh himself also knew of my relationship with President Diem, so he trusted my judgment. Eventually, he must have given word to his censors to just do their job pro forma and they started to approve everything that I published.

I was very happy that my attempt to publish the first English paper in Saigon was successful despite all the difficulties involved. I always felt that private business was interesting and had greater opportunity for initiative and innovation than did government service. I was glad to find that my hunch was right. After I left government service, I became more active in the community to get the widest possible exposure for the newspaper and make new contacts. I began lecturing on US Government and on International Relations at the National Institute of Administration. I also became a member of several civic organizations, among them the Rotary and the Junior Chamber of Commerce International (JCI). At the time, the JCI was trying to raise funds for Operation Brotherhood's medical care program for refugees from North Vietnam. They organized a speaking tour in the United States during 1956 for a selected group of Vietnamese JCI members and I was asked to participate. We toured several US cities and spoke to local civic clubs in an effort to raise funds for Operation Brotherhood. After visiting America, we also went to Edinburgh, Scotland, to participate in the International JCI Convention. Nineteen fifty-six was a busy year for me and I enjoyed my new freedom in private business.

Chapter 3

FROM THE VANTAGE POINT OF VIETNAM PRESS

One day in April 1957, I was summoned by President Diem to come to the Palace because he wanted to talk to me. Diem was very pleasant that day. He started talking with me about "the old times" in the United States, then he asked me how I was doing with my newspaper. I told him that I was doing fine and that the paper was doing very well. It seemed to be accomplishing its goal of providing better information on South Vietnam for the English-speaking community in Saigon, which was increasing in number every day. I said that I enjoyed my work with the newspaper and that I intended to expand my business into a publishing company that would produce books on the history and culture of Vietnam in English. I had plans to hire several more returnees who had been educated in the United States and Great Britain. At that point, Diem asked me if I knew anything about the national news agency, Vietnam Press. I said that I had heard many bad things about the agency and about its management. Former heads of the agency had taken advantage of its autonomous status within the government to steal funds and put relatives on the payroll as "correspondents." I told him the story I had heard of a doctor who was appointed Director General of Vietnam Press because of his political connections. He knew nothing about journalism and showed up at the agency only a couple of hours a day, whenever he was free from his medical practice. He hired a number of his friends and relatives as employees, but they did not do any work for the agency and he pocketed most of their salaries.

In short, from what I had heard, Vietnam Press was plagued by corrupt management and poor administration. Diem turned to me and said, "You may have to go over there and straighten things out." I replied that if he wanted me to do that, I had to be given some time to study the agency's problems in more detail and to prepare my exit from *The Times of Vietnam*. Diem did not say anything else and I thought nothing more about our conversation in the following days. Then on May 5, the very day Diem left for an official state visit to Washington, DC, Information Minister Thanh telephoned me and said that Diem had signed the decree appointing me Director General of Vietnam Press. He jokingly added that I had to take over the agency immediately because the President had left for America and, under the martial law prevailing in South Vietnam while Diem was away, I could be shot for noncompliance with direct presidential orders!

The sudden appointment surprised me, but I had no choice other than to accept it. I quickly went down to take control of the Vietnam Press office, which at the time included two separate buildings several blocks apart. This separation alone accounted for much of the disorganization of the agency and its lack of control over its personnel. At any given time I didn't know which employees were in what building, and it seemed that some employees were always "working in the other building" when needed. Another factor contributing to the confusion was the unchecked use of flexible time that was enjoyed by a number of privileged employees, who just came and went as they chose. My immediate response to this confusion was to install a time clock in each building and to require all employees to sign in and out with no exceptions.

This simple move of requiring employees to clock in, however, triggered a violent protest from those employees who were connected with the former Director General and other influential figures in Saigon. I soon received anonymous letters threatening harm to myself and members of my family because of my "arbitrary and dictatorial action against Vietnam Press employees whose personal esteem (*nhan vi*) had been violated." In those days, the word "nhan vi" (which vaguely meant personal esteem or personal worth) was a frequently used, ambiguous catchword coined by Ngo Dinh Nhu as part of his effort to build an ideological antidote to Communism. Some Vietnam Press employees also signed petitions requesting that I be replaced immediately by a new Director General who would respect their "nhan vi." I was not scared by these threats, though, in part because I did not really want to be the Director General of Vietnam Press in the first place.

Diem's departure for America left me with no possibility of protesting my appointment, and it also meant that I was taking the reins at a particularly important moment. It was Diem's first international trip as the South Vietnamese Chief of State and it was to South Vietnam's most important ally. The trip was filled with symbolic importance both within Vietnam and internationally. Diem had overcome his many political enemies in Saigon and was now being heralded by the US government as "one of the strongest personal bulwarks against Communist encroachment." President Eisenhower himself greeted Diem at the airport and praised him as a "staunch patriot" who had become a "truly very great" leader because of his "courage and statesmanship."[1] For such an important occasion, Vietnam Press, as the country's official news agency, was supposed to provide the best coverage possible.

At the time, Vietnam Press published three daily bulletins in both Vietnamese and French. All of the newspapers in Saigon, the National Radio Network, foreign diplomatic missions, and important business enterprises in the country subscribed to these bulletins. Obviously, time was of the essence for a news agency and there were constant deadlines. Everything was done under great pressure, yet mistakes had to be avoided and accuracy ensured. In my first days at Vietnam Press, however, I found some unusual and spectacular mistakes in the bulletins on Diem's state visit. These strange errors could be explained only as willful sabotage by the employees who were upset with my changes.

The first error would have been laughable under other circumstances. In the political context of the time, however, it could have been a disastrous mistake if it had not been caught and corrected immediately. In one of the news items on Diem's trip there was a typographical error and the name of Ngo Dinh *Nhu* was spelled *Ngu*, meaning stupid or imbecile. Nhu was already considered by many to be the most powerful person in South Vietnam as the Political Adviser to the President. He also controlled some of the much-feared secret operations of the regime under the Presidential Office for Political Research, so calling him an imbecile was unthinkable and perhaps dangerous. At the very least, for the official news agency of South Vietnam to publish such an error would have made Vietnam Press the laughingstock of Saigon and the world.

The second error was more subtle. Nevertheless, it could not be explained as a simple oversight due to absentmindedness and I attributed it to intentional sabotage aimed at discrediting me as the new Director

General of Vietnam Press. Beginning on the day Diem flew to the United States and continuing for the length of his absence from Saigon, Vice President Nguyen Ngoc Tho was supposed to be in charge of the government. Typically, Vietnam Press put news items involving the President or Vice President on the front page of its bulletins. This was a tacit sign of respect for these authorities and was a protocol that South Vietnamese newspapers followed as well. Somehow, on the day Diem left for America, however, the news about Vice President Nguyen Ngoc Tho's assumption of interim leadership was buried on the last page of the Vietnam Press bulletin. This unusual placement on the last page would have been interpreted instantly by many South Vietnamese political observers as a sign of disrespect and an attempt to insult the Vice President. That was particularly true because regional sensitivities were very important to the politics of Vietnam. Diem was from Central Vietnam, whereas Tho was from the South. Diem needed Tho's Southern political support, but some of Diem's family members tended to look down on Vice President Tho. Of course, Tho and other Southerners noticed that disrespect and resented it. In this political environment, the error in the bulletin could easily have been interpreted as a deliberate affront to Tho, especially when it was coming from a new Director General of Vietnam Press who was from Central Vietnam himself.

Luckily, I somehow spotted the errors in time, just before the bulletins were released for publication. Afterward, I called the Chief Editor into my office. I told him that as Director General I was not responsible for correcting every typographical error or other mistake in the bulletins; it was his job to spot and correct them. Whether they were intentional or unintentional errors was beside the point; if they had been released as they were, they would have been disastrous for Vietnam Press. I told him that I could not afford to keep him any longer and that he had to be fired on the spot for the errors. He knew he had been caught red-handed and did not object. Later, though, he tried to get himself rehired by lobbying many important figures, including my boss the Minister of Information. Nobody interceded on his behalf, however, and I was not forced to rehire him.

After Diem's state visit, I began making the necessary moves to clean house at Vietnam Press and to reorganize the agency. I fired all of the incompetent employees who had been hired due to their connections rather than their qualifications. I held exams for recruiting new, qualified employees. I found a larger building for the new office of Vietnam Press, replacing the two separate offices. I got rid of the head accountant, who was politically well connected but who did not know anything about accounting. This was an important matter, because every three months Vietnam Press, as an autonomous agency of the government (which meant that the Director General could hire personnel without the approval of the Civil Service Agency and could spend without the prior authorization of the Finance Ministry), was required to submit accounting details to justify its expenses of the past quarter and to request funds for the next. I found that the accountant had always been late in submitting those quarterly statements. I replaced him with another employee who was qualified for the job of accountant but who had previously been relegated to a minor editorial job because he did not have any connection with the former Director General.

Once these internal administrative moves were made, I requested USAID to supply Vietnam Press with new teletype and duplicating equipment, new Morse broadcast machines, new IBM typewriters, and a fleet of several four-wheel drive vehicles to be used by reporters in the field. I also asked the Americans to finance an accelerated journalism-training program for a number of qualified Vietnam Press reporters. Because I had cleaned up Vietnam Press and it was clear that the money would be properly spent, they were eager to assist. We sent the Vietnam Press reporters to Boston University for six months of training as a result.

As part of the reorganization, I created a new section to publish English bulletins, which were subscribed to by the increasing number of English-speaking customers in Saigon. I renegotiated contracts with other international news agencies to lower the rates Vietnam Press paid and to get a better balance of international news from more sources. In the past, Vietnam Press had been pressured by the pro-French Saigon governments to give the French news agency Agence France Presse (AFP) preferential status and a very expensive contract, limiting Vietnam Press financially. Without pro-French political pressures, I succeeded in obtaining better prices for AFP and reached deals with Associated Press, United Press, and Reuters. I also increased the number of our Morse newscasts to match that of other Asian news agencies such as Antara of Indonesia and Kyodo and JiJi of Japan. There was a large demand in Asia for news from South Vietnam, so these exchanges were quite productive. To get better domestic news coverage, I reorganized the network of Vietnam Press provincial correspondents and I reassigned some of the Vietnam Press foreign correspondents back home. Finally, I initiated a new exchange program to have seasoned journalists from English-speaking countries of Asia like the Philippines and Ceylon come to work at Vietnam Press to learn more about Vietnam while writing for their home newspapers.

It was a very busy time at Vietnam Press as I tried to reorganize and to initiate so many new programs. A few weeks after his return from America, I had a meeting with Diem. He asked me about the situation of Vietnam Press. I reported to him what I was doing, pointing out how my firings "to weed out the rotten wood" from the agency had provoked strong protests from some well-connected employees. I also told him frankly that I preferred my work in the private sector as Publisher and Editor of *The Times of Vietnam* and hoped to leave Vietnam Press after six months. That had been the average tenure of my predecessors and would have been enough time for me to point Vietnam Press in the right direction. Diem smiled, though, and told me that I had better make arrangements to leave *The Times of Vietnam* permanently. He wanted me to stay at Vietnam Press "for a while" to continue the work I had started. He told me that I had a free hand to do whatever I deemed necessary at the agency.

In those days I had the idealistic notion that, as a news agency, Vietnam Press had to improve its journalistic image. It had to become less of a government propaganda agency and more of an independent outlet capable of reporting news honestly and truthfully. That was a goal toward which Vietnam Press had to try to move. I knew it was going to be a very difficult and long process, however. I understood that as a government-subsidized agency operating in an underdeveloped country with an autocratic government, Vietnam Press would always have a hard time maintaining its journalistic independence. Over time, though, I was able to make Vietnam Press news coverage more objective. For the most part, the outlandish propaganda items that appeared before were dropped and we stuck to the facts. Ironically, I was able to create this distance between the government and Vietnam Press because I was known as being "close to President Diem."

My relationship with Diem may have given me the authority to carry out my reforms, but it also presented me with a dilemma because I did not want to appear to be taking orders from the President. I felt that as the head of a news agency I should personally keep my distance from Diem to preserve my independence. I did not succeed in that at all, though. I suggested to Diem that he should call on interpreters from the Foreign Affairs Ministry instead of me, but Diem did not get the message that I was trying to convey to him. He just smiled and did not say anything whenever I raised the issue. Later on, I found out that he did not agree at all with my idea to keep my distance, and of course he continued to call on me to translate for him. Part of the reason for this was definitely his comfort with having me translate. I think also that, in his mandarin way of thinking, he saw calling on me to translate for him as a big favor to *me*. As he seemed to see it, he was bestowing an honor on me as a "subject," and I should have felt grateful to be called upon by him, the "sovereign."

Because Diem expected me to stay at Vietnam Press for some time, I had to sell my shares in the corporation owning *The Times of Vietnam*. At first I asked Nguyen Lau to buy them. He was a former schoolmate of mine from Hue, and he had been to university in England. I thought that he would continue building *The Times of Vietnam* into a first-class English newspaper that would reflect a nationalist view of Vietnam (although after 1975 it was revealed that Lau had been a Communist agent). Lau did not have the money to buy my stake, however, so I sold him only a few token shares. The majority were sold to Gene Gregory, who had the money and who was eager to buy my shares. I had no idea then that Gene Gregory would end up pushing Nguyen Lau aside and taking full control of *The Times of Vietnam* to use it as the mouthpiece for Mr. and Mrs. Ngo Dinh Nhu.

I viewed Gene Gregory as a scheming man. He seemed to have seen that Ngo Dinh Nhu was his ticket to power and influence in South Vietnam, so both he and his wife took every occasion to get closer to the Nhus. At first, they volunteered to give English lessons to the Nhus' kids in the Presidential Palace. After a time, they were invited to accompany the Nhu family on frequent weekend trips to Dalat. Finally, in the early '60s when the Nhus were considered by the American government to be bad influences on President Diem, the Gregorys became anti-American propagandists for the Nhus through the pages of *The Times of Vietnam*. It was a case of profitable and convenient mutual exploitation: the Nhus wanted to use the American couple for their own ends and the Gregorys used the Nhus to promote their business interests in South Vietnam. Gene Gregory got rich by cleverly dropping the Nhus' names to scare local businessmen into doing his bidding. He even managed to get the free use of a big government villa in the heart of Saigon. From 1959 on, knowing that the Gregorys had become the American lackeys of the Nhus, I kept my distance from them and avoided seeing them anymore. By 1963, Diem was completely dependent on the Nhus, and the American government sought ways to detach them from Diem. The Nhus responded with increasingly anti-American editorials written by the Gregorys and published in *The Times of Vietnam*. During the last days of the Diem regime before the November 1963 coup, the Nhus also used *The Times of Vietnam*, as well as Vietnam Press, to publish inflammatory attacks against the Buddhists protesting the government. As a result, when the coup happened, angry Buddhist mobs ransacked the office of *The Times of Vietnam* on Gia Long Street.

THE VIEW FROM VIETNAM PRESS

As Director General of Vietnam Press I had a fairly comprehensive view of what was going on in South Vietnam. Although I had been excited after the initial successes of the Diem government, that enthusiasm soon faded. From the vantage point of Vietnam Press, I watched with unease as the regime made more and more political mistakes. I told myself that I had to stick through it, though, and that perhaps with time Diem would change course. In any case, I had little choice but to continue at Vietnam Press because of Diem's insistence that I remain there.

Due to my close relationship with Diem and his trust in me, Vietnam Press functioned not only as a simple national news agency but also as a discreet censor and a stealth public relations agency for Diem. The unique position of Vietnam Press allowed it to affect significantly the news both coming into and going out of Vietnam. With incoming news, local publishers relied on Vietnam Press to provide international news through our contracts with AP, UPI, Reuters, and AFP. Every day, these services provided Vietnam Press with thousands of news items. We would select the stories that were politically acceptable to the regime, translate them into Vietnamese, and then provide them for use by local publishers. Thus, Vietnam Press acted as the censor of international news for the people of South Vietnam. Local newspapers usually reproduced our domestic news bulletins verbatim as well. The Ngo family was so sensitive about news coverage that the local papers learned from experience that the safest thing was to run Vietnam Press dispatches word for word. If they deviated and it upset a regime member, the transgressing newspaper could be immediately closed down. In addition to this copying by the newspapers, Vietnam Press bulletins were used in all broadcasts by the government's National Radio Network.

Vietnam Press had less influence on outgoing news, but it still had a notable impact. We published our bulletins in French, English, and Chinese for international audiences. Diplomatic missions in Saigon found these Vietnam Press reports indispensable because our reports were one of the few means available for foreigners to find out what was going on in South Vietnam and because they often conveyed the official viewpoint of Diem's government. Likewise, the international news agencies relied heavily on Vietnam Press for their local news coverage even if they had their own reporter in the country (which was not always the case). Another important and influential function performed by Vietnam Press was to decide on whom or what to feature and put in the national spotlight of official approval. Because of this, the attention of Vietnam Press was in high demand and was assiduously sought after by foreign diplomats in Saigon as well as Vietnamese diplomats abroad.

Vietnam Press was frequently privy to the secrets of the Diem government. Almost every day, the President himself or somebody close to him would ask me to watch for some special news item and "play it" this way or that. Information was power and it had to be manipulated by those who sought to monopolize it. Sometimes these sensitive orders were passed to me by one of Diem's ministers, who had received instructions from the President. Most of the time, however, the secret instructions were relayed to me by Tran Kim Tuyen, the head of the Presidential Office for Political Research and a protégé of Ngo Dinh Nhu. It was not unusual for Tuyen to tell me ahead of time what the sentence would be in a politically important trial or when some kind of news event would occur. I was often told in advance about plans for "spontaneous public demonstrations" or even "spontaneous" mobs that were going to ransack an opposition newspaper. Tuyen would suggest that it would be "appropriate" for Vietnam Press to cover the news this way or that, as required by the interests of the regime.

I resented these secret instructions and the slanting of news published in Vietnam Press bulletins. I considered it my duty as a journalist to cover the news as objectively as possible. Despite that, I was resigned to the situation. I tried to convince myself that South Vietnam was still a developing country and its national news agency had to meet the requirements of its underdeveloped politics. I told myself that I was at Vietnam Press to help Diem and not to create more problems for him. I reasoned that I was being too idealistic and that I had to be more realistic and learn to adapt. As time went by, however, I reached a point where I could no longer justify these rationalizations for slanting the news.

Everyone in South Vietnam knew about the capricious whims of President Diem concerning news coverage, so nobody wanted to stick his neck out and risk the ire of Diem with undesirable news. As a result, they all relied on my judgment because I was regarded as the only one who understood Diem's mind and what he liked or disliked in news coverage. I could negotiate the dangerous minefields of Diem's preferences, so everybody else just followed the lead of Vietnam Press in order not to risk trouble with Diem. This was the heavy burden imposed on me as Director General of Vietnam Press.

I did not lose much sleep worrying about Diem's fits of anger when he read news he did not like, though. I had told him many times that I wanted to change Vietnam Press into an objective and unbiased news agency like AP or Reuters. He knew who I was and where I stood. Furthermore, he knew my father and my family and I think he was convinced that I was not the type of man to betray him. He could trust me as long as I was standing behind him. With that tacit, mutual understanding, Diem and I never had any major arguments with each other while I was at Vietnam Press from 1957 until the end of 1961. During that time, however, I saw Diem's government rapidly deteriorate to the point that my loyalty and faith in him were severely tested. I found the emergence of the Ngo family dictatorship underneath him unacceptable, and I was a firsthand witness to their many flaws and failings.

DIEM'S PERSONALITY CULT MOVEMENT

One of the first indications I had of the government's disturbing direction was the movement to "venerate President Ngo." The Information Ministry was the headquarters for this national campaign. They printed millions of posters and distributed them around the nation to promote this movement called "Suy Ton Ngo Tong Thong" (Let Us Venerate President Ngo). A hymn was also adopted to praise President Diem as the savior of the nation. It was played right after the national anthem and everybody had to stand up when it was played. In theaters and anywhere there was a public event, that presidential hymn was always heard. There were even dishes and plates inscribed with the motto and with Diem's picture, and they were on sale almost everywhere. The huge number of orders for printed materials that this cult of personality campaign required created opportunities for corruption and secret bribes for the high-level officials in the Ministry of Information.

The cult of personality was also very useful for the many sycophants in South Vietnam who sought to ingratiate themselves with the regime and move ahead through flattery. Their fawning over Diem was often so ridiculous it was funny, although the humor came at a high cost to the prestige and popularity of the government. One ludicrous incident in early 1958 encapsulated the sycophancy to me. I was in the Presidential Palace to see Diem about some Vietnam Press business when an ARVN (Army of the Republic of Vietnam) major came to report to Diem that there had been a severe "lèse-majesté" against the President. He said that there was a French-Corsican restaurant next to the port of Saigon that had a painting of a nice, big fish with the famous Latin saying "Carpe Diem" (seize, or enjoy, the day). This ignorant major told Diem that "those Corsican French need to be severely punished because they dare to insult you, the President, by saying that you are a carp." I could not help but intervene, so I told Diem that I had studied Latin and I was certain that the restaurant meant no insult but was only exhorting customers to enjoy themselves. Diem laughed at it, and the major kept quiet after that. Unfortunately, though, there were many other flatterers like that major and the cult of personality only encouraged them.

Personally, I thought that campaign to create a personality cult around Diem was counterproductive. It smacked of Communist propaganda tactics and it made people resent Diem more than anything. I wondered whether some secret Communist agent was actually behind the movement because it was a very good way to alienate people and make the government unpopular. I was concerned enough that I raised the question with Information Minister Tran Chanh Thanh. He dodged the issue, however, and Diem's personality cult continued to run its course in South Vietnam. Later, after the collapse of South Vietnam in 1975, I learned that one of Thanh's closest friends, Nguyen Van Thuan, was a Communist mole planted by Hanoi. That knowledge made me wonder whether Thuan had launched the unpopular cult-of-personality campaign in order to alienate the people. If that was the case, then he succeeded brilliantly as a Communist mole by helping make anti-Communism under the Diem regime very unpopular in South Vietnam.

In any case, Diem himself approved the campaign. He obviously saw nothing wrong with a cult of personality glorifying himself like a deity. Despite Lansdale's advice to remain close to the people, Diem preferred to emphasize his superior position. In all his pictures and for all public appearances, Diem was dressed in immaculate, white sharkskin suits with black neckties. His attire was not at all practical in the tropical heat of Saigon, but after 1957 he forced all other government officials to adopt his excessively formal wear. Even when the President and officials went on inspection trips of the countryside, walking in the hot sun through muddy fields, we had to wear these suits. It was ridiculously incongruous: we standing in our impeccable outfits next to peasants in their mud-stained black pajamas. Such a contrast was bad public relations in my view, and because of that I begged off accompanying Diem on any more of those inspection trips.

Diem was no democrat by temperament, and the better I got to know him the more it showed. When I first met him in the United States, he had appeared to admire democratic principles and institutions. Later on, however, when he was in power in Saigon, he became increasingly autocratic. It seemed to me that he wanted to forget his past connections and acquaintances, especially those who had known him in his time of need. In his view, the memory of his previous powerlessness was not compatible with the new image of himself as all-powerful chief of state. Especially after his May 1957 state visit to America, where he was received triumphantly, Diem seemed to get megalomaniac ideas about himself. Before, as a political exile in America, he had acted humbly. After 1957, however, he began to truly believe the boasts of American anti-Communists that he was indeed the "biggest little man in Asia."[2]

THE NGO FAMILY

By 1958, the government of South Vietnam was clearly monopolized by Ngo family members, each of whom left a unique imprint on the regime. Although Ngo Dinh Diem was the official repository of Presidential power, he never made an important decision without consulting his brothers. There were multiple power centers in the regime which meant that, to a certain degree, potential supporters had a variety of choices of whom they would like to serve. More important, though, as I wrote in my 1962 book on the regime, "this *illusion* of diversity of political views" and the differing tendencies within the regime helped keep the regime in control by confusing, dividing, and exposing potential opponents.[3] This dynamic helped to keep the Ngo family in power, but it also left the government disorganized and handicapped.

In my position at Vietnam Press and with my frequent trips to the Presidential Palace to visit Diem, I had many opportunities to observe the Ngo family members and detect how they operated. Of all the brothers, I thought Luyen clearly had the least detrimental, but also the weakest, influence on Diem. Consequently, he held the least blame for the eventual collapse of the regime. On the opposite end, Ngo Dinh Nhu and his wife held the most sway and had the most damaging influence, in my eyes. That was especially true toward the end of the regime, when the real power of the government could be thought of as a triangle. Diem may have formed the base, but Mr. and Mrs. Nhu made up two equal sides that gave the regime its complete form. Because of this, I believe that the Nhus deserve most of the blame for the political mistakes that precipitated the overthrow of Diem in November 1963.

Ngo Dinh Luyen: Ambassador in London. Ngo Dinh Luyen, one of Diem's younger brothers, had been instrumental in lobbying for Diem's rise to power. In 1953 and 1954, it was Luyen who lobbied for Diem among Vietnamese and French political circles in Paris. At the crucial moment in June 1954, Luyen was the one who arranged for Bao Dai to meet Diem to appoint him Prime Minister. Despite that, Luyen was removed from the Saigon political arena shortly thereafter by his more intrigue-prone brother Ngo Dinh Nhu.

I was very impressed with Luyen when I met him in Paris on my way back to Vietnam in 1954. Luyen was trained in France as a civil engineer and was well liked by other young, foreign-trained Vietnamese like myself. This appeal of Luyen to young overseas Vietnamese was important for Diem because his government desperately needed capable, well-trained officials. Similarly, Luyen was also very successful in mid-1954 at rallying some of the young military commanders in South Vietnam to Diem's side. For Diem's followers who resented Nhu's intrigues and secret schemes, Luyen's direct and open approach was appreciated. In the early days of the regime in 1954 and 1955, when Diem was struggling for political survival, Luyen was often in Saigon and his presence made a positive difference.

Many intellectuals and officials like myself wished that Luyen could have stayed in Saigon to counterbalance Nhu's influence. Unfortunately, however, soon after Diem's power was consolidated Luyen was removed from the scene. In the contest for political influence over Diem, Luyen was outmaneuvered by the more cunning Nhu. Likewise, Luyen's spouse was a conventional housewife with no political interests, whereas Mrs. Nhu was extremely ambitious. She intrigued to make life in Saigon personally unbearable for Luyen and his wife. As a result, Luyen was sent to London as a Roving Ambassador to Europe. Although this was an impressive title, the move was really more of an exile. In practice, the Diem regime regularly used those overseas diplomatic postings to banish their opponents and keep potential threats away from Saigon.

With Luyen removed from the local scene, Nhu's advice began to dominate Diem in Saigon. Diem had nobody to offset Nhu and was forced to rely more and more on the Nhus' ever-expanding clout in South Vietnam. From faraway London, Luyen could only watch the deterioration of his brother's government and could do nothing to help Diem avoid disaster. It was deeply regrettable that Diem, who was the President and older brother, did not exercise better judgment by keeping Luyen in Saigon to have the benefit of his sound advice and to counterbalance Nhu's scheming. Perhaps if this had happened the Ngo regime might have avoided its worst mistakes that led to the 1963 coup. As it was, after the coup Ngo Dinh Luyen lost his job as Ambassador and ended up living in France until he died in 1987.

Ngo Dinh Thuc: Bishop of Hue. After the death of Ngo Dinh Khoi, who was killed by Communists in 1945, Catholic Bishop Ngo Dinh Thuc was the only surviving older brother of Ngo Dinh Diem. Because he was "the Bishop" and the oldest in the family, all the other members of the Ngo family owed him respect and obedience. This was particularly true for Diem, who was devout and had considered a religious career for himself in the past. Within the regime, Thuc's prestige and the respect Diem had for him made him the mediator of family disputes. Although he had no official role in the government and was usually not publicly political, his role as arbitrator within the family gave him great influence on some of the most important matters.

Despite being a man of the cloth, Thuc did not remain strictly religious and was heavily involved in various lucrative business schemes. He did so for the benefit of the Catholic University in Dalat, which he founded, but he still became hopelessly mired in corruption and shady dealing. By the end of the Diem regime, Thuc even lost his sense of moral balance and his spiritual authority. He made many virulent attacks against Buddhists during the Buddhist crisis, contributing much to the protests that culminated in the overthrow and assassination of Diem. Had Ngo Dinh Thuc been a better religious man and kept himself removed from dirty politics he might have been able to save his younger brother's presidency and life.

Like many people in South Vietnam, I had heard that Ngo Dinh Thuc lobbied for appointment as the Cardinal and Archbishop of Saigon, which was the most important Catholic community in the country. The Vatican, however, seemed to know about Thuc's involvement in the Ngo family corruption. Despite Thuc's lobbying efforts, it instead appointed a non-controversial Southern priest. Diem and Thuc took unusual and extraordinary steps to try to reverse that decision, including preventing the Post and Telegraph office in Saigon from delivering the Vatican's letter. Thuc went to Rome to petition for a change in the Vatican's decision. When rebuffed again there, he and Diem still tried to stop the news of the appointment from spreading in South Vietnam. They only gave up and accepted the appointments when Diem was threatened with excommunication for his interference in church affairs.

Thuc was bitterly disappointed to be only the Bishop of Hue instead of the Archbishop of Saigon (although Hue was elevated to an Archdiocese eventually). In Hue, Thuc started the chain of events that sparked the dramatic protests of Buddhists all over South Vietnam. His unwillingness to compromise with Buddhist demands to be treated fairly and on the same footing as Catholics in South Vietnam eventually led to the violent overthrow of the Diem regime. When the coup took place, Thuc was already out of the country, having left for Rome in September 1963. In all likelihood, the Vatican had ordered him to leave in the hope that his absence might help defuse the Buddhist crisis. Even in exile from Vietnam, however, Thuc could not avoid controversial intrigues. He later got involved with a religious movement that challenged the Vatican's authority, leading to his excommunication.

Ngo Dinh Can: Warlord of Central Vietnam. Unlike his brothers who received traditional Confucian educations (Khoi and Diem) or Western training (Luyen, Nhu, and Thuc), the youngest of Diem's brothers, Ngo Dinh Can, did not receive any formal education. All his life, he stayed with his mother in the family's ancestral home in Hue. Can, however, was regarded by keen observers of South Vietnam politics as cruel but intelligent, a no-nonsense man who was the most practical brother of the President. He did not get lost, like Nhu, in ideology or nebulous concepts such as "personalism." Had he been listened to more, the regime would have been more effective at the very least.

Known with awe as "Cau Can" (Uncle Can), he wielded life-and-death power over millions of people in Central Vietnam. Through tacit agreement in the Ngo family, Central Vietnam was his unofficial dominion. He controlled the economic resources of the region and used them at his own discretion. The Province Chiefs were mostly his own handpicked men. Like Nhu in the South, Can also operated his own personal secret security network. Sometimes his secret service even competed with Nhu's network or with the official national security apparatus of the Saigon government. Although Can was known to be quite autocratic like his older brother, he differed in that he was *consistently* autocratic. Whereas Diem often confounded his subordinates by talking about democratic ideals and methods while giving autocratic orders, Can's followers suffered from no such handicaps. Furthermore, Diem often failed to reward loyal followers and instead took them for granted while promoting relative strangers. Can, on the other hand, always made sure to promote and pay those who served him well, creating a hierarchy that was far more responsive and effective in following Can's will.

As the unchallenged overlord of Central Vietnam, Can acquired a reputation as the most feared defender of Diem's rule. Anybody he considered to be a potential enemy of the regime could be jailed, tortured, or executed on his order. He was considered rabidly anti-Communist, but Can nevertheless did not hesitate to arrest people he suspected were anti-Communist opponents of the regime. Many members of nationalist parties like Viet Quoc (the Vietnamese version of the Chinese Nationalist Party) and Dai Viet (Greater Vietnam) in Central Vietnam were targeted by Can's feared secret agents. Only after the overthrow of the Diem regime were the infamous secret jails used by Can uncovered. Some of them were hidden in an elaborate estate on the outskirts of Hue that Can built using forced labor. He had spent a fortune there and was planning to create a famous landmark for himself, something like the elaborate tombs of the Nguyen dynasty emperors. Fortunately for the public treasury and the people of Hue, who had to contribute labor, the 1963 coup interrupted this lavish construction project. Can was arrested shortly after the coup and was executed in 1964.

Ngo Dinh Nhu: Political Adviser of the President. Incontestably, Ngo Dinh Nhu was the most powerful brother of Diem. There was a sharp contrast between Nhu and Luyen in their personalities, styles of operation, and backgrounds. Whereas Luyen was trained as an engineer and operated in an open and direct style, Nhu was trained as an archivist (at the École des Chartes in Paris) and preferred to operate in a secretive and scheming fashion. Nhu had remained in Vietnam and organized political support for his brother while Diem was in exile in America. Diem valued that contribution much more than he did Luyen's efforts in Paris. In many ways, Nhu had the right kind of personality to be the power behind the throne and *éminence grise* for Diem. He was adept at whispering convincing advice when asked, patient enough to endure Diem's bursts of anger, and discreet in executing secret plots. Nhu was also often rumored to smoke opium, and he certainly had the kinds of grand, visionary ideas that opium smokers indulged in. I never saw any direct or concrete evidence that he did so, however.

One of these grandiose ideas was the so-called doctrine of "personalism" (*nhan vi*), which was the official philosophy of the Diem regime and was supposed to be the ideological antidote to Communism. It was an adaptation on some French Catholic philosophy and was the brainchild of Nhu. While Communism sacrificed personal freedom for the good of the community, personalism, in theory, gave priority to the person and individual freedom. This was nothing new or groundbreaking, but nevertheless Nhu's many convoluted elaborations on this essentially self-evident premise became very confusing. Nobody, it seemed, really knew exactly what Nhu meant by personalism because of his vague and tortuous explanations. In the end, people in South Vietnam either ignored the doctrine completely or pretended to admire it in order to curry favor.

In my capacity as interpreter for the President, I saw repeatedly that even Diem did not actually understand his government's official doctrine. I tried to avoid interpreting whenever possible for a long time because I thought it improper for me to do so as head of the national news agency, but later in Diem's presidency I gave in far more, especially in 1961. I was ready to do anything to get myself in the good graces of Diem then to get his permission for me to leave Vietnam. Interpreting was one of the chief ways I gratified Diem, so I found myself in the Presidential Palace frequently. Diem had many important guests coming from the United States at the time, and I often heard him parroting the phrases of Nhu's personalist doctrine to them. I realized that it did not make any sense, but I would translate what Diem said verbatim. Naturally, his distinguished guests rarely comprehended these points. Instead of trying to explain or clarify for them, Diem would turn to me and whisper in Vietnamese with his Hue accent. He would tell me, "You check about what I just said with Mr. Nhu and you ask him to explain more clearly about this personalist doctrine. Then if our guest wants more clarification, make arrangements for Mr. Nhu to give it."

I think that Diem was very impressed with Nhu and with his personalist doctrine, even if he did not really understand it. Diem was at heart a simple and honest man, and he had a great respect for Nhu's Western erudition. Diem thought he needed that Westernized perspective to complement his own traditional Confucian thinking. In that and many other ways, Nhu filled in Diem's shortcomings. Diem was unorganized, but Nhu was methodical; Diem was unskilled as an orator, but Nhu could write beautiful speeches for him in French or Vietnamese. When Nhu, with his lofty air of superiority, spoke and used sophisticated-sounding words, Diem assumed that they were quite profound even if the meaning was not completely clear to him. Diem was very averse to admitting when he did not know or understand something, so he was prone to rely on what he saw as Nhu's superior intelligence.

Nhu's biggest advantage in influencing Diem, however, was that he lived in the Independence Palace with Diem and was available at any moment. Nhu and his family resided in the left wing of the Palace, less than a minute's walk from Diem's quarters in the right wing. Diem, in my observation, was the type of person who was easily persuaded by whoever last talked to him, so this was often a decisive factor in Nhu's favor. Nhu probably knew better than anyone his brother's bad moments and could easily avoid these and patiently wait to seize the right moment to persuade his brother. Others who came to the Palace were at a disadvantage because they had to face Diem no matter what mood the President was in. Nhu's presence also prevented contradictory information from reaching Diem. Nhu screened Diem's visitors to filter what Diem heard. Should anyone come to tell Diem something Nhu did not like, Nhu would typically sit in Diem's office throughout the meeting to monitor and intimidate.

Additionally, Nhu had a whole array of *his* own men on hand to come at a moment's notice and present Diem whatever Nhu wanted. Except for Diem's personal secretary Vo Van Hai, Nhu could count on everyone in the Palace to do his bidding. His men included the highest ranking officials in the Saigon government and the closest aides to the President. He could mobilize ministers of the most important agencies, generals, province chiefs, bishops, and even Diem's own bodyguards; all would do as Nhu wished and tell Diem what Nhu thought Diem needed to hear. Because of this ability to screen and filter who saw Diem and what they told him, along with his possession of the crucial last word with Diem, by 1958 Nhu had the whole government under his thumb. Everyone knew that Nhu could run circles around Diem and that real presidential power resided with Nhu. Diem, with nobody else to turn to for support, had no alternative to Nhu's overwhelming influence and had no choice but to take it.

Although Nhu's power was mostly derived from his personal influence over Diem and informal authority over most government officials, he also had substantial formal authority and his own political assets. The most formidable of these was his secret Presidential Office for Political Research, which was housed in an annex to the Independence Palace. This office came into existence shortly after Diem assumed power, after Nhu had become Diem's sole adviser by pushing aside Luyen. At that time, Diem had his personal secretary Hai to handle top secret, confidential matters, but Hai was too loyal to Diem for Nhu's liking. As a result, Nhu established his own secret service and staffed it with his own men. He selected a very discreet Catholic refugee by the name of Tran Kim Tuyen to head this office. Tuyen never practiced medicine, but he was called "Doctor" anyway because people were afraid of him and at the time in Vietnam it was a signal of deference to call someone doctor. "Dr." Tuyen, with his staff of secret operatives, quickly gained power and influence commensurate with the growing authority of Nhu.

Staffed with operatives loyal only to Tuyen and Nhu, and financed by the CIA, the Presidential Office for Political Research in many ways resembled the KGB in the scope of its power. It had the ability to infiltrate all government agencies and it often functioned as a *real* government that informally and secretly supervised the *official* government. Even among secretaries of state or ministers of agencies, there were few in the government with the courage to resist a secret order believed to be originating from Nhu or Tuyen. Because of the secrecy of Nhu and Tuyen, it was often difficult to tell if they had actually given orders. Nobody, however, wanted to check and risk being seen as questioning Nhu's or Tuyen's commands. All this meant that cooperation with their shadow organization was customary, even when they did not have their own loyal men in place. Not only was this office able to directly control many aspects of the government, but it also became another of Nhu's many tools to guide Diem. With its covert information sources, Nhu became practically omniscient and omnipotent. He could always supply Diem with exactly the right information at the right moment to sway the President. In addition to the Presidential Office for Political Research, Nhu controlled the covert Can Lao (Labor) Party. This was the secret core of trusted supporters of the Diem regime. Can Lao Party members were assigned to control other organizations or groups throughout the country. In order to reach the highest positions of power and trust in the government, it was almost required to be a party member. Can Lao Party membership was one of the three "Cs" that were often said to be the keys to advancing under Diem; the other two were being Catholic and being from Central Vietnam.

As a Catholic from Hue, I already possessed two of the "Cs" and in 1957 I was approached to add the third by joining the secret Can Lao Party. My sponsor told me that I would be eligible for the most important positions in the regime if I joined. I refused the offer, however. I told my sponsor that I was disgusted to see officials in the Diem government convert to Catholicism just to get promoted to higher positions and I would not behave similarly. I only wanted to work for President Diem as long as he lived up to his reputation of honesty; I had no interest in pledging allegiance to the entire Ngo family. I said that I was not pursuing any promotion to a high-ranking position and that I did not need Can Lao membership.

In hindsight, I think I made the right judgment in not joining the Can Lao Party and not working for Nhu. When I first met Nhu, I somehow felt that he was not dealing openly and frankly like Luyen. I instinctively sensed that Nhu favored intrigue and secret maneuvers. I realized that if I worked in that style, eventually I would be involved in shady deals that would compromise my sense of integrity. Furthermore, it would be impossible for me to pull away from Nhu's control once I started working for him and became enmeshed in his schemes. Of course, in those early days I had little idea of the extent of Nhu's misdeeds that included extreme corruption and the murders of political rivals like Trinh Minh The or Hoa Hao military leader Ba Cut, so it was fortunate that my gut feeling had prompted me to stay away from him. The fake riots to destroy opposition newspapers, predetermined court sentences, and corruption cover-ups I witnessed from Vietnam Press were all Nhu's doing and it was bad enough that I had to help hide them from the public.

Madame Nhu as "Mrs. Ngo." Toward the end of his rule, Diem seemed to be under the complete control of Ngo Dinh Nhu and Nhu's ambitious wife Tran Le Xuan, who was better known as Madame Nhu. That situation was unacceptable to the United States government, and Diem was under heavy American pressure to get rid of the Nhus in 1963. He mostly resisted but eventually gave in a little and sent Mrs. Nhu abroad. She embarked on her self-proclaimed "disintoxication" tour around the world in September 1963, just a couple of months before the overthrow of the regime. At the time, the Buddhist crisis in South Vietnam was reaching its boiling point and almost every day there were demonstrations or self-immolations to protest the Diem government. American public opinion and policymakers were increasingly alarmed by the protests and the Diem regime's apparent unpopularity, but despite that Mrs. Nhu still did not hesitate to use inflammatory language against the Buddhists while on her tour. Most infamously, she described the Buddhist self-immolations as "Buddhist barbecues" and offered to supply the matches in the future. Such insulting language by Mrs. Nhu only exacerbated the mounting protests in South Vietnam, greatly contributing to the eventual overthrow of the Diem regime.

Who was Mrs. Nhu, and how did she gain such power in the Diem regime? Born in 1926, she was a cousin to Emperor Bao Dai. Like many upper-class Vietnamese, she was educated in French-Catholic school where French was the only language used. At only 17 years old, in 1943 she married Ngo Dinh Nhu, who was 16 years her senior. This was a very traditional arranged marriage between two high-ranking Vietnamese families of equal status. Tran Le Xuan's father, Tran Van Chuong, was a well-known lawyer. He had met Ngo Dihn Nhu in France while Nhu was attending the École des Chartes and had promised to marry his daughter to Nhu. Family relationships and political power were still deeply entwined in Vietnam at the time. That was because of the legacy of Confucianism; the continuing (though dwindling) role of the royal family; and the difficulty of developing political trust through less intimate bonds during a time of colonial oppression, war, and revolution. The marriage of Tran Le Xuan to Nhu was every bit a political arrangement intended to link the two powerful families together.

As a consequence of the close connection between political power and family relationships, the behavior and reputations of individual family members were seen as a reflection of the family as a whole. That was particularly true for politically connected upper-class clans like the Ngos and Tran Van Chuong's family. That could mean that, fairly or unfairly, people were sometimes prejudged for the sins of their parents, siblings, and even distant family members or ancestors. Such was the case with Madame Nhu. There were stories about Madame Nhu's grandmother having been famous for scandalous behavior in the Emperor's court in days long past. Even worse, Madame Nhu's mother was widely regarded by foreign diplomats and Vietnamese political observers alike as having had numerous romantic affairs in connection with her husband's political maneuvers. French police and officials had even kept detailed records of the supposed liaisons in order to suss out the political implications. These family reputations followed Madame Nhu and her older sister, Tran Le Chi, who was accused of promiscuity by Diem himself at one point.

Such views of the importance (and impropriety) of these women's personal behaviors were not very enlightened, but in the political and male-dominated context of Vietnam at the time, they were a fact of life. All of this meant that Mrs. Nhu was going to be the subject of intense scrutiny and judgment — whether she deserved it or not — once she became the First Lady for her bachelor brother-in-law, Diem. There was little direct evidence of the sensational kind of sexual indiscretion committed by her mother (although I witnessed some odd things and heard credible rumors), but Mrs. Nhu courted controversy rather than trying to avoid it. Much of this controversy stemmed from her unwillingness to listen to or heed anybody, including her parents and President Diem. She acted in any way she pleased and made national decisions based upon her own self-interest or whims, often in defiance of both the proper authorities and the common good. Rather than apologize for or minimize her arbitrary and capricious power, however, she reveled in it and tended to add insults to the injury of her opponents.

To me and many others like me in South Vietnam, it was her usurpation of proper authority and her willingness to flaunt the usurpation that really were so distasteful. The rumors concerning her personal behavior that emerged were more a consequence of that dislike (along with her family's reputation, of course) than a cause of it. It seemed to me that Mrs. Nhu was so defiant and arrogant that she had no respect for anything or anyone. In fact, she cared so little about what others thought that she would use the scandals and rumors for her own ends. Sometimes, she seemed to deliberately play into the rumors or cause a new scandal to get her way. That was one of the sources of her unusual power and control over both her husband and President Diem. The Ngo brothers belonged to a very proud family and their good name was important to them. They were afraid of any scandal that would damage their reputation. Mrs. Nhu knew this was a weak point of the Ngo family, so she would threaten to bring shame and humiliation to them whenever she needed leverage over them. The Ngo brothers had no choice but to give in to her in order to keep everything quiet and avoid dishonor. Mrs. Nhu always came away from these confrontations with the upper hand.

Besides being defiant and daring to the point of recklessness, Mrs. Nhu's other prime characteristic was her ego. She enjoyed being the center of public attention and needed constant flattering. At times, this restlessness and her desire to get involved in any kind of action was useful to the Ngo brothers. With her cleverness, energy, and charm, she could be an asset. In the early days when Diem's power was shaky, her readiness to stage demonstrations with Catholic refugees supporting Diem was useful as these had some symbolic value. Although the demonstrations were not particularly significant in number or substance, they later served as examples of the "big contributions" Mrs. Nhu claimed to have made in the consolidation of the regime. She would point to them and narcissistically boast that she was capable of doing great things for the Ngo family, especially if she were given a free hand.

The United States government eventually regarded Mrs. Nhu's power as annoying and harmful to the prestige of President Diem, but the Americans were at least partly to blame for her prominence. It was the United States, after all, that introduced the idea of having an American-style First Lady for the bachelor Diem. For the Vietnamese, there was no precedent nor need for any First Lady in the Presidential Palace if the President happened to be single. In North Vietnam, the bachelor Ho Chi Minh was Chief of State, but he had no need for a "First Lady." On the contrary, Ho Chi Minh was admired by many Vietnamese people for being single and totally dedicated to the service of the country.

In South Vietnam, however, Mrs. Nhu was put in a position of honor and allowed to live in the Presidential Palace because of the perceived need for a First Lady. This defied Vietnamese tradition and public opinion, which found it hard to accept the concept of a First Lady for an unmarried President. Although this was a "protocol arrangement" at first, toward the end of the Ngo regime Mrs. Nhu even posed as the de facto wife of Ngo Dinh Diem. It went so far that some of Diem's aides suspected that there was a secret ménage à trois in the Independence Palace. Although I cannot say with certainty that this was true, I did observe some curious behavior in the Palace that led me to suspect there was indeed some kind of romance between Madame Nhu and her brother-in-law Diem.

In late 1961, weeks before I was going to resign as Director General of Vietnam Press and leave for America, Mrs. Nhu herself called me at my office. This was not out of the ordinary because she and President Diem both tried to personally control all press accounts of themselves. Her request for me, however, was unusual. She told me that henceforth Vietnam Press should refer to her as "Madame Ngo," rather than as Mrs. Nhu as had been done in the past. She added that foreign journalists should be instructed to do the same. I was shocked. I said that foreign journalists were free to write whatever they wanted and that they would do so. Furthermore, I said, "Madame Ngo" was rather misleading and unacceptable by Vietnamese conventions. She was apparently annoyed and surprised by my reply. At the time, almost nobody in South Vietnam dared to contradict her like that. I kept pointing out to her that "Madame Ngo" was not the correct Vietnamese way to refer to her and she knew that "it did not sound right." She stood her ground, though, and kept repeating her instruction. I ended up asking her whether she had checked with the President about the new "Madame Ngo" appellation. Exasperated by this question, she barked in anger, "My office will send Vietnam Press my new instruction." Then she hung up abruptly.

That same afternoon I drove to the Presidential Palace to see Vo Van Hai, Personal Secretary of the President and a close friend of mine. I wanted to compare notes with Hai and try to understand the relationship between the President and Mrs. Nhu. I began by telling him about my latest conversation with Mrs. Nhu and her new instruction about being called "Madame Ngo." Hai was shocked and appeared to be agitated by my story. He repeatedly mumbled "that prostitute" in reference to Mrs. Nhu. When I finished telling him, Hai sighed and said that I was lucky to be able to leave and go to America. I then asked Hai for a definite answer to the question troubling me: "Do you mean that the President and Mrs. Nhu are lovers?" At first Hai refused to answer this so I pressed him further. "If they are not lovers, how can she talk about 'Madame Ngo' and behave as if she has the President under her thumb?" Hai still did not answer, however, so I started telling him about two other strange incidents I had witnessed.

On a recent Saturday, the President had urgently asked me to come and see him at the Palace. I hurried over and found the President sitting behind Mr. Nhu's desk in the wing of the Palace occupied by the Nhu family. He seemed lost in thought. He threw a Vietnam Press bulletin on the desk and asked me, "Why do you publish this news item on Mrs. Nhu going to Dalat for the weekend?" I was surprised by the question and answered, "This is the standard version approved by Mr. Nhu for Vietnam Press to publish when he and Mrs. Nhu go to Dalat for the weekend." The President said nothing, his mind clearly wandering somewhere else. I said, "Mr. President, if there is nothing else for me to do here, I ask permission to return to my office." The President absentmindedly nodded and I left. Driving back to my office, I thought that this strange behavior seemed like that of a lovesick person longing for the presence of his absent lover.

On another occasion, I was at the Palace and saw Mrs. Nhu in an almost transparent negligee, sitting on an armrest next to the President. Mr. Nhu and Bishop Thuc were also sitting nearby, apparently having a casual conversation. The scene and the provocative apparel of Mrs. Nhu in the presence of the President and Bishop Thuc shocked me. I thought that there was something strange here among Mrs. Nhu and the Ngo brothers for this to somehow be considered acceptable and "normal."

I asked Hai, "How do you explain those two incidents I witnessed and this new matter of 'Madame Ngo?'" I told him that whatever secret he cared to reveal to me would be strictly confidential. Agitated, Hai spoke quickly:

> Good for you to leave! We are lost. The Old Man is under the spell of that whore. He has been a bachelor for too long and now she is giving it to him, so he is hooked. Do you remember Cat, my assistant here? He happened to see the Old Man with Mrs. Nhu, together...so he had to be fired. Now you know the truth and it is good that you can leave because here we are all doomed and that whore has messed everything up for the Old Man.

Hai seemed exhausted by the revelation of the secret. I left him, deeply troubled and saddened by what I had heard. Hai was closer to Diem than any non-family member, so this accusation was not some trifling rumor. Whether or not Hai was correct about there being a sexual relationship, the fact that he could believe that told me there was definitely something unhealthy and unusual about the dynamic between the President and Madame Nhu.

To me, the possibility that Mrs. Nhu was somehow holding President Diem hostage because they had a secret affair was less important than the hypocrisy of the Diem regime toward matters of family, sex, and personal morality. This alleged ménage à trois in the Presidential Palace was understandable and was only human, even if it was something to keep quiet. What made it so unacceptable, in my opinion, was that at the same time this arrangement appeared to possibly exist, the Diem government was constantly preaching that South Vietnamese must imitate President Ngo in his ascetic, pure way of life. Every citizen of the Republic of Vietnam was constantly exhorted to avoid the dangers of the four social vices: sex, opium, gambling, and drinking. This morality campaign was all double-talk and pretense, it seemed.

The most galling example of this revolting hypocrisy to me was the adoption, again initiated by Mrs. Nhu, of the Family Law. This law forbade divorce in South Vietnam, regardless of any circumstances. Not even the most puritanical or Catholic country would ever consider adopting such strict anti-divorce legislation. Divorce was extremely rare in South Vietnam and was not at all a problem at the time. Vietnamese family traditions and Confucian values already tended to prevent all but the most necessary divorces. There was no reason for this Family Law, except that Mrs. Nhu wanted to prevent one divorce in particular. She initiated the law in order to prevent Nguyen Huu Chau from divorcing her sister Tran Le Chi.

Chau was a rich lawyer in Saigon and was the Secretary of State at the President's Office at the time. He wanted a divorce because Chi had been so indiscreet that seemingly everyone in Saigon knew about her many lovers. Chi stood to lose out on Chau's family fortune if there was a divorce, so Mrs. Nhu endeavored to make that impossible.

In what nation has there ever been such a case when a new law was created only to solve one individual's personal problem at the expense of the whole society? Mrs. Nhu's creation of the Family Law demonstrated the full extent of her power in the Diem regime while also defying tradition and common sense. In a country where divorce was not an issue, the Family Law made it one by prohibiting even reasonable and justifiable divorces. Furthermore, it was part of the unreasonable effort to close dance halls and bars throughout the country. It even included regulations forcing hotels to check the status of couples to make sure only legally married husbands and wives shared rooms. It did not matter that all this would upset public opinion; Mrs. Nhu was determined and so she got her way. Not only could Chau not divorce his unfaithful wife, but he was also stripped of his position in the government. He was forced to escape in secret from South Vietnam, such was Mrs. Nhu's persecution of him. With the secret help of Cambodia's Prince Sihanouk (who had been a classmate of Chau's at Lyceum Chasseloup Laubat in Saigon), Chau hid in the Cambodian Embassy. From there, he was taken surreptitiously to Phnom Penh before going into exile in France.

Chau had been one of the brightest young supporters to rally to Diem in 1954, and the regime's harassment of him was a vivid illustration of the destructive power Mrs. Nhu wielded. He came from a prominent family, was well educated with a law degree from France, and was a native Southerner. He gave the government a good, respectable image and was an asset in attracting Southern support. He was well qualified when he joined Diem's first government in 1954 as the equivalent of the President's Chief of Staff, and he had served the regime loyally since then. His only mistake was antagonizing Mrs. Nhu by seeking a divorce from her sister. That alone was enough to bring the full wrath of the regime down upon him, forcing him into exile. If this could happen to Chau, who had been a key aide to Diem, what could happen to lesser-known victims of Mrs. Nhu's fury?

In the later years of the Diem regime, Mrs. Nhu was anything and everything she wanted to be. Although only an ordinary delegate in the

National Assembly, she effectively controlled it and was able to pass any legislation she wanted with nearly unanimous votes. She also created the "Women's Solidarity Movement" to show that she was as powerful as her husband, who was leader of several men's organizations. The Women's Solidarity Movement was no mere social or political group but also included paramilitary training for women, generously provided at government expense. Mrs. Nhu went so far in flaunting her influence that she began reshaping Vietnam's historical figures in her own image. In Vietnam's history the Trung Sisters, who led rebellions against Chinese occupiers in AD 40, were well-known national heroines. In 1961 Mrs. Nhu ordered government architects to erect statues of the Trung Sisters in the central square of Saigon. These monuments looked exactly like Mrs. Nhu and her daughter. The resemblance was so obviously deliberate that angry anti-Diem demonstrators demolished them after the successful coup in November 1963.

Undeniably, Mrs. Nhu gave the Diem regime its "character," molding it according to her own image just like the statues of the Trung Sisters. More than any other member of the Ngo family, Mrs. Nhu attracted the most attention and drew the most hate. She was aptly labeled the "Dragon Lady of South Vietnam," and she was the most responsible for the bad image the Diem regime gained. Her arrogance and complete lack of sense of her own limitations did irreparable harm by antagonizing both domestic and international opinion against Diem's government. In this, she greatly contributed to the eventual collapse of the regime. Nevertheless, ultimately the blame for her unacceptable and destructive influence rested squarely on Ngo Dinh Diem's shoulders. Mrs. Nhu was only his sister-in-law, with no official position other than being a National Assembly delegate, and he was the President. He had the authority to stop her and could have done so, but in the end he did not.

In retrospect, I realize that my father's warning in 1954 about the Ngo family was prophetically true. It came shortly after I returned to Vietnam to serve Diem. Although my father was obviously happy to see me again after my four-year absence, he felt it was important to caution me about the Ngo family. Usually my father was reluctant to say anything derogatory about anyone, but in this case he did not hold back. He told me that they were very proud, to the point of being arrogant and stubborn. I was still very idealistic and was hopeful about Ngo Dinh Diem's leadership, so I was somewhat shocked by my father's negative comments. Later, after witnessing the Ngo family up close for years, I saw that my father knew what he was talking about. The flaws my father warned of were much in evidence in the Diem regime, amplified by excessive power and authority. It was so unfortunate. I still believe that during those years Ngo Dinh Diem was President there was a golden opportunity to build a free, independent, and peaceful South Vietnam, thus averting so much conflict and tragedy. Diem did not rise to the demands of the time, however, nor did he live up to his reputation of honesty and integrity. Instead, the Ngo family proved that they were indeed too proud, arrogant, and corruptible. They dragged themselves and South Vietnam toward disaster.

Chapter 4

THE CONVINCING TEST—ELECTIONS OF 1959

By 1959, I had seen enough of the Diem regime to conclude that it was heading in the wrong direction. The signs of the Ngo family's corruption were everywhere. Their authoritarian predilections were also becoming more and more obvious, and Diem's previous reputation for honesty and integrity was in tatters. Like many of Diem's early supporters who had believed in that reputation, I was bitterly disillusioned. It seemed to me that Diem had lost control of his government and had abdicated presidential power to the Nhus. I was especially revolted by the strange power that Mrs. Nhu had over Diem. I could understand if he were emotionally attached to her in private, but for his relationship with her — whatever it actually was — to cloud his judgment and public leadership was unacceptable. As Vo Van Hai and I witnessed, Diem failed to remain rational when it came to Mrs. Nhu, thereby subjecting the fate of millions of South Vietnamese to her foolishness and selfish whims.

Diem's government had seemed promising to myself and many others in 1955 and 1956. Then, there had been successes and movement towards a relatively free and prosperous South Vietnam led by a non-Communist, nationalist government. Starting in 1957, however, alarming signs began to emerge of corruption, mismanagement of national assets, and waste of American aid. Even worse, the promise of democratic ideals that had led many like me to rally to Diem faded. Not only were Diem's early supporters being let down, but in many ways the Diem regime began to antagonize and assault the non-Communist nationalists who should have been its closest friends. From my position at Vietnam Press I watched these disturbing trends and the betrayals of the Diem regime for over two years. I began to get fed up with this Ngo family dictatorship. The last straw for me was the 1959 election for the National Assembly. The election definitively convinced me that the regime was doomed and unworthy of support. The sensitive knowledge I had of the regime meant that leaving government service was bound to be dangerous and difficult. I nevertheless became determined to remove myself from the regime and, if necessary, from Vietnam.

THE NGO FAMILY ABOVE THE LAW

Working at Vietnam Press, I witnessed many instances where the Ngo family appeared to be secretly engaging in corrupt and illegal business. They believed they were above the laws of the Republic of Vietnam and acted accordingly. Particularly later in my time at Vietnam Press, after the Communist insurgency grew significantly, the Ngo family even apparently colluded with the Viet Cong as part of their crooked business enterprises. Normally any citizen of South Vietnam suspected of even having contact with the Viet Cong could be arrested and imprisoned. If they were providing money, weapons, food, or anything that might help the enemy, the penalty could be death. The anti-Communist laws of South Vietnam were draconian and strictly enforced, except apparently with the members of the Ngo family.

Once, Vietnam Press received a news item about the firing of the Secretary General of the Public Works Ministry in Saigon. He was just the scapegoat for the real scandal, however, involving Ngo Dinh Can. Although all trade with the Viet Cong was forbidden, Can managed to organize a racket selling rice to Communists at a very profitable price. Somehow leaks about this secret rice deal occurred, but President Diem pinned the blame on an innocent official instead of punishing his brother. When the news release about this was given to me at Vietnam Press, I called Tran Kim Tuyen of the Presidential Office for Political Research. I told him what I knew about the true story and suggested that perhaps it would be better not to publicize and draw attention to the punishment of this poor fall guy. It would be better to keep quiet about it, I said. Tuyen agreed with me, but he said he "had orders" to release the story. He requested that I publish it verbatim, and so I had little choice but to comply.

Ngo Dinh Can was not the only member of the regime to deal secretly with Communists. Mrs. Nhu and Bishop Thuc also authorized some of their underlings to do business with the Viet Cong. They were workers from her women's organizations and his Dalat Catholic University. Secretly, they provided cash, medicine, and food to the Communists. In exchange, the Viet Cong gave free access to the forests they controlled so that Mrs. Nhu's and Bishop Thuc's agents could harvest the valuable lumber. These surreptitious deals with the Communists were carried out for years without much disturbance, but every now and then incidents occurred that disrupted them. In one case late in 1959, two battalions of ARVN paratroopers were engaged in an operation in a VC-infested area when they discovered the lumber outfit. They even found that there were two platoons of Special Forces from Dr. Tuyen's office tasked with protecting the lumber harvest and with assisting the Viet Cong in the area. The commander of the paratroopers, my friend Nguyen Chanh Thi, was shocked by his discovery but could do nothing about it. If he had spoken up, he would certainly have lost his command and possibly much more. He did not reveal what he saw until many years later in his autobiography.[1]

Not only was I forced to help cover up the Ngo family's corruption at Vietnam Press, but at times I was compelled to assist in the regime's underhanded political maneuvers. Once, I received a secret briefing from Dr. Tuyen on the covert operations that the regime was plotting against some opposition politicians. He told me that an opposition newspaper was going to "be ransacked by angry students," because of its "slanderous attacks against the President and his Political Adviser," Mr. Nhu. There was no real substance to these so-called "slanderous attacks," but the regime needed an excuse to silence the paper. Nevertheless, Vietnam Press was required to quickly break the news of the "spontaneous" demonstration and try to convince the public the newspaper was wrong.

As an idealistic journalist, I felt uneasy with such gross distortions of the truth. At times, I was tempted to quit Vietnam Press. I felt that I did not need the job, which required me to frequently compromise my conscience. I still rationalized, however, that I had to be patient and that these were minor annoyances compared to the bigger goal of helping President Diem develop South Vietnam. Another consideration that kept me at Vietnam Press could be summed up with the French saying "les absents ont toujours tort," or "those who are absent are always wrong." It might have been distasteful at times, but only by being "present" and part of Diem's government could I hope to influence it positively. While I held hope that the Diem regime could eventually become a more democratic and just government, this thinking sustained me. As time went on, however, I was forced to distort the truth more and more. Signs of improvement in the regime failed to materialize and so my doubts continued to grow.

Although I had to compromise much and was often unable to avoid involving myself in the repugnant acts of the regime, on some occasions I was more successful at keeping my hands and my conscience clean. One time, Dr. Tuyen wanted to use Vietnam Press as a cover for some covert operations in Cambodia. At the time, Tuyen's office was directing secret operations to help a rebel leader, Dap Chhuon, overthrow Prince Sihanouk as ruler of Cambodia. Tuyen wanted one of his secret agents to work under the cover of Vietnam Press, posing as its correspondent in Phnom Penh. I strongly protested this because I thought it was completely out of order to involve our news agency. Furthermore, I told Tuyen, this whole affair appeared to be doomed anyway because Prince Sihanouk was very popular with the Cambodian people, unlike Dap Chhuon and Tuyen's other Cambodian allies. I predicted the plot would backfire in all likelihood, badly damaging South Vietnamese and Cambodian relations.

I told Tuyen that he was going too far in trying to involve Vietnam Press in his coup plotting. I had been working hard to build up the good name of Vietnam Press as a news agency and it would be disastrous for its image if the coup failed and the role of Vietnam Press were exposed. Tuyen gave in to my arguments and dropped the idea of involving Vietnam Press in his coup scheming. It was a good thing, too, because the coup did fail miserably, just as I anticipated. It was a major blunder committed by the Saigon government that gave Hanoi an important strategic advantage. Sihanouk had previously adopted a neutralist but non-Communist position, but afterwards he became much more pro-Communist. He allowed the Communists to use Cambodia as a sanctuary and as part of the Ho Chi Minh Trail that brought men and supplies into South Vietnam. I had not been in a position to prevent this massive disaster, but at least I had kept Vietnam Press from being dragged down by the failure.

In another instance, I had to object to Tuyen's scheme to use Vietnam Press as a cover for secret agents he was sending to the capitals of various African and Asian countries. At the time, Ngo Dinh Nhu was very keen on projecting a good image for South Vietnam in neutralist, developing countries like India, Indonesia, and Egypt. To please his boss, Tuyen had the idea of sending his agents to New Delhi, Djakarta, and Cairo under cover as Vietnam Press correspondents. I protested, but Tuyen insisted that it was Nhu's order. I had to give in, but I asked Tuyen to at least send his agents to Vietnam Press for a few weeks to be properly trained. They needed to be taught how to be news agency correspondents and to be fully briefed about Vietnam Press operations so that they would not be so easily exposed. Tuyen agreed and sent three of his agents to Vietnam Press for training and briefing. When their training was complete, I told Tuyen that the agent he was sending to Cairo did not seem to be up to the task. I predicted that he would probably get himself in trouble with such a difficult assignment. Tuyen insisted on sending him to Cairo anyway. After only a week there, he had all kinds of problems, just as I suspected he would. He lost his wallet, money, and passport. Instead of relaying secret intelligence dispatches or even normal news reports, he had to send an urgent request for help through the Vietnam Press teletype network.

After witnessing such mistakes, along with the many signs of corruption, I really began to wonder where the Diem government could be heading. Both domestically and internationally, it seemed to lurch from blunder to blunder. I began losing all hope that the regime would change course. How much longer I could stay with such a government and why became major questions in my mind. As a result, in 1959 I began quietly discussing the situation with friends I could trust to be honest and discreet. I wanted to determine if my doubts about the regime were well founded and if I should remove myself from it.

The person whose advice I trusted and valued the most was Vo Van Hai, Diem's Personal Secretary. Hai was a sincere friend, and he knew more about what went on in the Presidential Palace than anyone. He had devoted his whole life to serving Diem, going back well before Diem had come to power. Their relationship started in the 1930s when Diem had resigned his position as Interior Minister and had continued on into Diem's exile. In 1954, when I returned from America, Hai had been one of Diem's few aides at the time and he was the one who greeted my group of students at the airport. Hai was nearly inseparable from Diem, always standing ready to do whatever Diem required. Despite this devotion and loyalty, however, Hai was not appreciated by Diem. I was shocked by how Diem treated Hai and took for granted Hai's service. One time, I was at the Palace and I saw Diem angrily yelling at Hai. Scornfully, Diem threw a stack of files at Hai, scattering them all over. Hai did not flinch, though, and instead calmly collected the files without saying a word.

This incident was one of many things I discussed with Hai while I was trying to decide what to do. I asked Hai why he did not quit if he was treated so badly. He lamented that "they would not let me!" As would be the case for many senior RVN officials in the later stages of Diem's rule, Hai feared repercussions like jail or worse if he tried to separate himself from the regime. That inability to escape only made him more pessimistic and depressed about the direction of the regime. He felt helpless and hopeless about the situation, it seemed. This was well before our conversation about the secret romance in the Palace, but already he despaired over Mrs. Nhu's growing power and the strange spell she had over Diem. I asked him, "Is there any hope that things will change for the better?" He doubted it very much and advised me that if I could find a way to leave Saigon I should do so. I should go back to America for further studies, he said, just to get away.

THE BIEN HOA ELECTION "TEST"

Leaving Diem was already precisely what I had in mind, and Hai's advice carried great weight for me. Still, I wanted to give Diem the benefit of the doubt and leave no stone unturned before I gave up on him. I decided also to consult two other friends, Huynh Van Lang and Bui Kien Thanh. Of the group of students with whom I returned to Saigon in 1954, they were the only two others remaining in the country. Both were high up in the secret Can Lao Party, so they knew a great deal of what went on in the regime. Lang was Director General of the Exchange Office, in addition to being the Treasurer of the Can Lao. Thanh was a high-ranking employee of the National Bank of Vietnam, and he managed a Can Lao business project involving the exploitation of mountains of seabird droppings, which were very rich fertilizers, on the Parcels and Spratley Islands.

I intended to compare notes on the Diem regime with Lang and Thanh. Although they were close associates of Nhu, I hoped that their different view might give me some more facts either to confirm my suspicions or to convince me that I should not give up hope yet. With that in mind, we three, along with our wives, met a number of times before the 1959 National Assembly election. In our conversations, Lang and Thanh consistently defended the regime. They advised me to be patient and not give up yet. Lang especially argued that Mrs. Nhu was not nearly as bad as Saigon gossip made her out to be. He said that maybe Mrs. Nhu just needed some other good women to help her, so we should encourage our own wives to work with her. Hearing this, I challenged Lang to cooperate with me in a test to see if what he said about Mrs. Nhu was true.

The test was to have my wife run for the National Assembly against one of Mrs. Nhu's followers. Under Diem, the National Assembly was just a rubber-stamp institution. Its delegates were handpicked by the regime and if you wanted to run you had to get the consent and support of a Ngo family member first. We were not going to consult the regime first, however. My wife would run as an "independent" candidate to see how democratic the election really was. We chose to run in Bien Hoa district, only about 30 kilometers from Saigon. The regime-backed candidate there was a protégée of Mrs. Nhu's who was running for reelection, so the test would show not only how fair the election was but also how much power Mrs. Nhu wielded. My wife and I did not care if she were elected. We only wanted to see how far Mrs. Nhu would go to ensure that her protégée was reelected.[2]

Lang would put up the money, which amounted to about 30,000 piasters, less than a thousand dollars. This would pay for the registration fees and other expenses of running. Lang, with his position in charge of the Exchange Office and the Can Lao's finances, was quite well off so the money was not an issue for him. Challenging the regime politically, however, was a significant risk, even for a trusted Can Lao member like him. Still, he agreed to participate in my test and so we set to work. The first step was to register my wife as a candidate with the Province Chief of Bien Hoa. When my wife came to the Province Chief with all the required documents, he was very surprised. It was almost the deadline for filing to run and a last-second, unapproved candidate was quite unexpected. He told my wife, "Madame, I know your husband, the Director General of Vietnam Press, works very closely with the President. Why do you want to register here in Bien Hoa? It is all arranged already!" He pleaded with her not to carry through with it: "Please go somewhere else; I know that your husband can arrange for you to be elected anywhere. I beg you. Do not give me trouble by registering here." My wife insisted, however, so he had to accept her documents.

After my wife registered to run, we visited some Catholic priests we knew near Bien Hoa. Their parishes were filled with refugees who had fled from the Communists in the North. They told us what they knew of the scheme for the *mandatory* reelection of Mrs. Nhu's protégée, Mrs. Huynh Ngoc Nu. Besides Mrs. Nhu, two other candidates had already registered. One was a Catholic school teacher in the Ho Nai refugee camp, while the other was the province's head of the pro-government Movement for National Revolution. These candidacies, however, were nothing but a ruse. It had already been arranged that these other candidates would withdraw from the race before the election. The teacher was to withdraw first, then just a week before the vote the other candidate would also excuse himself. Both of them were supposed to ask the people who had supported them to vote for Mrs. Nu, who would then be unopposed. The priests told us that this was all necessary because the people of Bien Hoa disliked Mrs. Nu. She had done nothing for them and they knew that she was in office only because of her connection to Mrs. Nhu. The priests thought that perhaps, if another candidate dared to run, the people of Bien Hoa might vote for that person as a protest against both Mrs. Nu and Mrs. Nhu. The priests asked my wife, "Do you think you can go against their will and sabotage their prearranged scenario?" She assured them that she was ready and willing.

My wife started going to Bien Hoa frequently, making speeches and other public appearances to promote her candidacy. She had a chauffeur to drive her, but he suddenly quit his job shortly after she started campaigning. She hired another, but by a strange coincidence he also told her that he had to quit after only a week. She had no choice but to drive herself, which she did. After that, she received a number of anonymous letters threatening that "accidents" might happen during her commute to Bien Hoa if she continued to campaign for office. Despite these intimidations, my wife did not give up.

One morning, only a week before the election, I received a call from the Minister of Interior, Lam Le Trinh. We had attended the same French-Catholic school in Hue, but I did not like Trinh because I saw him as one of the sycophants in the Diem regime. He was a protégé of Bishop Thuc and had a reputation for being arrogant and arbitrary as Diem's Interior Minister. In Saigon, Trinh was detested by many for frequently preventing theaters from showing movies on time. If he wanted to go to a movie, the theater had to wait for him no matter how late he was. If they started before he arrived, he would use his authority to close the theater. That's the sort of man he was. Naturally, I was not excited to get a call from him.

I asked him what was up and he told me, "I just came from the Palace and saw the President this morning." He said they had had "a long conversation about the election in Bien Hoa," and he asked me, "How come you let your wife run there and disrupt the government's plans?" Before I could respond he added, "The President was very angry with you. He wants me to let you know that." That upset me and I told him briskly, "I don't know what the President told you. In any case, though, if he has anything to tell me he can tell me directly. He has my phone number." I told Trinh I had nothing to discuss with him and hung up.

Two days before the vote, a lieutenant serving Colonel Do Mau, the Chief of Military Security and a friend of mine, came to my office. He said that the Colonel wanted to see me in his office as soon as possible to talk privately about something very important. I told him to go back and tell his boss I would be over shortly. When I arrived, I noticed that Do Mau was nervous and uneasy. He asked me to sit and then whispered to me:

> I saw the President this afternoon. I could *not* believe my ears. We talked, among other things, about the election in Bien Hoa district. I think that your wife has a good chance of winning because people there hate Mrs. Nu, the protégée of Mrs. Nhu. I had reports through my local contacts that people there were fed up with Mrs. Nu and did not want to reelect her for another term. I was shocked when I heard the President tell me that I had to do anything needed for the reelection of Mrs. Nu. Mrs. Nhu wants her reelected at any cost. Can you believe that? I don't know what to do!

I told him, "You have your orders from the President, your Commander-in-Chief, so as a military man you have to obey. Go ahead, do what you think is necessary. Don't worry about my wife not getting elected!" I explained to him that we didn't care if she was elected, that we were just using the election as a test to see "whether people like you and me, who have supported President Diem since before he even assumed power, should give up or not." I told him confidentially, "Between you and me, I think Mrs. Nhu is bossing the President around and all of us will have to leave him if we don't want to be her servants." Colonel Do Mau was much relieved to hear all this. He accompanied me to my car and we said a friendly goodbye.

On election night my wife received phone calls from the Catholic priests of the refugee camps saying that the great majority of the people there had voted for her. They were afraid that there was cheating going on in favor of Mrs. Nu though. At several voting stations, there were reports about sudden power blackouts, during which the ballot boxes were switched. The priests had also heard that soldiers of the Seventh Division, stationed near Bien Hoa, had been ordered to stand by and be ready to vote a second or third time if Mrs. Nu needed it. Their commander was a notorious sycophant of the regime, so this was not surprising. The priests asked my wife what they should do. They said that the young Catholic refugees were angry at seeing the cheating and wanted to protest. My wife wasn't sure what to tell them about this and asked me what I thought. I said, "Tell them to keep cool." I told my wife to explain that this was a test and to urge them to think carefully before protesting. That would probably lead them into unnecessary trouble and the election result would be the same anyway. The government was clearly bent on cheating for Mrs. Nu and no protest would change that. The most they should do, I told my wife, was to talk to the foreign journalists who were observing the elections and tell them about the cheating they witnessed.

The next day, I went to work as usual. The election results from the whole country were coming in that morning for Vietnam Press to publish. I looked at the election figures from Bien Hoa and was amused to see that the votes reported for Mrs. Nu alone exceeded the number of people living in the district. With the votes for my wife included, the total number of votes was about double the known population of Bien Hoa. The Ministry of Interior was in charge of coordinating the collection of election results nationwide and relaying them to Vietnam Press, so I picked up the phone and called Trinh. I told him, "I just looked at the election results of Bien Hoa district your office sent. Would you please double-check those figures carefully because they look ridiculous!" I asked him, "Did you notice that the number of votes for Mrs. Nu is one-and-a-half times the population of Bien Hoa? If I publish what you sent me, people will know for sure that the government is cheating. Please give me some figures that look *plausible* at least." Trinh said he would double-check and send me some new figures. A little later he gave me some revised numbers, having rearranged the "election results" to correspond more realistically to the population of Bien Hoa.

Meanwhile I looked at the international press coverage of the election in South Vietnam. The foreign correspondents were no fools and they saw the cheating of the Diem regime plainly. They cited Bien Hoa as one of the prime examples of electoral fraud committed by the government. I was disgusted with the whole election affair and the transparent duplicity. I asked myself, why was this fraud needed? All it did was dishearten former supporters of Diem and create new enemies. Was it truly necessary to cheat so blatantly just to get Mrs. Nhu's lackey reelected? Did this prove Mrs. Nhu was the true power in the regime? She had forced the whole government totally to disregard democratic principles, popular will, and common sense, all for one relatively trivial position in the impotent National Assembly. Pondering these questions, I realized that this meant the regime had definitively failed my test. I did not expect full and perfect democracy, but I did hope for progress in that direction and some respect for common decency. That progress and that respect clearly did not exist in the Diem regime. In my eyes, the Diem government was going nowhere but down and there was no saving it. I had to find some way to dissociate myself from it as soon as possible.

NGO FAMILY REACTION TO THE BIEN HOA ELECTION

After the election, I decided to forget about it completely. My wife and I did not really care about the office, and the affair had served its intended purpose of demonstrating the true nature of Diem's government to us. I was still in an awkward and delicate position because of the election, though. As Director General of Vietnam Press, I was supposed to help create the best possible image for the government. Instead, I had inadvertently engineered a major public relations black eye. I was not too afraid, however, because I thought there wasn't much the regime could do against me. I had my long personal and family relationships with Diem shielding me. Perhaps more important, I was prominent and had foreign friends, so there was no way to quietly punish me. At worst, I thought, I might lose my job. That would have suited me just fine, though. I no longer wanted to be the chief public relations man for a government I did not believe in. The best course, I decided, was to remain quiet and let the regime forget about everything. Once the regime had moved past the incident, I figured, I could start trying to find a way to leave its service. I thought I would try to leave South Vietnam for a while, maybe going back to America for graduate studies. Anything would be fine; I just had to get away until changes occurred in Saigon

Knowing the regime as I did, however, I probably should have been more concerned than I was. Thanks to Pham Xuan An, who was still my

Vietnam Press liaison with Tuyen's secret service, I eventually found out how the Ngo family members reacted to my Bien Hoa election test. An had learned through Ngo Dinh Nhu's Chief of Staff about a meeting of the family concerning the election and my role in it. It was a disturbing revelation for me.

Mrs. Nhu was furious at my role in the election. She considered me a "traitor" working deliberately against the government. She thought that I had intentionally brought the foreign correspondents to Bien Hoa and was responsible for the negative articles they wrote against the government. She also accused me of stealing money from Vietnam Press for my wife to run against the government-sponsored candidate. Mrs. Nhu insisted that I had to be punished and that sending me to jail was appropriate. President Diem listened to her accusations without saying much. The only point he raised was that I had "a bad wife, a Northerner," and I probably was under her influence. Diem did not trust people from Northern Vietnam like that, although in fact some of his closest and most sycophantic aides were Northerners. He may have been trying to excuse my actions by blaming my wife, but he also apparently believed Mrs. Nhu's story that I had stolen the money from Vietnam Press to finance the campaign.

It was Mr. Nhu who spoke up in my defense. He said that I was efficient as Director General of Vietnam Press and that Vietnam Press had improved a lot under my management. He argued that it was better to keep me at my job than to punish me. The government-supported candidate had won in Bien Hoa, he reasoned, so the matter should be dropped and I should be left alone. Why "open a can of worms" by publicly punishing me, which would only create a scandal and cost the regime a good worker?

After hearing about this discussion, I became concerned that a false step on my part could be dangerous, if not fatal. I already knew that publicly protesting the election would be unwise and would accomplish nothing positive with the regime anyway. Now I also knew that I could not even discuss the issue with Diem to try to quietly push him in a more democratic direction. He believed Mrs. Nhu and had no problem with her mockery of democracy. If I brought any more problems to his attention or rocked the boat further it would only confirm to him what Mrs. Nhu had said about me. That reaffirmed my belief that I needed to keep quiet about the election, but I no longer was so blithely confident that Diem or the rest of the Ngo family would just move on. I would have to actively work to regain their confidence and prepare my exit.

The climate of distrust was deepening by the day in Saigon, which made it impossible for me to discuss my problems with almost anyone else. I knew other Diem supporters had lost faith in the regime and were in about the same predicament as I was. Talking to them, however, would not help and would carry the substantial risk of someone telling the regime what I was planning. The only person I trusted enough to tell was Vo Van Hai. He shared my disgust with the corruption of the election and Diem's increasing dependency on the Nhus. He approved of my decision to leave Diem and once again urged me to do so as soon as I could. Aside from Hai, though, I told nobody of my plans. I did not even tell my wife what I was thinking.

At the time, it never occurred to me to discuss my secret intention to leave the regime with any of my foreign friends. I was close to some Americans, but somehow I felt that this was strictly my own problem and I had to deal with it by myself. In retrospect, that was a mistake. Discussing my problem with my American friends could have been very useful. They too were deeply concerned by this time with the deterioration of Diem's government. Talking to them could have helped them get a better understanding of the depth of the regime's problems, and there was the possibility they could have helped me leave. Without such discussions, however, they all believed the public façade I put on. Everyone assumed I was still a close and trusted aide of Diem and that I supported him without reservation.

GETTING SETTLED DOWN TO STAY?

Diem never did say a word to me about the 1959 Bien Hoa election. To confront someone directly was simply not his way. The election had made up my mind for me to leave him, but I had to wait for the right moment to raise such a delicate proposal. In the meantime, I wanted to make sure that nobody could have any suspicion that I was thinking about abandoning Diem. If the regime suspected that, I feared they would create major obstacles for my exit or punish me for disloyalty. I therefore planned to pretend that I was still doing my job and that I was settling down to stay in Saigon. People needed to have the impression that nothing had happened and that I was still in the good graces of President Diem. I would keep my decision secret and eventually I would quietly request to leave at an opportune moment.

The first move in this plan was, ironically, to cause trouble with some close friends of the Nhus. As the Director General of Vietnam Press I was officially entitled to a government villa, but I still hadn't gotten one for myself. I didn't care much for these material privileges and had never taken the trouble to press my case for an official residence. Now, however, it was the perfect way to demonstrate how much I appreciated my lofty position in the government. I looked for a suitable villa and soon discovered a good one located in a very desirable residential neighborhood, near the homes of several other high-ranking government officials. It was also already occupied by Gene and Ann Gregory, the Nhus' American friends and propagandists. For most people, this would have automatically made them forget about that location, but I was only even more interested in getting it for myself because of the opportunity to kick out the Gregorys.

I went through the standard channels to request that specific villa for use as the official residence of the Director General of Vietnam Press, but nothing happened for several days. I investigated and found out that the officials in charge of government housing did not want to antagonize the Gregorys. They were well known as good friends of the Nhus, so nobody dared to do anything even if the Gregorys were not really entitled to the government housing. It was just too risky to evict friends of the Nhus. I checked around some more and found out that the Gregorys had another private villa in town that they had just built for themselves. Knowing all this, I decided that the only way to get the villa was for me to tell the Gregorys personally that I wanted the villa that they were improperly occupying.

I thought I was probably about the only person in Saigon who could directly confront the Gregorys in such a manner and obtain satisfaction. They were treated like VIPs in Saigon because of their relationship with the Nhus and people were afraid to say "no" to them. I was not some anonymous civil servant they could bully around, however, because of my connection with them in the past and my personal relationship with the President. Armed with my knowledge that they were illegitimately occupying the villa despite having their own private residence, I planned to raise the issue with them at one of the many official cocktail receptions they attended. That way I could casually address the matter instead of making a big issue out of it. A short time later, during one of these cocktail parties, I met Gene and Ann just as I expected. After saying hello and exchanging some small talk, I told them nonchalantly, "I understand that you have a nice new villa built for you in Phu Nhuan District and it is already completed. As Director General of Vietnam Press I need the villa you are occupying now. Do me a big favor: please move out as soon as possible. Would you please?" Gene knew me well enough to know that I would not take no for an answer. He immediately said, "Of course, for you we will move out immediately. I think by next week we can get all our things out." The eviction was thus smooth and swift, just as I had hoped. The Gregorys knew that I was not at all afraid of their relationship with the Nhus, so they really had no choice but to comply with my request, which was proper and reasonable.

Kicking the Gregorys out of their government villa was quite satisfying to me. The move was a good camouflage for my secret plan to quit the regime because it gave the appearance that I was settling down for a long period of government service. I also felt that the Gregorys were "bad Americans" and needed to be put in their place. By 1959 they were using *The Times of Vietnam* to flatter the Nhus and to publicize the Nhus' views to the international community. That galled me because I had founded the paper to be an objective journalistic outlet, not a propaganda mouthpiece. Everyone was afraid of the Gregorys, so to be the one to stand up against them was gratifying.

After getting the big government villa to give everyone the impression I was in Saigon for good, I concentrated on getting into the good graces of President Diem and Ngo Dinh Nhu. With Diem, it was not that difficult. Over the years I had found that the best way for me to treat Diem was like he was just an elderly uncle of mine. He liked to make small talk with me and felt relaxed casually chatting with me. Previously, I had tried to avoid doing that because I thought he was the President and had millions who depended on him. His time was precious, so I tried not to waste it when he summoned me to the Palace. I would tell him about whatever important matters I had come for and then promptly excuse myself. Diem, however, with his mandarin outlook, was not much concerned about wasting time or being inefficient. He thought that as President he could do as he pleased. He also thought he was bestowing an honor upon me by asking me to come to the Palace and talk.

Several times over the years people had told me that Diem considered me "arrogant" for refusing to stay and chat with him for extended sessions. After making my decision to try to leave, therefore, I gave up my old thinking. Above all else, I needed to please Diem. There was no longer any question of trying to maintain the independence of Vietnam Press by staying away from the Palace. From now on, if Diem wanted me to interpret or to sit and make small talk for hours, I would be available anytime for as long as he wished. This change on my part apparently pleased Diem a great deal. I was soon called to the Palace almost every day, sometimes several times a day. Diem clearly felt at ease in my presence, and other people who worked in the Palace noted that he was usually in a good mood when I was with him. I would sit and talk for hours with him, interpret whenever he had important guests, and take care of many other matters that he entrusted me with, all in addition to my duties at Vietnam Press. Gossip in Saigon circulated fast, and soon everyone knew that I was spending much of my time at the Palace. The talk around town began to be that I was the "darling adopted son of Diem," which was perfect for me. I had gotten myself back in the good graces of Diem and everyone saw it, so there was unlikely to be more questions about my loyalty and intentions. Although I didn't like currying favor with Diem like that, it was still different in my mind from the many sycophants in the regime because I never flattered him or gave him insincere praise, I did not change how I did my job at Vietnam Press, and I didn't do it for some material gain like a promotion. I just did what Diem wanted me to do.

I also needed to make sure I was on good terms with Ngo Dinh Nhu, who was the real power behind Diem by then. Before, I had mostly avoided him. I had never acted as though he was in charge, because officially and legally he wasn't. I had dealt only with Diem, who was the true leader of South Vietnam as President. Now, though, I considered Nhu to be more important than Diem because Nhu did run things in reality. I began to regularly report to him about my activities and plans. Whenever there was an important decision to be made, I consulted Nhu. Again, I considered this different from the sycophancy I detested because all I was doing was enacting the standard practice for everyone else in the government, treating Nhu as the real leader. Nhu was clearly pleased with my changed attitude, which he saw as my finally recognizing his power and authority instead of resisting it as I had. He knew that I was not the type to kowtow to him just to ask favors or for other benefits, so he interpreted my change as genuine acknowledgement of his important presence in the Diem government. My outward change in attitude therefore seemed to be working well with Diem and Nhu, so I began to feel much more secure again. My plans were proceeding smoothly, and all that seemed to be left was to wait for an auspicious time to take my leave.

Chapter 5

THE ABORTED 1960 COUP D'ÉTAT

For almost a year, I kept my head down and worked to reestablish my good relationships with Diem and Nhu. That process went well, but there were forces out of my control that could derail my plans. The announcement of the Caravelle Manifesto denouncing the regime in April 1960 certainly did not help me because it once again drew the regime's attention to the possibility of dissidents in its midst. As that seemingly blew over, though, I started to think that it was time to make my next move. I was about to request permission from Diem to quit my job and leave for the United States, but then a coup attempt against Diem on November 11, 1960 put that idea on hold indefinitely. It was most certainly not the opportune moment I had been waiting for as it cast an unprecedented cloud of mistrust on Saigon politics. The regime became hypersensitive to signs of disloyalty, so I had to bide my time until that pall cleared and the regime was not in a defensive crisis mode.

The night of the coup, I was called at home by the security guard at the Vietnam Press office. Our office was only one street away from the Presidential Palace. The guard reported to me that he had seen ARVN paratroopers pointing their guns at the Palace, but he didn't know why that had happened. I told him to keep watching and to call me back if he saw anything else. After I hung up, I turned on Saigon Radio and I heard Colonel Nguyen Chanh Thi, the "Supreme Commander of Revolutionary Forces." He read an appeal from the "Revolutionary Council," which stated that the Army had overthrown the corrupt family dictatorship of

Ngo Dinh Diem. After he spoke, Dr. Phan Quang Dan, an opposition politician, took to the air and began to attack the Diem government. He repeatedly called on the population "to tear up Diem's picture," but he didn't have much else to say. My immediate reaction was that this coup appeared to be planned very badly and probably had little chance of succeeding. I thought the radio message, with its shrill exhortation to tear up Diem's picture, was petty, incoherent, and highly unlikely to secure public support.

Hearing the messages, I was concerned that the coup leaders might try to force me, as Director General of Vietnam Press, to assist with their propaganda. They clearly could have used help in that area. To avoid any problems, I quickly left my government house and went to a friend's apartment so they wouldn't find me. There, I sat and listened to the radio all night. The same statement by Dr. Dan repeated itself, over and over again. By the early hours of the morning, that convinced me that the coup was indeed in deep trouble. If it had been proceeding satisfactorily, surely they would have been able to put together an updated and more compelling message.

In the late morning a statement by Diem himself came on, confirming my guess. He said that, after negotiating with the coup leaders and consulting with the ARVN Chief of Staff General Le Van Ty, he pledged to reform his government as demanded by the coup leaders. In exchange and in order to avoid more bloodshed, the coup would not proceed any further. Later that day, Diem broadcast another statement saying that a small group of "rebels" had been crushed by loyal troops. Diem had used the negotiations and his promise of reform to buy time for those troops to come to his rescue while the coup forces sat idle.

WHAT HAPPENED?

Although many South Vietnamese might have been ready for a change of government, the 1960 coup failed for a multitude of reasons. Some of them were obvious immediately, while others took years to be uncovered. I was well informed and knew some of what happened at the time, but there was still a lot that I puzzled over. Even though I was close with some of the main participants, for years none would give me an honest or full account of their actions. Now, though, with the release of their memoirs combined with the information they provided me before, I can reconstruct a fuller picture of the coup and the roles of its participants, including my friend Vo Van Hai.

At its outset, the coup appeared to have a good chance of succeeding. The plotters took Saigon by surprise, and the elite paratroopers were able to easily seize the important positions in the capital. They had the Presidential Palace surrounded and the city under control before loyal troops could be alerted or brought in. The coup, however, lacked a unified command. After the initial moves, confusion and hesitation took over as it was not clear who was in control. Additionally, although the opening actions were successful, many aspects of the operation were not well planned or executed properly. The coup plotters overlooked such elementary military measures as setting up roadblocks in the city and severing the communications of the Presidential Palace. The coup participants were so disorganized that they did not have enough trucks to transport some troops, and they did not secure the support of key tank and artillery units.

In the political arena, the coup was even worse prepared, as Dr. Dan's improvised haranguing demonstrated. Not only did the rebels lack a plan to win the support of the people, they also neglected to secure American support or at least understanding. Given the dependence of South Vietnam on American aid for survival, this was a ruinous error. Finally, the plotters made a fatal mistake by not carrying the coup to its conclusion in a determined fashion. In a situation where there could be no half measures, the coup leaders halted their forces and negotiated while they were not yet in complete control.

Colonel Nguyen Chanh Thi had proclaimed himself the "Supreme Commander of Revolutionary Forces" on the radio, and for years after he insisted that he had planned and led the coup. Colonel Thi, however, was not in fact the leader and was not even initially a willing participant. Lieutenant Colonel Vuong Van Dong was the real initiator of the plot. Dong forced Thi to join the coup because he felt Thi's presence would be useful in rallying the elite paratroopers to the rebel side. Thi's decision to suddenly shift from being a reluctant participant to "Supreme Commander" created a very confused situation in which nobody was clearly in charge, severely handicapping the coup.

It was a shock to me when Thi proclaimed himself the leader of the rebels on the radio because everyone considered him a Diem loyalist. In 1960, Colonel Thi was the commander of the paratrooper regiment stationed near the Tan Son Nhut airport on the outskirts of Saigon. Thi was an uncompromising anti-communist and was from a village just south of Hue in Central Vietnam. He had joined the paratroops under the French and had fought against the Viet Minh. When Ngo Dinh Diem came to power as Prime Minister in 1954, Thi resigned as commander of the 1st Imperial Guard battalion and sided with Diem instead of with the military officers backing Bao Dai. In gratitude, Diem appointed Thi as the commander of the paratrooper regiment, considered one of the best units in the South Vietnamese army. The paratroopers were also a key component in carrying out or thwarting any coup attempt in the capital, so the Ngos clearly placed a great deal of trust in Thi.

Lt. Col. Vuong Van Dong, on the other hand, was one of the many disgruntled officers whom the Diem regime had antagonized and discriminated against. He was a Northerner, he had not joined the Can Lao Party, and he had not converted to Catholicism. Because he was missing the three Cs (Can Lao, Catholic, and Central Vietnam), Dong was overlooked repeatedly for promotions and was not assigned to command any troops. Instead, the regime sent him to Fort Leavenworth in Kansas for advanced training and then assigned him a non-command position upon his return, teaching at the Military Academy in Dalat. He was well regarded by his ARVN peers and American advisers, though, and was eager for a more active role.

Although he did have personal motives for resentment, Lt. Col. Dong was dissatisfied with the Diem regime mostly for valid reasons and he had good intentions. Like many ARVN officers, he was upset with the regime manipulating the military and promoting commanders for political reasons rather than based on merit. He also worried the regime was mishandling the war against the Communists and believed that a change was necessary for the ARVN to achieve victory. Dong and his associates, however, were reckless coup plotters who failed to make careful plans commensurate with the importance of their undertaking. His rebel group was only a collection of junior and field grade officers without many common bonds or dedication. His closest associates in the rebellion were relatives: his brother-in-law Lieutenant Colonel Nguyen Trieu Hong and Hong's uncle Hoang Co Thuy. With the initial core of the rebellion restricted to these relatives, it was bound to be difficult, if not impossible, to mobilize truly national support for the coup. In his memoir, Dong himself admitted that "a revolution is not a game and cannot be the work of a group of 'amateurs' who are not professionals."[1] For the most part, however, "amateurs" were precisely what Dong's group was.

Dong wanted to use Thi as a figurehead leader of the coup to demonstrate that all of the paratroopers were behind the rebellion and to rally other Diem supporters to their side. Dong and his associates debated at length whether or not to try to convince Thi to join in the coup plotting. Thi was one of the three key officers in Saigon whom Diem relied on to defend the regime, along with the Commander of the Capital Region, General Thai Quang Hoang, and Chief of Military Security Col. Do Mau. Lt. Col. Dong wanted to include Thi, but Dong's co-conspirators all objected. It was a big risk to approach such a regime loyalist and so they decided that they should not place their trust in Thi.

On the many later occasions I asked Thi about his role, he always claimed that he was the leader of the plot and that the other officers came to his house that night to get his orders. His story never made much sense to me, however. He neither explained satisfactorily what exactly the actual plan for the coup was nor revealed who else had been part of the planning. On these counts he was vague and inconsistent. I strongly suspected that he was misrepresenting his role in the coup leadership to make himself look better. The reality was that he knew nothing of the coup until the other officers showed up at his house. He claimed that the coup was to start on November 12, but that Lt. Col. Dong and the others showed up at 8 p.m. on November 11 because the coup had been discovered. According to him, the other officers were seeking his permission to begin early while they could still achieve some surprise. "Confronted with a fait accompli situation," he wrote in his memoirs, "I could not do anything else," and so he gave his approval to initiate the operation.[2] Again, this was clearly not the truth as it was a known fact that Dong and his associates went to Thi's house at 11 that night, not at 8.

What really happened was that the rebels came to Thi's house to arrest him and force him to follow along with the operation. They told the sentry outside Thi's house they had urgent business with Thi and gave orders for the platoon guarding the house to return to base. Thi was asleep already and was awakened by their knocks. He was surprised when he opened the door and saw the other officers, but before anything was said they pushed into the house and closed the door. Dong told Thi about the plan and asked him to follow them. According to Dong's memoir, "at first Thi objected and refused to go."[3] Already at that point, a paratrooper battalion commander had been killed by accident when he refused to join the rebels. Dong assured Thi as a friend that he would be safe, however, so long as he came along. Thi was forced to dress and follow the rebels. On their way to the assembly point, Dong kept Thi with him both to protect Thi and to send the message that Thi was with the rebellion.

Once the coup was under way, Thi was allowed to move about freely. He apparently decided to change his role from reluctant participant to "Supreme Commander" when, by chance, he got hold of the Appeal from the Revolutionary Council to the Armed Forces. This statement was written by the main political sponsor of the coup, Attorney Hoang Co Thuy, and was meant to be delivered to Lt. Col. Dong so that he could broadcast it over Radio Vietnam. In his claims to have led the coup, Thi later explained that he had transformed from a loyal Diem supporter into a rebel because of the increasing unpopularity of the Ngo family dictatorship and the widespread disillusionment with Diem. Whether that was exactly his thinking at the moment he got his hands on the Appeal to the Armed Forces or whether he was merely acting opportunistically is not clear. In any case, Thi jumped at the chance and rushed to the radio station to read the message and proclaim himself publicly as the coup's leader, creating a very confused situation.

From a military standpoint, the lack of unified leadership created a number of problems while exacerbating the issues of the coup's poor planning and organization. Rather than prompting other commanders to rally to the rebels, Thi's proclamation that he was in charge actually gave uncommitted officers more reason to hesitate. Because it was unclear who and what they would actually be supporting, most officers decided to wait to see which way things went. Thanks to the many mistakes made by the rebels, the coup stalled out, allowing uncommitted officers to opportunistically rush to Diem's defense after it was clear what the outcome would be. The prime example of this was Brigadier General Nguyen Khanh. General Khanh was supposed to be arrested by the rebels, but he had recently moved to a new house so they could not find him. Awoken by gunfire, Khanh was able to rush to the Palace unhindered and climb over the wall of the besieged compound. There, he joined Diem and helped coordinate the regime's defense. Such was the incompetence of some of the key coup officers that this was allowed to happen. In almost every area of the operation there were unacceptable delays, confusions, and irresponsible blunders like failing to block the roads into the capital. Perhaps the worst executed aspect of the coup was the attack on the Presidential Palace itself, which was commanded by a major who was clearly not up to that important task.

Although there were many military mistakes made by the rebels, the political side of the coup was even more troubled. According to Dong, the political leadership of the coup was entrusted to Attorney Hoang Co Thuy, who was the uncle of Dong's closest co-conspirator, Lt. Col. Nguyen Trieu Hong. Thuy was a member of the Coalition for Democracy (*Khoi Lien Minh Dan Chu*), which was supposed to enlist popular support for the coup. During the coup, however, there was poor communication between Dong and Thuy. Dong was on the move constantly, so they missed meeting each other several times as the coup progressed. Even more important, Lt. Col. Hong was killed in the first few minutes of the coup operation, severing the main link between Dong and Thuy. The result was that Thuy was not where he needed to be and was not able to broadcast the appeals he had prepared over Radio Vietnam.

It was Col. Thi who invited Dr. Phan Quang Dan to replace Thuy and join the rebels as their "political adviser." Dr. Dan was a prominent opposition politician who had been barred by the regime from taking a National Assembly seat he won in 1959. He had also been involved in a number of Bao Dai's governments before Diem. According to Thi, Dr. Dan was a last-second replacement for Tran Van Dinh, a diplomat from Central Vietnam. Thi claimed that Dinh was supposed to fly back to Saigon from Rangoon, but instead of doing so Dinh informed Nhu about the coup. Thus, Dr. Dan had to be invited to the coup at the last moment because of Dinh's defection. Nobody else ever mentioned Dinh as concerned in the plot, however. For my part, I never believed what Thi told me about Dinh being involved. In any case, Dr. Dan ended up being the one to broadcast the political message of the revolt. It was a task that he was unprepared for and apparently incapable of satisfactorily executing. His calls to tear up Diem's picture seemed more petty than anything and reflected badly on the coup group. I suspect that Thi's story of Dinh's involvement was merely an attempt to excuse his misstep of inviting Dr. Dan to appeal to the people instead of Thuy.

The inclusion of Dr. Dan was an impulsive mistake by Thi, but the most significant political weakness of the coup was the result of Lt. Col. Dong's own miscalculation. Even after the failure of his plot, Dong was proud that there was no foreign hand in it. He had not contacted any Americans during the planning of the coup because he wanted to avoid the appearance of being subservient to a foreign power. It was understandable for a nationalist like Dong, but at the same time it was also completely unrealistic to ignore the Americans' influence. Without some assurance of American support or at least acquiescence, no coup plot in Saigon could have much hope of succeeding.

As it was, Dong was forced by circumstances to deal with the Americans anyway. Instead of carefully planning how to approach them and win their support, Dong had to deal with them in unfavorable conditions that gave him less leverage. When the coup started bogging down, Dong had to request the intervention of American Ambassador Elbridge Durbrow and Military Assistance Advisory Group (MAAG) commander General McGarr. Dong asked them to help ensure that Diem honored the promises he was making and to guarantee Dong's own safety. Without prior communication and with the coup looking like it was in trouble, however, what Dong got was evasive answers at that crucial moment. Durbrow was no great fan of Diem, but when Dong asked directly what the American attitude towards the coup was, Durbrow told him, "We support this government [Diem's] until it fails."[4] It was simply too late at that point for the United States to offer any sort of assistance or encouragement.

These mistakes made it likely that the revolt would fail, but the truly fatal factor was the lack of determination to carry out the coup to its conclusion. Dong and his associates wavered in the crucial moment and opened negotiations with Diem rather than continuing to secure the capital. At the time, Dong and the rebels still had enough respect for Diem that they believed that the nation could be rescued merely by removing the Nhus while keeping Diem. In reality, however, Diem was already wholly dependent on his brother and was not at all amenable to being "saved" from the pernicious influence of the Nhus. As the negotiations went on, Diem waited for the loyal forces that would rescue him. Diem's most loyal aide, Vo Van Hai, played an instrumental and ironic role in all this. Hai jumped to offer his assistance to the rebels because he agreed that Diem needed to be freed from the Nhus. He served as the intermediary between Diem and the rebels, thereby leading to the coup stopping midstream and the inadvertent salvation of the Diem regime.

ROLE OF VO VAN HAI

When I later asked Hai about his role in the 1960 coup, he did not want to say anything about it. It was as if the experience was too painful for him to recall and had to be completely forgotten. From various accounts, though, it was clear that Hai had inadvertently helped to preserve the regime as it was. Col. Thi claimed that Hai had some role in the planning of the coup and had offered money for the operation's expenses. Thi himself was not actually part of the plotting, however, so this was undoubtedly another invention on Thi's part. In reality, Hai's involvement in the 1960 coup seemed more impulsive than premeditated.

In his radio broadcast, Thi as "Commander in Chief of the Revolutionary Armed Forces" proclaimed that "the Ngo Dinh Diem government, after six years in power, has proved itself ineffective in the task of national salvation and reconstruction, while every day Communists are increasing their pressure." He further added, "Ngo Dinh Diem has imposed a family dictatorship, which is feudalistic and blindly selfish, putting its own interests above those of the nation." Hai already completely agreed with such arguments. Although Hai thought changes were needed in the government, he was still unconditionally loyal to Diem himself. He thought that the best solution was to deliver Diem from the bad influences of the Nhus. This coup attempt seemed to present an opportunity to do just that. Oblivious to any potential danger or trouble for himself, Hai rushed to volunteer his services negotiating to achieve this solution and to avoid any further bloodshed. He drove over to the area near the Presidential Palace, which was surrounded by rebel paratroopers, to meet Thi and offer to help.

When Hai found Thi, Thi told him to go see Lt. Col. Dong, "who had the authority to decide." At that moment, Dong was on his way to see the ARVN Chief of Staff, General Le Van Ty, in order to convince him to join the rebel side. Hai managed to intercept Dong in front of General Ty's residence. Hai informed Dong, "I have met Thi and he told me to see you. I agree with what you are doing. The Independence Palace should not be occupied by a bunch of prostitutes." These were unusually strong words from the typically mild-mannered Hai, but they reflected his anger and frustration with the regime. As he would later reveal to me, he had come to the conclusion that Mrs. Nhu was a real "prostitute" who was seducing Diem, and he was equally disgusted with the flatterers around Diem, whom he considered political "prostitutes." Having made his support for the rebels clear, however, Hai then told Dong that "in the present circumstances, prolonging the fighting only benefits Communists." As such, Hai offered to Dong "to serve as intermediary between President Diem and you," in order to help "find an acceptable solution which avoids giving any advantage to the Communists while satisfying the demands of the rebel side."[5]

What Hai considered "an acceptable solution" and what he proposed to Dong was essentially the preservation of Diem's leadership but the removal of the rest of the Ngo family. He told Dong they would temporarily keep Diem "as head of state without any executive power," while they went about "reforming the government." Most important to Hai, they would remove the Nhus and Mr. Can from the political scene. Hai was expressing what most loyal Diem supporters, including myself, believed in late 1960: that the salvation of South Vietnam could be achieved only by eliminating the nefarious influence of the Nhus. They were the predominant members of the Ngo family dictatorship and the ones who concerned people the most. Although Diem seemed unable or unwilling to dissociate himself from them, many South Vietnamese desperately hoped that he could still be a real national leader if he were forced to govern without the Nhus.

Dong agreed to have Hai serve as intermediary and to negotiate with Diem. He concurred with Hai's thinking and believed Hai could influence Diem. Additionally, Dong hoped that the negotiations might rescue his sputtering coup. Although Diem's side was not yet aware of it, the rebel military operations were not going well. Dong thought he could perhaps negotiate his way to success before the weakness of the revolt was recognized. Diem mistakenly still thought that the rebels had the ability to shell the Presidential Palace with artillery and that the paratroopers might storm in at any moment. Dong wanted to negotiate while those phantom threats still weighed over Diem. This was not entirely flawed thinking on Dong's part, but the simple fact was that time was not on the rebels' side. Every moment gave regime loyalists the opportunity to organize and come to the rescue, while at the same time, without clear momentum and control over key points, the rebels stood little chance of winning more supporters.

The result of the negotiations between Dong and Diem, with Hai serving as intermediary along with General Nguyen Khanh, was two proclamations broadcast over Radio Vietnam. The first was an order from General Ty to ARVN troops. He announced that "in order to preserve the unity of the army," Diem and the rebels had reached an agreement so "all units must immediately cease fire." The agreement was that Diem would dismiss the current government and the Revolutionary Council would be allowed to form a provisional government. Diem confirmed this agreement with his own proclamation, which stated:

> Following the uprising in the capital tonight, in order to preserve the unity of our armed forces in their fight against Communists, as President of the Republic of Vietnam, I have decided to dismiss the current government. I am appealing to ARVN generals to form a provisional government in order to continue the fight against Communists and protect the nation. At the same time, in coordination with the Revolutionary Council, I will form a coalition government. In order to avoid further bloodshed and to reassure people, I have instructed the generals to find the necessary means to stop all propaganda and false rumors and to cease fire: Ngo Dinh Diem.

Diem did not have much choice but to make this proclamation, believing as he did that the rebels had the upper hand militarily. He added the last portion about stopping "all propaganda and false rumors" because he was quite annoyed with Dr. Dan's verbal attacks against his "family dictatorship." With the agreement, both the propaganda and the rebel attacks ceased.

Although Diem may have negotiated and accepted the rebels' proposals, he was not acting in good faith. He was merely buying time. Even as his pledge to form a new coalition government was broadcast, he was sending out another urgent, secret message from the Presidential Palace to his Corps Commanders. His message to them read quite differently than his public announcement:

> Tonight, around 3 a.m., a group of field officers have betrayed and lied to soldiers to entrap them into joining their coup in the capital. At this moment communication is temporarily disrupted between the General Staff and the Capital Military Region as well as among some of the high-ranking officers. Consequently, the Military Corps Commanders have to remain calm and vigilant while waiting for instructions from liaison officers sent from the Presidential Palace. Colonel Tran Thien Khiem of the 5th Military Corps must dispatch the My Tho Armored Group to proceed to Phu Lam and to wait for orders. And Colonel Tran Thien Khiem should take a battalion and proceed to Phu Lam to wait for orders.

Diem himself read this message, and it was repeated again and again. It was eventually received and its orders carried out by Colonel Khiem, who saved the day for Diem. For his role, Khiem was proclaimed the "Hero and Savior of the Regime" and was promoted to Brigadier General.

Vo Van Hai, ever the faithful aide to President Diem, however, trusted Diem's promises made over Saigon Radio. He thought Diem had solemnly given his word to the nation as a Confucian gentleman, so there could be no duplicity. Hai helped to convince Dong that all rebel military operations had to stop, as had been agreed to, even though Diem was not halting his own military operations. As the rebels stopped their maneuvers and waited idly, the troops from outside Saigon that Diem had contacted began arriving. Had the situation been more uncertain, they may have sat on the fence uncommitted, but there was no need for that. They could see the disarray of the coup forces and so they enthusiastically seized the opportunity to prove their loyalty to Diem by crushing the rebels. The leaders of the revolt, including Dong and Thi, had to escape in a C-47 cargo plane, commandeered from the Tan Son Nhut airbase at the last minute. Interestingly, the pilot was supposed to be Major Nguyen Cao Ky, the future Prime Minister of South Vietnam in 1965, but he convinced the rebels to leave him be because he "had a French wife and small children." They found another pilot and took off for Phnom Penh, Cambodia, at 1 p.m. on November 12. They took Gen. Hoang, Commander of the Capitol Region, as a hostage.

Hai had meant to help the coup rid South Vietnam of the Nhus, but instead his involvement directly contributed to the failure of the revolt and the continuation of the regime as it was. Instead of being grateful to him for helping save their lives, however, Diem and Nhu made life miserable for Hai afterwards. He was suspected, investigated, and persecuted by the regime. Because he knew so many of Diem's secrets and was considered irreplaceable, they did not fire him or attempt to dispose of him, though. Hai had no choice but to continue in his job despite his bitter disillusionment with Diem. He vowed, however, that the next time Diem needed his help he would not provide it. He kept that pledge later on November 1, 1963, the day Diem was overthrown and killed. When Diem appealed to Hai for help then, Hai did not respond.

Deeply depressed and disgusted with politics, Hai languished in the years after Diem's downfall. I saw him again in Saigon a few times during the late 1960s and early '70s. He would tell me his thoughts about South

Vietnamese politics, but he was not involved at all anymore. Mostly, he told me about how he filled his days playing tennis at the Cercle Sportif or reading Chinese novels. Somehow, Hai did not leave Saigon when it was falling to the Communists in April 1975. Based on my conversations with him, I think he just may not have cared anymore. He was also not the kind of person to ask for any special favors, like a helicopter ride to escape, from his American friends. He was arrested by the Communists when they took over, and sadly he died in jail a few years later. His wife did make it to the United States, however. She contacted me from the house of a relative one time, but regrettably we never had the chance to meet face to face again. I would have dearly liked to have talked to her about the ordeals of her honest and brave husband.

In hindsight, I wish that Hai had talked to me about his desire to pressure President Diem into making reforms and getting rid of the Nhus. We were two of Diem's longest-serving and most trusted aides. Together we might have been able to organize and help implement a better solution. At the time, the American government had the exact same thing in mind, but without Vietnamese help — particularly from insiders like Hai and myself — they could not find the right way to convince Diem. Had those of us who wanted reform worked together, things may have been different. Instead, the disorganized 1960 coup only resulted in a worsening of the situation in Saigon.

Like myself, though, Hai kept quiet with both his Vietnamese and American friends about his desire to force Diem to reform. It seems clear to me now that it would have been better to have been more open and to have coordinated with the Americans to try to find a solution. In the political climate of Saigon at the time, having such a discussion seemed implausible, but looking back I can remember several opportunities when I could have discreetly talked to my American friends.

In 1960, Ambassador Durbrow very much desired to push for reforms and reduce the Nhus' influence. I was on good terms with him and saw him frequently at various diplomatic and social functions. One time, I invited him to my land on the Saigon River for a picnic and an afternoon of water skiing. I also invited my neighbor Vu Van Thai, the Director General of Budget and Foreign Aid, and Francis Cunningham, who was then the Deputy Ambassador. Francis had been the one who had suggested that I apply for an American scholarship in 1950, so he was a very close friend. In such a group of friends and in that private setting, I could have easily taken the initiative to discuss the problems of the regime and what we could do about them. Had Vo Van Hai confided in me his thinking about pushing for reforms, it would have been an excellent opportunity to initiate a coordinated campaign to achieve meaningful change in the government. I think that kind of direct and discreet communication between the American government and two close aides of President Diem could have been an important step towards a solution to the growing crisis in Saigon. Certainly, it would have had a much better chance of succeeding than the bungled 1960 coup attempt and, even if it failed, it would have had much less disastrous consequences. Unfortunately, it was an opportunity I let slip by unrealized.

LESSONS AND CONSEQUENCES OF THE 1960 COUP

The 1960 coup had very important political implications for South Vietnam. The handwriting on the wall was very clear and Diem should have seen that he had lost the confidence of even South Vietnam's anti-Communist nationalists. Diem should have seriously reflected on what had happened between 1954 and 1960 that led his staunchest supporters to turn against him. What had happened in those six years to destroy the great expectations that so many had previously had of Diem? Why had he grown so unpopular? Why had he been unable to check the growth of the Communist insurgency, despite having the generous support of the most powerful ally in the world? These were questions Diem needed to ask himself and that he also needed to ask Vo Van Hai. If Diem had been a good and fair leader, he should have asked Hai to frankly tell him what had gone so wrong. Why had Hai, who was Diem's most faithful aide and who had dedicated his whole life to serving Diem, become so alienated that he had tried to help the coup? Diem never did ask Hai, however. Instead, Diem persecuted Hai, and consequently he failed to learn anything positive from the coup attempt.

If Diem had been a real patriot and statesman, the 1960 coup could have provided him with a useful warning about the deterioration of his government and its popularity in South Vietnam. Had Diem learned anything from the 1960 coup he would have realized he needed to reverse course and initiate reforms to abolish the family dictatorship. I thought he should have offered to resign or at least hold new elections with the goal of creating a more popular and responsive government. Diem should not have needed a coup attempt to tell him that, considering that the US government and his American friends were telling him much the same thing already. What most South Vietnamese and Americans wanted was for Diem to build a broader nationalist, anti-Communist coalition behind and within his government that would better reflect the nation's politics. Had he done so, and thereby demonstrated his dedication to his country above all else, his prestige would have skyrocketed again. I thought that people would have begged him to stay on as leader of a new and more democratic government. Instead, Diem behaved as a despotic dictator, bent on hanging onto power and preserving his family's corrupt influence above all else.

Diem had solemnly guaranteed reforms over Radio Saigon, but it was a lie. Only hours after pledging to reform in order to avoid unnecessary bloodshed, Diem reneged on his promises and had the rebels crushed despite the ceasefire. Diem's reputation for honesty as a Confucian gentleman had always been his most important political asset, but that reputation had already eroded significantly by 1960. This latest and most blatant deceit cost Diem what little legitimacy and prestige he had left in the eyes of the South Vietnamese people. I didn't expect him to work with the coup leaders afterwards, but he could have easily carried out the reforms and expanded his government with many respectable and honest anti-Communists who were being excluded from the government at the time. There were still plenty of people who would have lent a hand to Diem if they were given real responsibility in the government and did not have to respond to the Nhus, but the regime continued to push aside and alienate these capable individuals instead.

Diem did not learn any of the necessary lessons from the 1960 coup, leading the regime in precisely the opposite direction it should have taken. Rather than becoming more inclusive and democratic, the government became more insular and centralized. Instead of listening to more and better people, Diem himself became even more isolated. Diem's dependence on his corrupt family only deepened as a result of the coup attempt. The political climate of Saigon, already unhealthy and distrustful, now became poisonous. That atmosphere only further empowered the worst intriguers and sycophants in the regime at the expense of the honest and competent.

The coup and its aftermath also set a dangerous precedent for the military of South Vietnam. It showed ARVN officers how they could capitalize on national crises for personal gain. It paved the way for ambitious and conniving officers like Nguyen Khanh and the "Hero and Savior of the

Regime," Tran Thien Khiem, to get promoted to positions of power and trust. Although they had acted as loyalists to Diem at that moment, in reality their only loyalties were to themselves. Khiem, for instance, had cleverly stationed himself on the outskirts of Saigon. He waited for the coup to founder and only then drove triumphantly into the capital. These were dangerous individuals who sought to promote their own selfish interests at every turn, even to the detriment of the nation's welfare. After 1960, they saw how easy it was to stir up trouble and exploit it for their own ends. They also learned what it would take for a coup to succeed in Saigon: an avoidance of half measures dictated by scruples of national interest or morality. Afterwards, these two were constantly conspiring in various coup plots, sometimes as the leaders and sometimes secretly behind the scenes. Their scheming was influenced heavily by the advice of their aide and confidant, Colonel Pham Ngoc Thao. Unbeknownst to them and everyone else in South Vietnam at the time, Thao was a Communist mole who reported directly to the Secretary General of the Communist Party in Hanoi, Le Duan. He was tasked with destabilizing South Vietnam and, thanks in large part to the unscrupulous Khanh and Khiem, he succeeded. South Vietnam was soon plagued by coups and countercoups, one after another, from 1963 until 1966. The rapid succession of coups completely undermined the political stability of South Vietnam and destroyed all credibility in the Saigon government.

Chapter 6

LEAVING DIEM

The aborted coup of 1960 spoiled my plans to request permission from Diem to quit my job and leave for America. The regime was busy throwing many people it suspected of disloyalty in jail, so I had to be very careful not to make any gesture or statement that would be interpreted as evidence of my dissatisfaction with Diem. Thanks to the 1959 election situation, the regime was already suspicious of my loyalty and armed with a plausible pretext for punishing me. I worried that asking for my leave would be too risky because the regime would clearly see it as a sign that I no longer supported Diem's government, which was basically true. I decided, therefore, that I had to postpone my plans to get out until a more favorable moment arose. As it turned out, I lost over a year waiting for that moment. During that time, I had to continue the charade that I was a content and loyal follower of the regime. Nobody could know what my real intentions were, not even my own wife or family.

I also had to stay on the good side of Diem and Nhu. I continued regularly coming to the Presidential Palace whenever Diem wanted and people around Saigon continued to say that I was Diem's "favorite adopted son." Despite my having gotten back in Diem's favor, however, the task of telling him that I wanted out was still going to be a difficult one. I wanted to tell Diem why I was leaving because I thought it might help him to understand why people were losing faith in him, but I had to be very careful. Bluntly telling him that I wanted to quit because I was fed up would have served no purpose. Diem did not respond well to such direct confrontations and

I would have risked provoking a hostile response from the rest of the Ngo family. Somehow, I had to find a subtle way to convey my critical message and yet still secure Diem's approval to depart.

FOREIGN TRIPS APPROVED BY NHU

One of the ways I tried to keep up the impression of my loyalty and satisfaction with the regime was by traveling extensively to represent Vietnam Press and South Vietnam. In 1960, I requested to make a number of such trips. I wanted to go to Germany, India, and Japan to increase contacts between Vietnam Press and the national news agencies in those important countries. I was also going to attend a UNESCO conference on mass media in Bangkok, Thailand. Diem was always slow responding to such requests, both because that was how he worked and because he did not like my leaving him. I had already discovered, though, that Nhu was really in charge of the government. Additionally, my experience with the 1959 election taught me that Nhu was the more rational and less emotional of the two brothers, contrary to many portrayals of the regime. Diem accepted Mrs. Nhu's impulsive desire to punish me without much consideration, whereas Mr. Nhu had been reasonable and had defended me. As such, I made sure to ask Nhu and not Diem about the trips. My requests to travel were sensible ones, so Nhu quickly approved them.

I felt at the time that West Germany was an excellent model for South Vietnam, especially because it was another country divided by the Cold War. I went there with the intention of expanding the working relationship between their national news agency, Deutsche Presse-Agentur, and Vietnam Press. West Germany was becoming more important economically and politically, so I thought South Vietnam could benefit from more news and information on how they tackled the problems of the Cold War and reconstruction from World War II. I had good relations with the West German Embassy in Saigon, including with the Ambassador, so they arranged for me to meet with Berlin Mayor Willy Brandt and to tour the cities of Bonn, Cologne, Stuttgart, Munich, and Frankfurt. I was impressed with what I saw of their recovery and economic growth, especially in comparison to what I saw during a short visit to Communist East Berlin. Mayor Brandt himself was even more impressive to me. He was not afraid of increased contacts between East and West Germans and counted on eventual reunification of the country. His conviction that Communism could be defeated if people had a free choice between dictatorship and democratic government struck a chord with me. As I admired his vision and patriotism, I wished that South Vietnam could have similarly inspired leadership.

My trip to New Delhi, India, was also a successful one. Politically, India was very important to South Vietnam for a number of reasons. Not only was India another underdeveloped country struggling with its fledgling democracy, but it was also the main advocate of neutralism in the Cold War. South Vietnam had many of the same problems as India, albeit on a much smaller scale. Additionally, there was a special connection between the two countries because of India's membership in the International Control Commission supervising the peace in Vietnam after the 1954 Geneva Conference. Despite all that, there wasn't yet any working relationship between India's national news agency, Press Trust of India, and Vietnam Press, so I went to establish one. In addition to New Delhi, I got to see the Taj Mahal and Calcutta, although I regretted that I did not have the opportunity to visit Bombay.

In Japan, my purpose was mainly to renew contacts with the two main news agencies in Tokyo, Kyodo News Agency and Jiji Press. Kyodo was the national news agency of Japan, while Jiji Press specialized in economic and financial news. Both agencies were very receptive to my ideas for increased cooperation and news exchanges with Vietnam Press. We had no problem reaching agreements and I was lavishly entertained in Japanese style by my counterparts. While I visited Japan, I also was invited to have a look at some of the rapidly growing Japanese companies like Sony. I left with a sense of awe and admiration for the tremendous dedication of the Japanese people to rebuilding their country and remaking it into a first-rate economic power.

The 1960 UNESCO Conference on Mass Media of Asian Developing Countries in Bangkok was the first of its kind. Up until then, mass media issues were generally considered important only in developed, Western countries with democratic traditions. Newly independent Asian nations had new and unique issues that needed to be discussed, however, especially because journalists in many of these countries faced excessive restrictions and political control. The UNESCO conference was intended to provide a forum for journalists in these less-than-free nations to discuss how they could improve the situation and find ways to report the truth as objectively as possible. I had made a good reputation for myself with all my work on improving relations between other national news agencies, so I was elected as one of the vice presidents of the conference. Because Thailand was the host country, its representative was named the president, and the representative of India was named a vice president also. The selection was a great honor for South Vietnam and for myself. Personally, however, I had mixed feelings about being honored like that at such an important international gathering. I was there, after all, representing a government that I did not really believe in and was trying to escape.

Although I had made up my mind to leave Diem and to do so as properly as possible, I was still tempted to try to get out of my predicament in any way I could, no matter if it was right or wrong. Physically, it would have been possible for me to leave illegally in a number of ways. My international trips were obvious opportunities when I could have simply not taken my return flight to Vietnam and stayed abroad. Another way I could have easily made my escape was during the flight lessons I was taking at the time. Sometimes, while flying, I thought about how easy it would be just to fly west toward the Cambodian border and out of South Vietnam. It was alluring enough that I told my instructor, a French pilot, to make sure I never inadvertently made the mistake of crossing the border. I found the idea of such easy exits from my situation enticing in some ways, but I also believed they were morally unacceptable. I had to leave Diem legally and with his permission because I needed to convey to him my belief that his government urgently needed change.

TELLING DIEM

By early 1961, I knew that Harvard University was ready to offer me an Associate Nieman Fellowship in Journalism, something I found out from the Director of the Asia Foundation in Saigon. I had been offered the same fellowship before, but I had declined it because I had not yet decided to quit the regime at that time. Now, though, the fellowship was not only a tremendous opportunity for me but it was also a nearly perfect excuse to escape Saigon. Every year, only three non-American journalists were selected, and I was the first person from Vietnam to have been offered this prestigious fellowship. Nieman Fellows were treated like faculty at Harvard, but I would also be able to audit any course I wanted during the yearlong fellowship. After that, I hoped to stay in the United States another year or so to complete a doctorate. Of course, even with such a compelling reason to leave I still needed Diem's approval.

I spent many sleepless nights debating the best way to approach Diem about leaving. My determination to not escape illegally without telling him left me with no alternative but to confront him with my request, but still I agonized over it. Even if I only raised the issue of my leaving and left my criticisms implicit, I still feared Diem might treat me unfairly. Diem would not fail to see my request to leave as a serious reproach of his government, and I already had seen how he could lash out emotionally in reaction to such perceived attacks. There was also the possibility that I might be thrown in jail on some trumped-up charge, as Mrs. Nhu had urged Diem to do to me after the 1959 election.

In the end, I calculated that given my situation, my friendships with many Americans, and my relationship with him, Diem would be forced to grant my request and let me leave. It was a dangerous, high-stakes bet, but I had no choice. I had to trust my own judgment and Diem's as well. I was counting on him to recognize that it would be politically unwise to move against me. My American friends would think very badly of him and his regime if I were punished arbitrarily. Everyone knew that I had done nothing wrong and had served Diem loyally, so I had to hope Diem would not dare to throw me in jail or to "liquidate" me just because I asked to go study at Harvard for a few years.

Finally, after months of waiting for the right moment, in April 1961 I had my auspicious day to ask Diem. It was the day after his reelection as President, and I knew he would be in a good mood. I gathered up some of the AP and UPI news stories on his reelection before I headed over to the Palace, knowing that these would please him even more. Before seeing Diem, I stopped by Vo Van Hai's office to ask him how the President was that morning. Hai confirmed that Diem was very happy about the vote, so I knew that this was probably going to be the best opportunity I could have. I went into the President's office and started by congratulating him about the election and showing him the positive news articles. Then, while Diem was still all smiles, I took the plunge. I told him:

> Mr. President, now that you've been reelected for a second term, I have a request to submit to you. You remember that when I left the US to return here with you in June 1954, I left in a hurry. I would like to go back to the States for advanced training in journalism. Harvard University has offered me an Associate Nieman Fellowship in Journalism for one year, beginning this coming fall.

As I explained what an honor the fellowship was, Diem listened quietly. I also informed him that I wanted to stay in America not just the one year for the fellowship but for two full years so that I could complete my PhD.

Diem looked pale and shocked by what I told him. He clearly understood that I was dissatisfied and that I wanted to leave him more than anything. After he had thought for a moment, he fired a series of questions at me. He demanded to know when I would leave, who would replace me at Vietnam Press, and many other details. He seemed to be grasping for a reason to deny my request, but I had anticipated all of his questions and had answers at the ready. Following my responses, he looked sullen and depressed. He had nothing more to say, it seemed, so I asked for permission to exit the office. As I was reaching for the door, however, Diem had one last question. He asked me, "When you go, will you take your family with you?" I sensed trouble at this. In his typically indirect way, Diem seemed to be asking me, "Are you leaving me for good because you are dissatisfied with me?" Not wanting to push him too far, I hedged in my answer. I told him, "Mr. President, it is only April. If I have your approval, I will notify Harvard now and, if everything is okay, I will leave in August or September to start the academic year. By then, I'll decide about my family. It's too early now to think about it."

After telling Diem about my decision to leave, I still kept my plans a secret and continued to behave as if I was very happy with my job. I kept going to the Palace and interpreting for Diem or chatting with him any time he wanted. I noticed, however, that Diem started calling me less than he had before. I did not mind, though, and I felt I had accomplished my mission. In the most polite and obedient way I could manage, I had signaled to Diem that I found it impossible to keep working for him. I thought that he understood that message clearly, especially when he made it a point to ask me whether I would take my family with me. Even though I thought the conversation was successful, I could not talk about it or my plans with anyone. I could not have others talking about my departure, which would be pouring salt in Diem's wounds. Only he knew that I wanted to leave, and it was up to him to give me permission. As such, I continued to keep everyone — including my family — in the dark.

After my meeting with Diem, I assumed that I had been authorized to leave because he had not said otherwise. I told the local Director of the Asia Foundation to notify Harvard that I would be coming before the beginning of the fall semester. In the meantime, I continued working at Vietnam Press as if nothing had changed. One day in early summer, though, I was suddenly summoned to Nhu's office. I did not know the reason for this unusual meeting, but I guessed that it had something to do with my secret request to leave. Nhu was very pleasant and nice to me when I sat down with him. He informed me, "The President told me you wanted to quit your job and go to Harvard. I know you have done good work at Vietnam Press. You are probably tired." He then suggested, "Why don't you make a trip by yourself to clear your head, and at the same time contact some Afro-Asian countries to establish better relations with them?" He concluded the meeting, telling me, "You have my authorization for that trip. Just send me a list of places that you want to visit. Go as soon as you want."

I could see this was an attempt to forestall my departure, but I could not argue against it. All I could do was thank Nhu for everything. I got up and told him I would submit a list of the countries I would visit. I added that I would also visit Paris and Hamburg because I needed to contact the news agencies in those cities. The next week, I sent Nhu my full itinerary. It was a lengthy one, including stops in Indonesia, Singapore, Hong Kong, Taiwan, Tokyo, Hamburg, Paris, Tunisia, Morocco, Senegal, and Côte d'Ivoire. Nhu approved it right away and notified the South Vietnamese diplomatic missions to give me any assistance I needed. At the time, Nhu was very much into solidarity with other underdeveloped countries of Africa and Asia, so this kind of diplomacy was something he was enthusiastic about. Additionally, of course, the trip would potentially delay or interfere with my plans to leave the regime, which I think was the real reason Nhu proposed it. After I got back from the trip, it was already July and my anticipated departure was rapidly approaching.

My plan was for Truong Buu Khanh to replace me as Director General of Vietnam Press. He was the Counselor at the Vietnamese Embassy in Washington, DC, but Diem had already recalled him to Saigon by the time I returned from my trip. Khanh's brother Dien was in charge of the Presidential Press Bureau, but Diem thought Dien was incompetent and so he was going to have Khanh replace his brother. I suggested that instead, Khanh should replace me at Vietnam Press. That way, I explained, the two brothers could work closely together at these two collaborative offices and Khanh could help his brother improve. Diem agreed to this but he didn't follow through. Instead of sending Khanh to Vietnam Press, Diem gave him various assignments that kept him away from our office. Khanh was in Saigon, but Diem made it impossible for me to get Khanh acquainted with the agency so that we could have a smooth transfer of authority in time for me to leave for Harvard. After a few weeks of this, I reminded Diem of our understanding that Khanh would replace me. He looked annoyed at me and just cryptically said, "We shall see about it later."

INFORMATION JOB ASSIGNED

As September came, I once again reminded Diem about the need to appoint my replacement, and once again he only gave me a cryptic reply. I was annoyed that Diem had not kept his word. I was already late for the fall semester at Harvard and I was getting very worried that I would not be able to leave at all. Then, one day, Pham Xuan An came to me with some troubling information. By that time, An was working as a stringer for Reuters news service, but we had an informal arrangement that An continued to cover the Palace — including Nhu's and Dr. Tuyen's offices — for Vietnam Press. Of course, An was still secretly working as a Communist spy as well. He told me that Nhu's Chief of Staff had prepared a decree appointing me as the new Director General of Information (the Ministry of Information had been downgraded to a Directorate General in 1960). If the President signed the decree, I would assume this new job while also keeping my current one managing Vietnam Press. I asked An whether he was sure about this information. He said he was "one-hundred percent" certain, but added that he could double-check for me if needed. I told him to do so. The next day, An came back to report that Nhu's Chief of Staff had shown him the decree and had asked An to tell me congratulations. Objectively speaking, it was a big promotion for me, and it showed how much Diem and Nhu appreciated my talents. It was a trap, however, even if it was a flattering one. If Diem signed the decree and I became the Director General of Information, there would be no way for me to leave.

I could definitely see a pattern now. The regime was unobtrusively doing its best to keep me in place through a combination of rewards for my service and delays to my departure. Nevertheless, there was no turning back in my mind. I had to maneuver fast to stop the new appointment. I decided to go and ask for help from Bishop Ngo Dinh Thuc and Ngo Dinh Can. With Diem and Nhu seemingly set on keeping me from leaving, I thought that only the considerable influence of their brothers could change things. First, I went to see Bishop Thuc. I brought him a proposal for a venture with Sony that I thought could raise some money for Dalat Catholic University, his pet project. After presenting the business opportunity, I asked for his help in stopping my new appointment to the Information Department. I explained to Thuc that Harvard was waiting for me and that it would look bad for me and South Vietnam if I did not show up. I told him that I had asked Diem for permission in March and Diem had agreed to let me go, but clearly Diem had not kept his word. Thuc said that it was good of me to suggest the Sony project to help Dalat Catholic University and he told me he would help with my situation. As I left, I thanked Thuc profusely for his help while also reminding him of the urgent need to stop the decree before it was signed.

Next, I flew to Hue to see Ngo Dinh Can and seek his help suspending the decree. I explained to him that I needed to get away for a while to "recharge" myself so that I might be more useful to President Diem later. Can was notorious for disliking Northerners, especially because of his competition with Nhu and Dr. Tuyen's secret police network, which was mostly made up of people originally from the North. Knowing this, I told Can that I had endured working with many Northerners at Vietnam Press for years and was in need of a respite. Can said he understood my situation and he promised to help stop my new appointment.

Having done all I could, I returned to Saigon and waited anxiously. I had gotten the promises I sought from Thuc and Can, but that did not mean anything was guaranteed. If, despite their assurances, they did not do anything or did not act quickly, the decree would be signed and I would be doomed. I asked Pham Xuan An to check again if anything had changed. He came back to me and reported that the decree was still on Nhu's desk. That could have meant one of two things. Either Thuc's and Can's interventions had delayed its release or it was still about to be released at any time. I could not be sure which it was, so I had to nervously wait and see. Several days passed, and then weeks, without the decree becoming official. That was very encouraging, but still I had not been given permission to go.

By that point, it was already October, and I was more than a month late for the semester at Harvard. I was getting desperate to leave Saigon, but it was impossible to go until Diem appointed my replacement at Vietnam Press. I suspected that Diem and Nhu were trying to corner me. By withholding the appointment of Khanh to take over Vietnam Press and making me late for the academic year, they hoped to force me to postpone my departure indefinitely and leave me with no choice but to stay. It would be another year before the start of school gave me another excuse to leave again, and I strongly felt that I could not wait that long. I was determined, then, to leave as soon as possible no matter what.

Once more, for the third time, I came to Diem and reminded him about naming Khanh as my replacement so I could leave. In order to convince Diem that his delays could not trap me, I explained to him that although I was late for the beginning of the semester it was not too late yet. If I left now I could show them I was serious about keeping my commitment and they would hopefully make an exception and accept me. When I had asked Diem about leaving before, he had been a little upset and annoyed. This time, he was clearly quite angry that I had once again raised the matter. He irately told me to "go see Secretary Thuan about it." I was not pleased with that at all. Nguyen Dinh Thuan was the Secretary of State at the President's Office and was known to be a "yes man" placed by Nhu to watch over Diem. He was also the type of sycophant I despised. I had personally seen Thuan pretend to take notes when Diem was talking about trivial matters like the weather. Although Diem liked that sort of thing because he thought it meant his aides were giving him their utmost attention and respect, such fawning served no real purpose and disgusted me. I had no regard for Thuan or trust in him, but I also had no choice but to go see him.

Previously, anytime I needed to talk with Thuan, he received me immediately and he always tried to show that he was very glad to see me. On that day, however, I had to sit and wait for him for more than an hour. When we finally met, I quickly and directly told him, "The President told me to see you. I have only two things to ask you to do for me: first, get Truong Buu Khanh, my replacement at Vietnam Press, appointed so that I can make the official transfer of service and leave; second, notify the Police and Security Directorate General to issue me and my family passports." Thuan sternly replied, "The appointment of Khanh will be made. But the President said that your family would not be issued passports." I thought to myself, "Damn, they are trying to scare me into staying on at Vietnam Press since my family cannot go with me. I must not fall for the bluff." I told Thuan, "I have not heard the President say anything about not issuing passports to my family. Anyway, if that is what he has decided, then I will leave by myself if needed. Please report to the President and have him sign the decree appointing Khanh as soon as possible. I must leave, no matter what."

The next day, the decree appointing Khanh as Director General of Vietnam Press was made public. I immediately arranged to meet him to make the official transfer of service, as required by government regulations. I signed off on the accounting books and Khanh signed on, proving that everything was in order. I made sure to keep a copy of the official transfer to prove that I had left office legally and properly. With the memory of Mrs. Nhu's allegation that I had stolen money from Vietnam Press during the 1959 electoral campaign in the back of my mind, I wanted that document badly. After getting that taken care of, I said goodbye to the staff. I told them to keep on working for the new boss the same way they had for me, thanked them for their help, and left the office.

Once the transfer of authority at Vietnam Press was complete, I called the Acting Director General of Police and Security, Nguyen Van Hay, and asked him to issue passports for my family and me. I told him I had to leave as soon as possible and he said, "No problem; just have someone bring the passport photos." I had my secretary bring Hay the photos and wait for the passports. I planned to leave Saigon the next day. Thankfully, Hay issued the passports immediately, for my family and me, without any problem. I never found out for sure whether he did that on his own as a favor to me or if he had the approval of Diem and Nhu. Normally, Diem and Nhu personally kept tabs on the comings and goings of every important person in South Vietnam, so I believe that they must have finally decided to give in. After all, they had signed the decree appointing my replacement at Vietnam Press. My determination to leave, even without my family, seemed to have been the decisive factor. I had called their bluff and made it impossible for them to stop me without taking drastic actions that would have brought public trouble for the regime. Once they decided it was better to let me go, keeping my family separated from me accomplished nothing for them and so they issued passports to my family, despite their previous threats that they would not.

With the passports in hand, I made a quick call to a friend who was the local director of Trans World Airlines (TWA). I made reservations for the next available flights to Hong Kong, Tokyo, and Los Angeles. That afternoon, I got calls from John Anspacher, Director of the US Information Service (USIS) in Saigon, and from Bill Colby, the CIA station chief. They both asked me if I could attend a send-off cocktail reception. Aware that they were in the business of immediately knowing such political developments, I jokingly asked them how they knew that I was leaving. I thanked them for the offer, but I told them I couldn't attend a reception because I was leaving so soon. They said they understood.

I hurriedly packed my suitcases and then said goodbye to my parents. We did not have much to say, but my father definitely approved of the decision. As a mandarin under the French, he too had served less-than-ideal governments under trying circumstances, so he understood my dilemma well. He said it was the right time to leave everything, that it was good for me to forget about all the trappings of high office. I did not need the nice government villa, the chauffeured cars, the servants, or the impressive titles if it all meant serving a corrupt government that I did not believe in. Likewise, my wife understood my decision even if it was a surprise. She accepted our sudden life change without objection or protest.

The next day, October 11, 1961, I left Saigon. It was an immense personal relief finally not to have to serve a regime I had become disgusted with, but I still worried about the fate of my country. It was somewhat gratifying that I had been proven right in my expectations of Diem and Nhu. Although I had spent an inordinate amount of time thinking and worrying about how I might leave, in the end I had not had time to plan anything carefully. Instead, I had navigated more by instinct, by what I knew of the characters of the Ngo family members, and by what I knew to be right. That Diem had let me go, despite my apparent disapproval of his government, without taking any drastic, regrettable actions gave me some slight hope for the future. I had made it known to him that I believed his government was going in the wrong direction, but I had not burned my bridges entirely. Two years in the United States would be a long time and perhaps Diem eventually would be convinced of the necessity of reform. Realistically, I knew the chances of that were slim. Still, I hoped that when I returned to Vietnam I could once again serve the man of integrity I had met in America rather than the petty despot I had come to know.

Chapter 7

BACK TO THE UNITED STATES

For months, my overriding focus had been how to get myself out of Vietnam. That would be an immense improvement and would end my dilemma of having to publicly support a government I saw as hopelessly corrupt and immoral. Beyond that, I had not contemplated much of what might happen next or what I might do. Leaving, as it turned out, raised a completely new set of unanticipated dilemmas.

Although my message to Diem was clear when I left him, I did not burn any bridges with him. I had made sure that I appeared to be a loyal supporter of his government, refraining from any public criticism of the regime. That step was made out of necessity. Even without raising any trouble, Diem and Nhu had tried several strategies to keep me from leaving. If I had not been so determined they probably would have succeeded in trapping me. Considering the arbitrary character of the regime, I was already lucky. Many others had already been punished for the crime of showing insufficient support for the government, but I had not been treated harshly. Had I spoken out, though, no amount of luck would have helped me. I would have been declaring myself an enemy of the regime, all but guaranteeing that I could not leave Saigon and making it quite likely that I would be thrown in jail or secretly eliminated. Once in the United States, though, things were different. There would be much more opportunity to speak out and much less danger of retaliation, although that still definitely existed.

I was not sure yet if publicly criticizing the Diem regime was right or if it was what I wanted to do. Actually, it was tempting to simply withdraw into silence and wait to see how things went. Why should I stick my neck out again just after removing myself from immediate danger? At the time, most of the Saigon intelligentsia believed that the fate of South Vietnam was a problem that would be solved primarily by the US government, so why shouldn't I adopt that same noncommittal attitude? If the Americans were making all the decisions anyway, it would be futile to bother taking a stand. It seemed unlikely that I could accomplish anything other than causing trouble for myself. Although being separated from the regime by an ocean afforded some protection, speaking out still carried risks and I stood to lose much. The regime could still prevent me from ever returning to Vietnam or, even worse, it could revoke my passport and force me to return for punishment. If I did not rock the boat, on the other hand, I would be able to go back to Vietnam after my two-year break and continue to pretend to support Diem. That way I could retain my privileged position within the regime and all the advantages that went with it. Despite that, my conscience inclined me to try to do something, no matter the risk and no matter how slight the chance of making an impact.

I resolved that I would avoid any rash decisions and take my time to think over the situation and its new dilemmas. I would carefully explore the options open to me before I took any definitive stand against the regime. Such a decision would have major consequences for my own future and for others as well, something I was deeply aware of and concerned about. Additionally, I wanted to be as fair as possible to Diem and give him the benefit of the doubt. I had hoped that my departure might serve as a wake-up call for him, so I needed to give him a chance to change on his own. In the meantime, I intended to seek out the advice of anyone who might have more information on the state of affairs in South Vietnam or who could give me a different perspective.

COMPARING NOTES ON THE DIEM REGIME

Shortly after my arrival in the United States, I went to New York City to meet some old friends who were also early Diem supporters. There, I ran into Vu Van Thai, who had been Director General of Budget and Foreign Aid. We were each surprised to discover that we were both no longer with the government. Thai told me he had just quit his job because he was "fed up with the Diem regime." That was quite the revelation to me. It was also reassuring that we had separately reached the same conclusions and had both decided to leave Diem without ever discussing it together in Saigon.

It was somewhat of a coincidence that we met in New York after deciding to leave the regime, but it was also symptomatic of the deteriorating situation with the government. In Saigon, people had said before that we were the "two Thais who tolerated no nonsense" in the government's business. We were both considered good administrators, and Americans had held us up as examples of the kind of efficient, modern management that other agencies in South Vietnam needed. The Michigan State University Group in Saigon had even published case studies of our two offices as models for effective reorganization in an underdeveloped country.[1] We had worked hard to eliminate nepotism, waste, and inefficiency, but we discovered that the Diem regime had little place for such ideas of meritocracy and competence. The sycophants and schemers were gaining more and more ground in the government, to the point that dedicated, capable people like Thai and me were repulsed.

Thai and I were neighbors and friends before, but we had never talked about the 1959 Bien Hoa election. Now in New York, Thai had some revelations to share with me about its aftermath. He told me that, shortly after the election, President Diem called him to the Palace and ordered him to send an inspector to check my accounting books at Vietnam Press. Apparently, Diem believed Mrs. Nhu's allegation that I had stolen money without any doubts or questions. Thai said that Diem gave the definite impression that he wanted the inspection to prove that I had stolen the money, regardless of whether or not that was true. He even went so far as to tell Thai that it was his job to slant the outcome of the inspection! Thai was shocked to hear Diem give such an order, especially directed against me. Diem clearly thought that Thai would be a servile bureaucrat who would blindly obey, but he grossly misjudged Thai. Thai was determined to do only what was right. He simply told Diem that he would send an inspector to check my accounting, leaving out his intention to clear me of wrongdoing if the inspection revealed nothing wrong.

Thai did send someone from his office, and everything was found to be in order with our accounts. At the time, I believed that the inspection was just a standard, periodic one and I had no idea that it was connected to the election. I had welcomed the inspection because I had nothing to hide. Had I known that Diem intended for Thai to find me guilty of malfeasance no matter what, I would have been much more fearful. What Thai told me was extremely disturbing. Not only did it reveal the true extent of the danger I had been in, but it also showed how far Diem had fallen from his reputation for integrity. I wondered how Diem could have been so corrupt as to give such unethical orders. Hearing the story, I felt renewed sorrow for Diem and my shattered expectations of him.

After New York, I went to Washington, DC, to seek the counsel of some American experts on Vietnam. The first two people I decided to talk to about my dilemma were Edward Lansdale and Sherman Kent, both of the CIA. I had known Lansdale from when he worked closely with Diem in the chaotic early days of Diem's government. Sherman I did not know personally, nor did I know that he was with the CIA. I went to see him because his nephew Ken, who was then working in Saigon as the local Director of CARE (Cooperative for Assistance and Relief Everywhere, had given me Sherman's address and insisted that I make time to see him.

Lansdale had been a central figure in Vietnam early in Diem's rule, but by 1961 political adversaries in both Washington and Saigon had pushed him aside into a sort of official exile from Vietnamese affairs. His unorthodox methods and individualism had created enemies within the American government who resented both his success and his routine flouting of the bureaucratic pecking order. President Kennedy had briefly considered sending Lansdale back to Vietnam as Ambassador, but that idea was quickly shot down by Lansdale's more powerful rivals. Instead, he was kept in a desk job at the Pentagon. Lansdale was also kept away from Vietnamese issues because, although Diem had relied on him when his government was in peril, Ngo Dinh Nhu sought to maintain a monopoly on advice to Diem. That meant keeping the meddling Lansdale away, especially because Ed did not approve of Nhu's devious ways. Lansdale consistently pushed for Diem to be more open and democratic, so the politics of corruption adopted by the Ngo family appalled him. When I arrived in the United States I was already somewhat aware of Lansdale's banishment from Vietnam issues, but I sought him out anyway. He was someone I deeply respected and I knew he still had substantial connections to Vietnam even if they were unofficial.

In his typically cryptic style, Lansdale did not say much when I talked to him. It was clear, however, that he was also disturbed by the course of events in South Vietnam and the evident changes in Diem. He hinted about his troubles with political rivals trying to keep him away from Vietnam, but he also told me that the Kennedy administration continued to quietly seek his input. He disclosed to me that he had been ordered by President

Kennedy to make a trip to Saigon in 1962 and that he would try to see Diem again then. I saw that as perhaps another opportunity to reach out to Diem and encourage changes. I suggested that I would write a confidential analysis of the regime's problems and asked Lansdale if he would look at it and share his thoughts about it. I told Lansdale that I would like him to personally bring Diem a copy of the analysis as well. I hoped that someone, be it Lansdale or Diem, could convince me that I was wrong about the problems I saw. Lansdale said he would be glad to take Diem whatever I wanted to entrust to him confidentially.

When I met Sherman Kent in Washington, he was in the house that had belonged to Allen Dulles, the former CIA Director under Eisenhower. Sherman was very friendly and casual with me, never mentioning anything about the important position he held at the CIA. At the time, I was not aware of Sherman's high prestige as a "father of the US intelligence community," but I still thought he was an impressive man.[2] He struck me as unassuming but also thoughtful and knowledgeable. I told him about the analysis of the Diem regime that I was writing and asked him if he would take the time to read it and give me his comments. I added that it had to be kept absolutely secret between us because I had not decided if I would publish it or not. He agreed and said he would be pleased to read it. We talked for some time about Vietnam and he told me that it was the current dilemma of the Kennedy administration. The US government, he said, was divided about whether to stick with Diem or dump him. It was a dilemma I understood well.

AT MICHIGAN STATE UNIVERSITY

It was November 1961 when I arrived in America, and Harvard's fall semester had been underway for two months already. Unfortunately, there was no way for me to start my Associate Nieman Fellowship for the 1961–1962 academic year because I was so late. Harvard understood my circumstances, though, and they agreed to postpone my fellowship until the next year. It was a nice arrangement that I appreciated very much. I had been afraid that my delays might cost me the fellowship for good. In the meantime, I had much to keep me occupied until the next school year rolled around. Of course, I was still very worried about how I could support myself until then because I had only a limited amount of savings with me.

Fortunately, Dr. Wesley Fishel was able to help me out with an academic assistantship at Michigan State University. He was a professor of political science there and had been an early supporter of Diem. I had met him while I was studying in America, and we were quite close friends. In fact, he had even stood in as the "father of the bride" at my wedding before I returned to Vietnam in 1954. Early on in Diem's rule, Dr. Fishel had spent a great deal of time in the Presidential Palace with Diem as the Chief of the MSU Assistance Group, so he was very familiar with the personalities of the regime. I was glad both for the support and for the opportunity to discuss South Vietnam extensively with another knowledgeable early supporter of Diem.

My priority while at MSU was to put in writing everything that I had been carrying in my head all those months. I wanted to answer for myself several key questions I had been wrestling with: What went wrong in the Diem regime? Could it still be saved? Could South Vietnam itself be saved, with or without Diem? After all that I had witnessed of Diem, his family, and his government in the last few years, I had a lot of thoughts but needed to organize and analyze them all. I was highly motivated to write everything because I felt I owed it to myself and anybody else who was concerned about South Vietnam. With a deep sense of responsibility, I told myself that this was not merely an academic exercise but an important political commitment. It would affect my own life and those of many others, possibly influencing major decisions on Vietnam. Although I was emotionally involved, I constantly reminded myself that I had to be as objective as possible.

I was acutely aware that by explicitly writing out my criticisms of the regime I ran a real risk. Not only was I likely to be put on the black list of the regime, but I was also possibly putting my life in danger. It was conceivable to me that Mrs. Nhu would be so enraged by my critique that she might order someone from the South Vietnamese embassy in America to silence me. If she could pressure Diem as she had in 1959 to throw me in jail when I had done nothing wrong, who knew what she might do now that I was actively engaged in writing a scathing critical analysis? I was certain that the punishment could be much worse than just jail, but nevertheless I decided to carry on. I thought it was the right thing to do, so that was that.

Nobody else had systematically examined the regime's structure and practices, and I was the only one who could do so with a perspective from inside the Palace, with all the facts and information. Many South

Vietnamese politicians residing abroad, especially those in Paris, had already criticized Diem extensively, but they did so based on hearsay and second-hand information. They had also focused on the regime's lack of democracy and disregard of human rights. Although I saw those issues as significant and I had personally stopped supporting Diem because of them, I still believed that they were actually secondary problems for a few reasons. For one thing, I believed that the American government was most concerned about the issue of the regime's effectiveness. If Diem had been even less democratic but more effective in fighting the Communists or limiting their growth, it seemed to me that the Americans would be fine with that. Because any South Vietnamese government was going to rise and fall based on its American support, the US government's appraisal of just how important democracy was mattered a great deal.

More important, I believed the regime's disregard of democracy to be a symptom of its fundamental flaws and inner rottenness, not the root cause. Whatever the form of government, Diem and the Ngo family were unwise and ineffective leaders who were incapable of moving the country forward in a determined and consistent fashion. As I wrote in my analysis, much of the regime's problems stemmed from the basic fact that Diem's regime was "neither democratic nor totalitarian." The regime frequently erected democratic façades with institutions like the National Assembly or with its rhetoric, but then it made mockery of the idea of democracy with its blatant election fakery and intolerance of even loyal opposition. The result pleased nobody. The failure to live up to its democratic rhetoric angered many people while the attempt to create the democratic façade added dysfunction to the government, undermining the consistency and effectiveness totalitarian rule might bring. I believed that in South Vietnam — a developing country beset by Communist enemies and the debilitating legacies of colonialism — people would have accepted a more totalitarian government if it was effective at improving people's lives and bringing development; if it showed discernible progress toward democracy; and if it was, above all else, fair and consistent. Diem's government was none of those things, and the root problem was that the Ngo family's rule was arbitrary, inconsistent, and unreliable. Thus, the lack of democracy was important (and I especially worried that Diem's sham democracy would discredit true democracy in the future for many South Vietnamese), but there were deeper problems that other critics of Diem were not addressing.[3]

MY FATHER'S REPORT ON DIEM'S VISIT

I finished writing my analysis of Diem's government and the causes of its shortcomings in a few short months. As promised, I sent copies to Sherman Kent and Ed Lansdale. Sherman said he found it most interesting because it was the first time he had seen such an objective analysis of the situation, backed as it was by revealing facts from someone who had personally witnessed the regime in action. I did not hear anything directly from Landsale about my writing, but a few weeks after his trip to Saigon I received a long letter from my father that I suspected was connected to Ed's reading of my work. My father wrote that Diem had come to Dalat (a cool-weather mountain resort in the Central Highlands) to see him and they had a long talk about me. Diem told my father that he had given me the best job in his government. He said that my salary as Director General of Vietnam Press was higher even than that of a cabinet-rank minister; that I had more autonomy than anyone else in the government when it came to hiring and spending; that I was allowed to travel abroad more often than were most ministers; and that all my perks and benefits were better than those of other government officials. He said that I had done a good job at Vietnam Press and that he had not wanted to replace me, but he had let me leave for America anyway. Diem told my father that he had heard that I was in a financial bind because of missing the academic year and my fellowship. He offered to have Mrs. Nhu buy a piece of land I owned in Saigon to help me out, saying that she would use it for a social project to help veterans. Last and most important, my father wrote that Diem told him that "he had heard that I was writing a book to criticize his government." My father ended the letter advising me, "That's what Diem told me. You do what you have to do."

Judging from my father's letter, it was apparent that Lansdale must have given Diem a copy of my analysis or at least spoken with him about it. Otherwise, how could Diem have known "that I was writing a book to criticize his government"? I had not discussed politics with my father when I said goodbye to him in Saigon, but he still understood why I was leaving Diem. His message to me was very succinct and straightforward, but I knew he was saying much more than he wrote. My father, like Diem, had been a high-ranking mandarin trained in the Confucian tradition. They had both worked for Diem's mentor, Nguyen Huu Bai, and knew each other well. My father understood Diem and realized that, in Diem's way of thinking of himself as a Confucian sovereign, it was a very special gesture to take the trouble of coming to Dalat to visit and talk about me. This was a big deal for Diem and he was going out of his way to show he still cared about me. His reference to my financial problems was an offer of help, an indirectly extended olive branch to me. Diem, of course, had not explicitly said that accepting the olive branch required me to halt my writing, but that message was clear for anyone who knew Diem like my father and I did.

My father knew that I had to follow my conscience and that I would have to do what I thought was right. Although the opportunity to wipe the slate clean and once again enjoy all the benefits of being in Diem's good graces was tempting, it was not enough. The offer showed that Diem was bending to try to satisfy me personally, but that flexibility did not extend any further to changing his way of governing. Maybe in Diem's way of thinking this was a big concession and a generous offer, but I needed to see him being more straightforward and open. He did not take the initiative to address any of the issues I raised in my analysis. Instead, Diem's offer was for me to just forget about my criticisms and once again enjoy the material benefits of my position in his government. To accept, I just had to remain silent and reach out to him to renew our friendly relationship. If Diem had only gone a little further, if he had responded more "democratically" by offering to seriously discuss and consider my analysis, it would have been very difficult for me to say no. Unfortunately, his response gave no indication that he would ever do so. It was very regrettable, but I had to accept that it was basically useless to try to find a solution to South Vietnam's problems that involved Diem. I also had to accept that the man I had respected and followed before with such great hope no longer existed, if he ever truly had. Diem was not going to change, so there was no saving him from the disastrous path he was following. It looked to me very much like a Greek tragedy in which the main character was heading inexorably to his preordained fate.

AT HARVARD

Before I knew it, September 1962 came and I had to be at Harvard for the beginning of the academic year. The Nieman Foundation of Harvard selected about a dozen "promising journalists" in the United States every year and invited them to Harvard "to broaden the scope of their knowledge for better journalism." In addition to these twelve American Nieman Fellows, three foreign journalists were selected to be Associate Nieman Fellows, although the program was the same for both groups. I was the first Vietnamese Associate Nieman Fellow at Harvard, joining a South Korean and a South African in the non-American group for 1962. I found housing in one of the university-approved buildings near campus. We lived on the fourth floor of an old building at 34 Irving Street in Cambridge. There was no elevator in the building, so it was very hard for my two-year-old daughter to climb the four flights of stairs several times every day. Compared with the privileges I had enjoyed as Director General of Vietnam Press, with the government villa, chauffeurs, and servants, life in Cambridge was a great hardship. I did not mind, however. I reminded myself that I had an important purpose and that I had to make the most of my year at Harvard. Very quickly, I adjusted to my new life in Cambridge. The weekly seminar sessions and guest speakers of the Nieman program were outstanding, and I relished taking advantage of the tremendous library resources available to me. It was also great sharing the company of so many interesting students and faculty at Harvard and at nearby MIT.

Although I was enjoying myself at Harvard, I could not keep South Vietnam out of my mind. Because the program allowed Fellows the freedom to do whatever they wanted, I took the opportunity to travel to New York and Washington frequently to make contacts with people associated with Vietnam. One person I was especially glad to see again on one of these visits was Nguyen Van Thoai. Thoai was a relative of Diem's sister and had been with me at the Bandung Conference in 1955. He had left Diem in 1956 and had been working as a research scientist at the Collège de France in Paris since then. When I saw him, he was in New York for a scientific conference.

Thoai told me everything he had been hearing in Paris and said that he was worried about the fate of the Diem government. He was surprised that Mrs. Nhu had gained so much control over the regime. His main concern, however, was the lack of alternative leadership for South Vietnam after Diem. Because he lived in Paris, the home of many Vietnamese exiles, he was well acquainted with that problem. He deplored the ineptitude of the Vietnamese opposition politicians residing in France along with their lack of unity. He asked me what I knew about American policymakers' thinking concerning South Vietnam and I told him that finding out about that was my goal while I was in America. I expressed my concern, though, that the Diem regime might not last much longer. I worried that its precipitous collapse might mean American leaders would not have time to plan for an adequate government to replace Diem's.

Another interesting contact I made in New York was with Joseph Buttinger. He had written one of the first histories of Vietnam in English, *The Smaller Dragon*, and had been one of Diem's early supporters in America. He had influential lobbying contacts and had been instrumental in creating the American Friends of Vietnam, which provided public relations support for Free South Vietnam. Buttinger told me that he was concerned about the direction Diem had taken, and he lamented the bad image the Nhus were giving the government. He realized that many Vietnamese might be looking to America for solutions, but he stressed to me that the South Vietnamese had to solve their own problems through their own efforts. Foreigners, he said, were likely to suggest or impose unsuitable solutions for the country and support the wrong leaders, so it was better for Vietnamese not to rely on outside help. He added that, in any case, American policymakers were so divided about what to do in South Vietnam that they wasted most of their time fighting among themselves rather than planning what to do. If they ever did decide to remove Diem, there would be no time left to organize the right kind of government to replace him. I told him that that was precisely my main concern, that there was no thought being given to what might come after Diem. Our concerns turned out, unfortunately, to be all too prescient.

MEETING THE DAI VIET PARTY

One cold winter day in 1962, I got a telephone call from Milton Sacks, a Yale professor I had met once before. He had been with the Office of Strategic Services (OSS) during World War II and was interested in Vietnamese affairs. Sacks said to me:

> I have with me here Huynh Sanh Thong, who was with you at Cornell before. Do you remember him? I also have with me Dr. Nguyen Ton Hoan, the Dai Viet leader whom you probably know. Dr. Hoan just came from Paris. He would like to see you today if this is possible.

"This is very strange and sudden," I told Sacks. I asked him, "Why didn't Thong call me a little bit in advance? We could have talked in Vietnamese together! Anyway, I have about an hour to spare before I have to go pick up my kids after school. Please come to my apartment here at 34 Irving Street."

When the three of them arrived at my apartment, I turned to Thong and said to him in Vietnamese, "How are you? Really long time no see! What happened? Why didn't you call me instead of Milton Sacks? We are all Vietnamese and we knew each other, so why let a foreigner get in between?" Thong gave me an explanation that I found most surprising: "You see, I have become a member of the Dai Viet Party, so I have to obey our leader Dr. Hoan. He wanted Sacks to make the call to you." It was quite unexpected for me to learn that Thong had joined the Dai Viet Party. When we first met at Cornell, he was teaching Vietnamese-language classes. He appeared then to me as the most "apolitical" guy in the world. He was easygoing, sloppily dressed, open-minded, and friendly toward everyone. It was a big turnaround for him to go from that unregimented way of life to becoming a member of one of the most rigid, sectarian political parties. I also still wondered why Dr. Hoan prevented Thong from just calling me and why he had involved Sacks at all.

After the introductions and small talk, Dr. Hoan apologized to Sacks and started talking to me in Vietnamese. I had heard about him before, but I had never met him. He had briefly been a Minister of Youth in one of the many pro-French governments before 1954. He was the leader of the Southern faction of the Dai Viet Party, which had splintered into many blocs that fought among one another. Besides being disunited, the Dai Viet had a bad reputation for being the most venal Vietnamese political party. The only thing that really interested them, it seemed, was to get into power and to use that power to make money for themselves. I had also heard that Dr. Hoan was not very highly regarded by the other Vietnamese émigrés in France. When he wasn't engaging in political intrigues, he operated a Vietnamese restaurant there.

Dr. Hoan told me that he was receiving many reports from his Dai Viet comrades in Vietnam. They stated that under Diem, democracy and human rights were not respected. Diem's police treated his Dai Viet members very harshly, he said, commonly subjecting them to surveillance, arbitrary arrests, and torture. He added that he was happy when he learned through his American friends that I had left Diem in protest. He also asked me if I knew about any changes in American policy concerning South Vietnam. I was not at all impressed with Dr. Hoan and could tell he was quite uninformed and naïve for someone who claimed to be a leader. His simplistic complaints about the lack of democracy in South Vietnam irritated me, so I responded sarcastically to his inquiry. "When you were Minister of Youth under Nguyen Van Tam," I asked, "did the French Sûreté (Security) and Tam's police do the same thing as Diem today or was it democratic? As for US policy changes in South Vietnam, maybe you should ask Dr. Milton Sacks here!"

Everybody felt uneasy because the meeting was leading nowhere. Dr. Hoan did not respond to my mocking question and instead moved on. What he did next definitively confirmed my poor first impression of him. He pulled a thick book out of his briefcase and showed it to me. It was one I was familiar with, a text on public administration written by J. de Galembert in the 1920s. To my astonishment, Hoan told me, "You see, this is a book which shows us how to organize the next government in South Vietnam." In fact, this book described how the French colonial administration of Indochina was organized, and here Hoan was suggesting it as a blueprint for independent South Vietnam. How he could imagine that such an outdated and discredited system was still applicable at all, let alone the answer to South Vietnam's plague of problems, was beyond my comprehension. It went to show that, if anything, what Nguyen Van Thoai had told me of the incompetence of the opposition politicians was an understatement. This was a leader of one of the more important political parties, one that would indeed come to power, unfortunately, in 1964. His *vision* for the future of a free and independent Vietnam was *to ape the practices of the defeated and despised colonialists.* My conversation with Hoan left me even more concerned about who might replace Diem and reminded me of the urgent need to get American policymakers thinking seriously about what was to come when Diem inevitably fell from power.

CIA CONTACTS

With hindsight, I can see that in my younger days I failed to fully recognize the importance and power of the CIA, although I worked quite closely with many of its officers. In 1954 and 1955, as one of Diem's closest aides, I participated in a number of missions to consolidate Diem's power that were orchestrated by Edward Lansdale. One of the most important of those missions was when I was sent to contact General Trinh Minh The to rally him to Diem's side. Another time I was sent to contact a Hoa Hao general in the Mekong Delta when Diem needed that sect's support. Many other times while Lansdale was trying to prevent coups against Diem, I went on trips to Manila that he had arranged to remove key aides of the coup plotters. I got to know Ed rather well during that time when we were working together to help consolidate Diem's power, and we became very good friends. We remained close friends over the years, all the way until Ed's death in 1987. In fact, after the collapse of Saigon in 1975, I even settled down in Newport Beach in part because Ed's older brother Phil Lansdale lived there. Despite our close friendship, or perhaps because of it, I never quite realized Lansdale's importance or the influence that the CIA had.

Besides Lansdale, I also had dealt with many other CIA officers and agents in Saigon. They worked as Embassy staff, Foreign Broadcast Information Service employees, members of the Michigan State University Advisory Group, or even as employees of airlines like TWA. One person I got to know well was William Colby, who was CIA Saigon station chief from 1959 to 1962 and who later went on to become the CIA Director in the 1970s. We were close enough that he attended the christening of my oldest son at the Saigon Cathedral in 1956. Although we got along well personally, however, Colby never talked seriously about South Vietnamese politics or policy with me during my time working for Diem. I am sure it was because he regarded me as being too close to Diem and therefore as someone who would not be able to have a frank and confidential discussion about South Vietnam's problems.

By 1962, however, I had dropped my charade of loyalty to Diem and was trying to speak with everyone I could who was concerned with Vietnam. Colby had also just returned to the United States at that time to become the chief of the CIA's Far East Division, so I arranged for us to meet. It was late in 1962 when we met and I already had the manuscript of my book, *Is South Vietnam Viable?*, ready. I brought a copy so Colby could give me his thoughts on it as well as his assessment of the situation in Saigon. I wasn't sure if he was trying to play devil's advocate and probe my thinking, but I was surprised that he kept defending the Diem regime. He argued that removing Diem would not solve any problems and would only create instability. I said that he surely must have realized that Diem's government was so unpopular and ineffective that it would not last very long, regardless of America's immense support. Both disaffected South Vietnamese and Communists, I told him, desperately besieged Diem's government. Perhaps he conceded this point, but still he insisted that there was nobody to replace Diem. He kept asking me whom I wanted as Diem's replacement.

My reply to his inquiries was that I thought it was more important to decide "what to do" after Diem than "whom to install." I explained that because there was nobody of prominence to replace Diem individually, any post-Diem government should have some sort of collegial leadership made up of capable and patriotic men. At that time there was no single leader who could steer South Vietnam in the right direction, but there were many good men whom Diem had cast aside or driven away. Together, focused on implementing a range of obviously necessary new policies and reforms, such a group could put South Vietnam on the path to peace and democracy. That was the surest way, I believed, to restore the popularity of the government and give it the moral authority to be respected and effective. Colby listened attentively but still held fast to his opinion that the United States needed someone strong to work with. Our conversation was thus inconclusive, but I walked away from it more convinced I was right. Americans were thinking that South Vietnam needed a strong leader first and then popular support would follow. I was convinced, however, that first and foremost it was popular and correct policies that were needed and out of those a stable, healthy leadership would naturally grow. A change of leadership by itself would not magically solve South Vietnam's problems, so I was mostly concerned with what would be done. In some ways, my thinking was probably much too hopeful, especially considering what I knew about Saigon's many selfish intriguers. Nevertheless, it was the only remotely practical solution I saw to the dilemmas of Diem's failed leadership and the lack of obvious alternatives.

At least Colby was thinking about what might happen after Diem, even if he was approaching it in what I thought was the wrong way. Most of the rest of the US government was stuck in prolonged hesitations about whether to "sink or swim with Ngo Dinh Diem" or to dump him, giving little attention to the crucial matter of what would come after Diem was gone. Too few recognized the reality that whether they wanted it or not, Diem was on his way out. One way or another, he was bound to fall by that time, and until that happened South Vietnam would suffer through endless political crises. In hindsight, it is clear that the Americans' priority should have been considering what needed to be done in Saigon after Diem was gone (and, to a lesser degree, by whom), not whether or not it was right for the United States to try to get rid of Diem. The result was that eventually America did support a coup against Diem on November 1, 1963, but it did so without any plan for how to proceed afterwards, whom to support, and what to do in South Vietnam. President Diem and Nhu were assassinated unexpectedly, and South Vietnam soon lurched closer and closer to defeat under the inept leadership of a series of "strong" but unpopular generals.

HELPING NGUYEN CHANH THI IN CAMBODIA

While at Harvard, I was contacted by Dr. Ted Britton about a sensitive matter. Dr. Britton was a Canadian, but he had been in the United States for a long time and was teaching education at Sacramento State University in California. He told me he had been in touch with Nguyen Chanh Thi, who had been in Cambodia since the failed 1960 coup. Dr. Britton offered to relay letters between myself and Thi. I thought that was a little strange and suspected Dr. Britton must have been connected in some way with the CIA. For a professor of education, he certainly took an unusual interest in Vietnamese politics. Nevertheless, I accepted his offer because Thi was a friend and someone I thought should be part of a post-Diem South Vietnam.

Relations between Cambodia and South Vietnam were not good, so Thi and his fellow rebels had been granted political asylum by Prince Sihanouk. Although they were allowed to stay in Cambodia and were not returned to Vietnam for punishment, they were not exactly free. They were kept in house arrest, under constant police surveillance. In his letters, Thi told me that life in Phnom Penh was very hard for him. The hardest part, he said, was coping with the many attempts by North Vietnamese agents to persuade him to defect to the Communist cause. One of his best subordinates had already been swayed into joining Hanoi, and all the others faced similar temptations to switch sides rather than continuing to uselessly languish in exile.

After hearing from Thi about his difficulties, I thought that he deserved to be helped. Compared to the other South Vietnamese generals, Thi was much better. He was a good commander and, more important, he was not corrupt like most of the others. His biggest weakness was his political impulsiveness, which led him to jump into dangerous adventures without thought of the consequences. In his letters to me in 1962 he acknowledged that fault and admitted that he had been foolish getting involved in the

1960 coup the way he did. Although he did not tell me the full story of the coup then, I thought that he was genuinely contrite and had learned his lesson. If he could stay out of politics, I believed, he could still be useful to South Vietnam as a good soldier. Through Dr. Britton I sent Thi money, medicine, and reports on Vietnam news. I was convinced that someday Thi would be able to return to Vietnam and once again serve his country. It was gratifying when he was recalled almost immediately after Diem's overthrow on November 1, 1963. Although I still believe I was correct in helping him, my judgment that he had learned his lesson about staying out of politics was later proved wrong, unfortunately.

DECISION TO PUBLISH *IS SOUTH VIETNAM VIABLE?*

The more I talked to people about Vietnam, the more I realized that there was extreme confusion and misunderstanding about the Diem government, among both Americans and Vietnamese. A fierce debate was growing, but nobody seemed to have a complete grasp of the situation and all its aspects. The defenders of the Diem regime contended that despite its shortcomings, the regime was doing a good job against the Communists militarily. They felt that it was too dangerous to change leadership and that, for better or worse, the United States had to "sink or swim with Ngo Dinh Diem." As such, they tended to play down the political struggles of the government. They were unwilling even to consider the growing reality that the regime's political ailments were terminal.

On the other hand, critics of the regime argued that Diem's government was too corrupt and undemocratic, and hence incapable of rallying people away from the Communists. Most of the Vietnamese critics, however, were exiles in France or America and consequently had few of the necessary facts, while American critics mostly lacked the necessary understanding of South Vietnam's society and politics. Even worse, none of the critics seemed to have any real alternative plan of action. They called for Diem to be replaced as soon as possible, believing that the removal of his ineffective and misguided leadership by itself would cure most of South Vietnam's ills. Thus, they failed to realize that without a significant change in policies whoever succeeded Diem would end up in largely the same position. What was necessary, I believed, were policies centered around the rule of law and de-escalation of the war against the Communists. Without those two major changes, the Diem regime's worst practices would be repeated because the underlying dynamics would still be at work. With or without Diem, a system of government based on arbitrary personal power combined with limitless American aid for an all-out war on the Communists would inevitably lead to the same problems.

The American government itself was split equally between pro-Diem and anti-Diem factions. President John F. Kennedy was puzzled and did not know whom to listen to among his divided advisers. At the time, I had some journalist friends who were close to the President and his brother Robert. They told me that the Kennedys had been hesitating for months over the conflicting recommendations they were receiving. What troubled the brothers perhaps the most, I was informed, was the absence of Vietnamese voices in all of these arguments over South Vietnam. The President believed that any solution to South Vietnam's problems must come primarily from the Vietnamese people, so the silence was quite confounding.

Hearing of the President's concern, I resolved to speak out. The Kennedys and others in the American government needed to hear what I, as a well-informed South Vietnamese, thought about the current debate on the regime. It was no longer the time to keep quiet. I had given Diem the benefit of the doubt, I had checked and double-checked my arguments, and I had sought out contrary views to try to sway me, so there was no longer any doubt in my mind. To continue to remain silent, I was now convinced, would have been cowardly and irresponsible. I decided not only to publish my manuscript but also to raise my voice in other public venues. I did interviews with local papers and news stations and published a piece in the influential liberal magazine, *The New Republic*. My article, "A Vietnamese Speaks Out," argued that "Americans had been taken in by Diem's bluff," not realizing that his anti-Communism was "primarily for export" and his only real interest was preserving the Ngo family's power. For those Americans who still believed Diem could be pressured into reform, I pointed out that Diem had already failed to initiate reforms many times before and under much better circumstances than existed amidst the Communist insurgency that raged in 1963. It was "nothing more than wishful thinking" to expect that Diem would ever change, I contended. The choice by then was clear: either the United States could help South Vietnam move toward finding a new leadership based on merit and the rule of law, or it could sit by and accept "collapse through deterioration of the status quo."[4]

Another factor behind my decision finally to speak up was my growing alarm over the dangerous and unbearable strain that the best elements of the ARVN were under. They were faced with the choice of either sacrificing themselves on the battlefield while the regime's political blunders undercut them or getting themselves involved in conspiracies against the regime. Already there had been the one coup attempt in 1960, and again, in 1962, some of the ARVN's most capable officers made a move against Diem. Two ARVN Air Force pilots actually bombed the Presidential Palace in an attempt to kill Diem and Nhu, hoping that would spark a general uprising against the regime. Such foolhardy actions could lead nowhere good for the country, but they demonstrated how desperate the military was. Twice now, some of the most elite and highly trained professionals — the paratroopers and the Air Force pilots — had attempted to eliminate Diem largely out of the conviction that the regime was interfering with the war against the Communists. With the regime and its sycophantic top commanders focused more and more on coup prevention rather than fighting the Communists, it seemed likely that the ARVN's frustration was bound to grow. With such frustration came an increasing risk of yet more dangerous and drastic coup attempts that could tear the country apart. Thinking about these menacing possibilities made me even more determined to publish my manuscript.

I thought that my analysis of the regime could helpfully inform the debate on South Vietnam taking place in America and perhaps point the way to some sort of solution. I hoped that it might tip the then-balanced scales toward the side that advocated dumping Diem, ending the hesitations within the American government. If the United States acted quickly and decisively, it might forestall a more dangerous alternative such as the regime abruptly collapsing of its own accord or ARVN officers again attempting to take matters into their own hands. Furthermore, if the debate on whether or not Diem should continue to receive American support could be resolved, American policymakers could turn to the more important matter of planning an alternative government and developing new policies. It was clear to me that eventually Diem was doomed, so it was urgent to get everyone to see that and begin to think of the future rather than continuing to squabble over the present and past.

Once I made up my mind to speak out, it was a race against time to get my manuscript published. To be of any use at all, my book had to be published as soon as possible. At first I contacted Praeger in New York because they had already put out several books on Vietnam. They told me that, because of prior commitments, the best they could do was to schedule my book for publication in late 1963, almost twelve months later. I believed that there would probably be another coup before then, so I told them that my book would be useless if it took that long to come out. I checked around and discovered that there was no way that any American publisher could accommodate me and publish my book in the matter of weeks I believed necessary.

In need of advice, I contacted a friend of mine, Henri Pascal, who had been a United States Operations Mission (USOM) official in Saigon and who was also friends with Lansdale. His in-laws owned one of the biggest publishing houses in the Philippines, Carmelo and Bauermann, so I thought he could help. He told me to rush my manuscript immediately to him, which I did. A few days later, he called back and said that he had read my work with great interest. He concurred that it needed to be published as soon as possible and said that he could put it out in just a couple of weeks for me. Henri asked me how many copies I wanted to print. I said that I wanted enough copies to go to Saigon as well as to Washington, but I was not sure how many that should be. He suggested four thousand copies, which I agreed should be enough.

A few short weeks later, I received the first copies of my book, *Is South Vietnam Viable?*, and I sent them along to my friends who were interested in Vietnam. Henri had arranged to have copies sent to Saigon via Hong Kong, and he told me that all four thousand books sold quickly. He also reported to me that Diem's Ambassador to the Philippines had approached him when the first prints of my book came out in Manila. The Ambassador wanted to negotiate to buy all of the copies of the book so nobody would see it. Henri jokingly told him that he would have to pay for "*forty* thousand" copies if he wanted to buy them all. The Ambassador had to ask for permission to make such a large purchase. A few days later he returned to Henri and said that the regime could not afford to buy up the "forty thousand" copies, and so my book was available to the public.

I was surprised and gratified that the four thousand copies we printed were distributed so quickly. When I returned to Saigon a year later, after the 1963 coup, the first thing any of my friends wanted to talk about was my book. It was amazing to me that they had all somehow managed to read it. Everyone told me that I had a lot of courage to expose the truth about the Diem regime so publicly. They said they especially admired my decision to give up all my privileges and leave Diem while everyone still regarded me as “Diem’s favorite adopted son.” It gave me some sense of vindication, but I remained humble and reminded myself that I had only been one person out of many and I had merely done what I believed was necessary. I told my friends that I just did what I had to do, and I hoped that my book had indeed made some small contribution to the overthrow of a regime that most South Vietnamese wished had never existed.

Author (center) at 5 years old with brother Dzien (left, 13 years old) and sister Loc (right, 8 years old). Oldest sister Tran, 16, not pictured.

Le Thieu Huy, Liberation Army Officer and fiancé of Loc, in Laos, 1946.

Picture taken by author in 1952 at Maryknoll Monastery in Lakewood, NJ. Diem and unnamed Maryknoll Brother.

Author (left) with the Group of Six in Cholon, 1954.

Author (far right) with General Trinh Minh The (second from right) in 1954.

President Diem (left) with Vice President Nguyen Ngoc Tho (right) and General Trinh Minh The (center) in 1954.

President Diem on an inspection trip in 1955, when he mingled with local citizens.

Author (far left) with Philippine President Ramón Magsaysay (center) at Presidential Palace in Manila during one of the Manila trips organized by CIA Colonel Lansdale to prevent coups against Diem. On the far right is Rufus Phillips, one of Lansdale's closest aides. Next to him is Captain Man, right-hand man of the pro-French General Hinh, who plotted against Diem.

Author (right) with President Diem in 1955.

Official portrait of President Diem in his white sharkskin suit. The message reads: "To all my compatriots nationwide."

The first office of *The Times of Vietnam*.

General "Iron Mike" O'Daniel, first head of MAAG in Vietnam, visiting *The Times of Vietnam* in 1956.

Author (left) with Nguyen Van Thoai, Minister of Planning and Reconstruction (second from left) and Vo Van Hai (second from right), President Diem's personal secretary.

Author (left) at American Society for Public Administration Conference in the Philippines, 1958.

Author at his desk as Director General of Vietnam Press in 1957.

Diem (center, under picture), the author (second from left), and founders of the non-profit Popular Cultural Association in Saigon, which promoted literacy and practical technical training.

Author (far left), with Vo Van Hai (far right), 1963. Also pictured are Mr. Gene Gregory (second from the end on the left) and Mrs. Ann Gregory (end of the table, right) who used *The Times of Vietnam* as Ngo Dinh Nhu's mouthpiece.

Author addressing Vietnam Press employees after his resignation in 1961.

Ngo Dinh Diem (second from right) and Bishop Ngo Dinh Thuc (third from right) in Japan, August 28, 1950.

Author saying goodbye to the Dean of the School of Journalism at the University of Missouri in late 1963.

Christmas card from Soichiro Honda, founder of Honda, to Mr. Thai. The note reads: "I thank you very much for your card and letter dated December 5, 1967, the content of which had my careful attention. I am quite in agreement with you as to what you say about business developments of Honda motorcycle in South Viet-Nam. I sincerely hope that you will recover from your injury and get back to normal activity in no distant future."

Author in front of the Caravelle Hotel. Picture taken during a return trip to Vietnam in the 1990s.

Author (left) with General Nguyen Chanh Thi in America after the Vietnam War.

Former Honda executive Ted Kumamoto and the author in Hong Kong in 1998.

CIA Operative Edward Lansdale in front of his home circa 1980. Lansdale helped Diem consolidate power in 1954 to become the first President of the Republic of Vietnam.

Foreign Minister and former Information Minister Tran Chanh Thanh and his wife visiting the author in Newport Beach in 1970.

Author (right) visiting Hanoi's super-spy Pham Xuan An in Ho Chi Minh City in the 1990s.

The bamboo crest, Diem's personal symbol. Image from the front cover of *Deuxième Plan Quinquennal, 1962–1966,* Nha ton giám-doc ke-hoach. République du Viet Nam, 1962.

Republic of Vietnam coins, circa 1960. The heads side bears Diem's likeness while the tails side bears his bamboo crest. Images from: Anthony LaRusso Collection, The Vietnam Center and Archive, Texas Tech University, 1508museum1515.

Chapter 8

DIEM'S OVERTHROW

When I asked Diem to let me go to Harvard in the fall of 1961, I expected his regime to last only two more years at best. I didn't say that to anyone, of course, but kept it to myself. By coincidence, the South Vietnamese government gave me a passport that similarly expired in two years, in October 1963. That short validity was normal because the regime liked to be able to control its citizens even when they went abroad. In my case, that practice did cause me some difficulties. In November 1962, I needed a one-year extension of my US visa in order to be able to stay through the fall of 1963 for my Nieman Fellowship. To get that visa extension, my passport had to be valid for at least six months beyond the visa, so I needed to have my passport's original two-year validity extended by the Vietnamese government. Thanks to my decision to speak out against Diem, I worried that the normally simple paperwork was going to be a problem for me.

With the publication of my book and my other articles and TV interviews, I knew that I was surely on the regime's political "blacklist" for my criticism. I tried to have the South Vietnamese Embassy in Washington extend my passport's validity anyway, though. I hoped that it was such a routine procedure that the politics wouldn't matter. I sent in my passport to the Embassy with my request for the extension, explaining that I needed it because the United States required my passport to be valid beyond the period of my visa. Weeks went by, however, and I did not even receive a reply. The US Immigration and Naturalization Service (INS) contacted me during that time to remind me that I had to have my visa extended. All

I could tell them was that I had done everything I could already. I sent reminders to the Embassy to try to get a response to my request and still heard nothing from them.

Finally, I received a short official note from the Embassy early in 1963. It said, "According to instructions from higher authority in Saigon, the Embassy will NOT extend the validity of your passport as you requested." Tran Van Dinh, who was Chargé d'affaires at the Embassy, signed the note. I was surprised that Dinh had signed the note but had not added any personal explanation. We had been on quite friendly terms before, and at Vietnam Press I had done a lot to give him good coverage while he was the Consul General in Rangoon. I was sure that his hands were tied in the matter because it had been done with instructions from a "higher authority in Saigon," but I thought the least he could have done was to explain the circumstances.

I had no other choice but to forward the South Vietnamese Embassy's note denying the extension of my passport to the INS to explain my awkward situation. Luckily, the INS did not deport me back to Saigon because of my illegal status. On the contrary, although I had not applied for it, the INS gave me permanent resident status in the United States. I thought perhaps that nice gesture from the INS was connected somehow with my previous contact with Attorney General Robert Kennedy at Harvard. I had met him when he came to Cambridge as one of the guest speakers at the weekly meetings of the Nieman Fellows. That afternoon, the conversation focused on the critical situation in South Vietnam and the debate over American policy. I spoke up and described the situation in Saigon as I saw it. The Attorney General said that he was pleasantly surprised to hear my views and asked why other South Vietnamese had not been heard, even though there were a good number of South Vietnamese students in America by that time. I explained that they were afraid to speak up against the regime because the South Vietnamese Embassy could refuse to extend their passports and put them at risk of deportation. I told Kennedy about my own case and personal experience as an example. He said that he was surprised that the Diem government was acting in such an "undemocratic way." He told his aide to take note of the situation and to try to help any South Vietnamese students who might be in trouble with the INS because of their political problems with the Diem regime.

I never did find out if Robert Kennedy intervened on my behalf specifically, but the helpful arrangement by the INS turned out to be unnecessary in the end. The coup in November 1963 rendered it irrelevant. Right after the coup, the new Prime Minister, Nguyen Ngoc Tho, cabled me to return to Saigon as soon as possible. I was teaching at the University of Missouri Journalism School at the time. Such was my rush to return to Vietnam that I ended my semester early and finished grading my students' term papers in early December instead of late January as scheduled. Before I left, however, I took the time to write to the INS Regional Office in Kansas City to thank them for granting me permanent residence in the US while explaining that I did not need it now.

Upon returning to Vietnam, I discovered that it had, in fact, been Mrs. Nhu who had been the "higher authority" that ordered the denial of my passport extension. She had not only done that but had also published a series of newspaper articles attacking me as "the ungrateful aide of President Diem who bit the hand that fed him."[1] After I returned to Saigon several local journalists came to apologize to me for those editorials, which they had been forced to write by Mrs. Nhu. I understood their position and accepted their apologies. The whole situation was uncannily reminiscent of my experience in 1954. Both times, I had passport problems because of Vietnam's politics, only to have those issues instantly resolved by the urgent recall of a new government.

WATCHING THE BUDDHIST CRISIS FROM MISSOURI

In July 1963, my one year as an Associate Nieman Fellow at Harvard came to an end. I could not travel anywhere outside the United States because of my passport issues and there was no question of my returning to Saigon as long as the regime remained. Judging by the current news coming from South Vietnam, however, I expected that Diem would be overthrown within months. I thought the regime would collapse by the fall of 1963 at the latest, but I still needed to find a job in America to help me get by until that happened. Fortunately, the University of Missouri Journalism School offered me a job for the fall semester teaching a graduate seminar on the problems of journalism in developing countries. I accepted and left Cambridge for Columbia, Missouri.

The University of Missouri Journalism School was the oldest journalism school in the United States and had a reputation of being one of the best in the world. I was well aware of that reputation already. When I was at Vietnam Press, I had looked into many American journalism schools because I planned on sending some of my employees to America for advanced training. The University of Missouri had stood out to me then due to its emphasis on the practical side of journalism training, whereas most of the other top journalism schools like Columbia and Northwestern focused more on theory. I ended up sending the Vietnam Press employees to Boston University for their training, based on the recommendation of USOM advisers in Saigon, but the University of Missouri Journalism School had seemed ideal to me. After reading and hearing so much about it before, I was glad to have the opportunity to teach there.

During my stay in Columbia, I received a friendly welcome from everyone, from the President of the University and Dean of the Journalism School to the students in my seminar. The Journalism School was affiliated with the Freedom of Information Center in Columbia, which researched problems of press freedom around the world. The Director there invited me to be a Consultant to the Center, something that I gladly accepted in addition to my teaching duties. I was also happy to find that one of my former classmates from Cornell was teaching in the Department of Political Science, so we teamed up to share an apartment together.

Overall, I had a nice situation and was enjoying my stay in Columbia, but my mind was still focused on Vietnam. There, the Buddhist crisis had erupted earlier in May and was still spiraling out of control. It was typical of the political ineptitude of the Diem regime that a minor, local incident in Hue was allowed to develop into a major calamity with religious overtones. Diem's older brother Bishop Ngo Dinh Thuc should have been a conciliator when the incident started in his Hue diocese, but he was the one who added fuel to the fire and turned it into a national crisis. Although the Diem regime was strongly Catholic, South Vietnamese Catholics in general did not support the regime and there were many who were quite dissatisfied with it. The relationship between the Buddhist and Catholic communities, furthermore, was not particularly acrimonious in South Vietnam at that moment prior to the outbreak of the Buddhist crisis. It would later become so, in large part thanks to the Buddhist crisis itself, but the primary origin of the crisis was Buddhists' *political* dissatisfaction with the regime and its policies and not a *religious* clash between Buddhists and Catholics.[2]

The crisis started in May 1963, when pagodas in Hue hoisted Buddhist flags to celebrate a holiday. Bishop Thuc objected to the display of these flags and ordered the Province Chief to forbid them. Buddhists protested the prohibition and claimed religious discrimination, pointing to the fact that Catholic flags had been allowed — government buildings had even been bedecked with them — during the recent celebration of the 25th anniversary of Thuc's ordination. The Buddhists held a public demonstration in front of the local radio station in Hue, but the Province Chief declared the protest to be illegal and ordered its dispersal. Tanks were used against the crowd, some shots were fired, and a grenade exploded, leaving several demonstrators dead and more injured. Unsurprisingly, this heavy-handed action escalated the situation and sparked nationwide protests. Diem and Nhu suspected the Buddhist demonstrators were Communists, while Mrs. Nhu accused Americans of manipulating the Buddhists in order to overthrow Diem. Then, one day in June at a busy Saigon intersection, the Buddhist monk Thich Quang Duc burned himself to death in protest. Associated Press reporter Malcolm Browne was tipped off ahead of time and captured the self-immolation in a series of photos that dramatically captured the world's attention and won Browne the Pulitzer Prize. Not only did Diem face growing protest at home, but he also had global public opinion aroused against him after that.

The United States urged Diem to be conciliatory to defuse the Buddhist crisis. Diem did convene a committee of inquiry led by Vice President Nguyen Ngoc Tho to investigate the "Buddhist incidents." Diem, however, ignored Tho's advice and eventually ordered the committee to slant the final report to blame Communists instead of the Province Chief for the casualties at the initial Hue protest. Infuriated by Diem's stubbornness and distortion of the truth, Buddhists organized several more self-immolations in protest. Mrs. Nhu, who was becoming more and more vocal and controlling, took an outrageously provocative stance toward the crisis that only made everything even worse. She publicly ridiculed the protest suicides of the monks and said that she would applaud if more "Buddhist barbecues" were forthcoming. All over South Vietnam, pagodas were raided and Buddhist activists were arrested, and some were even killed. In the middle of the night on August 21, Special Forces troops loyal to Nhu stormed and ransacked the largest Buddhist pagoda in Saigon, Xa Loi. Knowing this latest and most brazen act of belligerence would anger yet more South Vietnamese while further alienating the United States, the regime tried to pin the blame for the Xa Loi pagoda raid on the ARVN high command. The government, with the support of the ARVN generals, had declared martial law the day before because of the unrest in Saigon, which helped Nhu pretend that the generals had made the decision to raid the pagoda. Nhu had his Special Forces troops disguise themselves in standard army uniforms during the operation to make it appear that the ARVN was behind it all. In reality, the ARVN generals had not known about the plans for the pagoda raid and did not support the action at all.

Throughout the Buddhist crisis, Mrs. Nhu seemed to be the ultimate decision maker in the regime. She accused Diem of being a weakling and giving in too easily to Buddhist demands. Reportedly, during a lunchtime argument at the Presidential Palace she threw a hot bowl of chicken soup at Diem in a fit of anger over his lack of aggressiveness against the Buddhists. Diem quietly took the abuse and did not react to her furious tirade. It was a complete reversal of a similar incident almost ten years earlier. Then, during the Binh Xuyen crisis, Diem had erupted in anger and had thrown an ashtray at Mrs. Nhu, who gave up her argument and meekly retreated to her quarters. Their relationship had obviously changed quite a lot from 1954 to 1963. In addition to privately lobbying the Ngo brothers for a tougher stance, Mrs. Nhu kept publicly escalating tensions. Not only did she make inflammatory statements of her own, but she also ordered her American "servants," Gene and Ann Gregory, to write incendiary editorials in *The Times of Vietnam*. They echoed her disparagements of the Buddhists while also attacking the US Embassy for supporting the Buddhists, who were supposedly "Communist agents."

WORKING WITH MRS. NHU'S FATHER AGAINST HER

Vietnamese are not usually a very religious people, but they rallied in support of the Buddhists. The country was already filled with resentment that made it a tinderbox, and Diem's uncalled for and repressive reaction against the Buddhists was just the sort of thing to spark it off. The outrage against Diem's brutal attempt to squash the protests extended from the bottom of society to the top, including within the regime itself. Diem's respected Minister of Foreign Affairs, Vu Van Mau, shaved his head and resigned his post in protest of Diem's actions. Even more dramatically, Mr. and Mrs. Tran Van Chuong, Mrs. Nhu's own parents, resigned their posts as Ambassador to the United States and South Vietnam's Permanent Observer at the United Nations.

Mr. and Mrs. Chuong came from prominent families from Central and Southern Vietnam. They had not always approved of the actions of their daughter or son-in-law Nhu, but they had been part of the regime since its very beginning. Diem appointed Mr. Chuong as Ambassador to the United States when he came to power and made Mrs. Chuong the UN Observer shortly thereafter. With their daughter making sickening statements that exacerbated the Buddhist crisis, however, they decided to resign to show that most South Vietnamese disagreed with the anti-Buddhist policy foolishly adopted by Diem and the Nhus. After he resigned, I got in touch with Mr. Chuong to see what we could do to tell the other side of the story that Mrs. Nhu was then spinning. He volunteered to give speeches to civic groups all around America to set the record straight.

The American government wanted Mrs. Nhu out of Vietnam to prevent her from aggravating the situation further with her comments, so she left Vietnam in mid-September. Instead of remaining quiet, however, she turned her temporary exile into a global speaking tour, which Mr. Chuong described as "an all-out propaganda campaign on behalf of the South Viet-Nam family regime."[3] She spent a number of weeks saying outrageous things around Europe before bringing her show to the United States on October 7. She had dozens of publicity events scheduled over the course of three weeks, so we planned to have Chuong give opposing appearances on the same days his daughter was speaking. With the help of Richard Dudman, the Washington Bureau Chief for the *St. Louis Post Dispatch*, we organized a series of speaking engagements and press coverage for Mr. Chuong in cities around the United States.

The most memorable incident of the tour was the night that Chuong was supposed to speak in St. Louis, Missouri. He was severely delayed because Mrs. Nhu unexpectedly went to his home in Washington, DC, along with dozens of reporters. He had not wanted to confront her, so he had been unable to get out of his house. The next morning all the newspapers carried a picture of Mrs. Nhu standing at his door, waiting as nobody came. Chuong said afterwards that his daughter had "gone wild" and was "uncontrollable." He believed it was impossible to reason with her anymore and that she had been "spoiled" by her husband and Diem, who gave her too much power.

While the United States was urging Diem to be conciliatory, the regime was intensifying its repression and Mrs. Nhu was continuing with her extreme rhetoric. Mrs. Nhu's speaking tour was supposed to be her campaign of "disintoxication," which would help Americans understand that Buddhist monks in South Vietnam were only "hooligans in robes" who were in collusion with Communists, as she claimed in her press interviews. Her provocative accusations, however, did nothing to win support in America and only further infuriated the Buddhists at home in South Vietnam. The members of the regime, especially Mrs. Nhu, did not know when to restrain themselves. They did not care about — nor understand — public opinion, and they were driving even their staunchest supporters into opposition. In short, the Diem regime was digging its own grave.

THE NOVEMBER 1, 1963 COUP D'ÉTAT

The coup began in Saigon at 1:30 p.m. on November 1, 1963, which made it 1:30 a.m. for me in Missouri. I had friends working at the AP and UPI news agencies, and in anticipation of the imminent action I had told them to contact me when they heard the coup begin. One of them from the AP called and woke me in the middle of the night when the news started coming in. He said, "I just saw the first flash about a coup in Saigon," and asked me, "Do you happen to know who the leader of the coup is?" I told him that my best guess was that it was General Duong Van Minh because I had received reports from Saigon that he would be the rallying point for the different factions cooperating on the coup. After hanging up, I tried to go back to sleep but it was impossible. There was so much to think about, but I also started to worry about potentially being misquoted by my AP friend. If I was wrong, it could mean trouble for me. I decided to call my friend back and ask him not to quote me. My friend told me, however, that he had just received more details confirming my suspicion. General Minh, or "Big Minh" as he was commonly known, was indeed the leader. He, along with General Tran Van Don and General Le Van Kim, were the key members of the new military junta, which included most of the ARVN command. Reassured, I thanked my friend for updating me and we promised to continue exchanging information about the coup as it progressed.

It was nerve-racking sitting there as the coup played out on the other side of the world, but it was also somewhat of a relief that it finally had come. Saigon had been roiling with coup rumors for weeks, if not months, and I had been expecting one for some time. By the fall of 1963, anybody who was anybody was scheming against Diem. There were at least three separate groups with their own plots in the works. Such was the level of intrigue that one group was led by Nhu's formerly loyal espionage chief Dr. Tran Kim Tuyen while another was led by a man whom some already suspected of being a Communist double agent, Colonel Pham Ngoc Thao. Tuyen, however, was exiled as Consul General to Egypt before his plot could develop very far. Thao, meanwhile, was too controversial and shady a figure for the United States to embrace, and he lacked support within the ARVN, so his plot did not go far either.

The third plot, the one that actually came to fruition, originated within the top ranks of the ARVN itself. Although Generals Minh, Don, and Kim initiated the planning, the United States was in close contact with this group. President Kennedy had reluctantly given Ambassador Henry Cabot Lodge Jr. the green light to help the coup plotters, and Lodge had CIA operative Lucien Conein acting as a liaison between the generals and himself. The actual planning and execution were left to the generals, but the failure of the 1960 coup had demonstrated that American acceptance of a coup plot was a necessity. Minh, Don, and Kim did not directly command any troops themselves, but the Americans' approval helped them convince most other ARVN commanders to join their coup.

The one obstacle the plotters faced, and the key man who had to be won over, was General Ton That Dinh, Commander of the Capital Region. Gen. Dinh had been handpicked by Diem and Nhu for the pivotal command in the hopes he would foil any coup attempt. Dinh owed his position to his close loyalty to the Ngo family, and as long as he remained faithful it was impossible for a coup to succeed. Dinh was, however, an ambitious and vain man. The coup plotters flattered him while nurturing Dinh's resentment that Diem had never named him Interior Minister as Dinh wanted. The promise of that job was enough to win him over, and with his support Big Minh's plot was almost guaranteed success.

Ngo Dinh Nhu, like everyone else, had expected a coup and devised two secret schemes in response. Code-named "Bravo I" and "Bravo II," these operations were designed to unmask and destroy the plotters. "Bravo I" was a fake coup that would be followed by phony "mob" violence, which was a favorite trick of Nhu's. During the bedlam, Nhu's men would assassinate Diem's opponents as well as anti-Diem Americans. To make it appear authentic, Diem and Nhu would flee Saigon and a "revolutionary government" would be formed, calling for eviction of Americans from South Vietnam and negotiation with the Communists. After a few days of eliminating Diem's enemies under the cover of chaos, loyalist Special Forces troops would move to crush the fake rebel soldiers in Bravo II. Diem and Nhu would then return from their secret hideout in Vung Tau to kick out the pro-Communist "revolutionary government." Nhu hoped this scheme would not only help flush out the regime's enemies but would also make the United States so grateful to have an anti-Communist government back in place that Americans would cease to demand reforms. At the very least, the scheme would make neutral ARVN commanders reluctant to join a genuine coup plot for fear of actually joining a doomed sham. Nhu revealed all of these top-secret schemes to General Dinh in a meeting at the Palace. Nhu had received a report that one of Dinh's deputies was part of a coup plan and had summoned Dinh to question him. Dinh pretended to be a loyal defender of the regime in the meeting, swearing "to behead" his subordinate for the betrayal. Nhu thought he could fool everybody all the time, but he was fooled himself by Dinh.

At the auspicious hour of 13:30 p.m. (some of the rebel generals were very superstitious and they had to consult astrologers before making a move), the coup started. Dinh had already moved the rebel troops into place so they were well positioned for the attack. Diem and Nhu had received reports of unusual troop movements around Saigon, but they were not too concerned because they believed that their man Dinh was executing Bravo I. Very quickly, the rebels seized key positions like the Saigon Radio station and the National Police headquarters. Telephone service in the city was cut, and rebel troops surrounded the Presidential Palace, poised to attack. A number of diehard regime loyalist ARVN officers, including the commander of the Special Forces, were arrested or killed.

While the coup was progressing, Diem and Nhu were initially overconfident and misjudged their true danger. Diem was unrealistically proud and refused to give in even while it was becoming apparent that he was in trouble. When he called Ambassador Lodge to ask for help, Diem talked as if he were still a Chief of State in full control of the situation. Instead of being specific about seeking protection or asylum, Diem was vague and got a vague reply from Lodge as a result. After his futile conversation with Lodge, Diem placed calls on his secret radio network, hoping to find loyal commanders to come to his rescue as they had in 1960. This time, however, he received no responses, so he fled the Palace. Escorted by his aide-de-camp, the Director General of Youth Cao Xuan Vy, and a few bodyguards, Diem and his brother were driven to Cholon. Vy was a protégé of Nhu and the leader of the "Republican Youth," which was a paramilitary loyalist group that was supposed to help defend Diem and Nhu if the military betrayed them. Nhu was unable to rally his organization's help, however, and none of the other pillars of the regime — the Movement of National Revolution and the Can Lao Party — did much to rescue the Ngo brothers. Diem and Nhu had to seek refuge in the house of Ma Tuyen, a wealthy Chinese businessman who had been an early Diem supporter.

By midnight, Diem succeeded in contacting General Dinh at the General Staff Headquarters where the rebel generals had gathered. Dinh answered the phone in front of the other generals and, to prove his loyalty to them, he cursed Diem and Nhu in the most obscene language. Shortly after that, in the early hours of November 2, rebel troops succeeded in storming the Presidential Palace. They, and the Presidential Guard, thought that Diem and Nhu still occupied the Palace. By 6 a.m., Diem talked by phone with General Don and agreed to surrender. In exchange for the surrender, Don promised Diem that he and Nhu would be allowed to safely leave the country. Diem revealed that they were at the St. Francis Xavier Church in Cholon and then waited for the generals to send a car to pick them up.

KILLING OF DIEM AND NHU

Following the events from Columbia, I was relieved to learn that the coup succeeded quickly and without too much bloodshed. It was clearly welcomed by most South Vietnamese, who celebrated in the streets of Saigon. People hoped this would be a healthy change in government. After all, it seemed that there was nowhere to go but up.

The news that Diem and Nhu had been killed, however, quickly erased much of my own sense of hope. The first reports said that the Ngo brothers had committed suicide following their surrender. It was a blatant lie and one that everyone saw through. Realizing the coup leaders had obviously killed Diem and Nhu, I felt they had made a huge mistake and that this was an ill omen for the future of South Vietnam. The truth, of course, eventually did come out. Big Minh and the former head of Military Security, General Xuan, had secretly ordered Diem's assassination without the knowledge of the other generals. Both feared that Diem and Nhu might outsmart them and somehow recover power if left alive, so they decided to leave nothing to chance. Perhaps more important, though, they both held grudges against Diem and Nhu for mistrusting them and sidelining them for years. Reportedly, Big Minh had been angered by Diem's arrogant tone when they had discussed the surrender. He ordered his aide Captain Nguyen Van Nhung to join the party sent to fetch the brothers, and Captain Nhung killed the tied-up captives in the back of an armored personnel carrier. General Don had promised Diem safe conduct and had assured Ambassador Lodge that he would allow the Ngo brothers to leave the country, so Big Minh's action put the junta in a bind. There was nothing Don or the others could do, however, to undo what had been done. Big Minh's act of cowardice and treachery tainted the new leadership of South Vietnam from the beginning.

Mrs. Nhu was still on the last leg of her publicity tour when the news of her husband's and brother-in-law's deaths reached her. Defiant and provocative to the bitter end, she blamed the United States for the deaths and cursed President Kennedy. President Kennedy, however, was shocked and appalled by the killing of the Ngo brothers. The United States had indeed been in close contact with the generals as they planned the coup, but assassination of the brothers had not been part of those plans. Still, as critics of the coup and America's role in it argued, the United States had to be held at least *indirectly* responsible. The American government may not have had concrete knowledge that Big Minh planned to kill Diem, but it was not at all an inconceivable event. After all, the United States was fully aware of the personal animosities at play and should have remembered that the failed 1960 coup had taught the ARVN generals that coups were all-or-nothing affairs. A repeat of 1960 was precisely what Big Minh feared, with Diem and Nhu talking their way out of trouble. Knowing that, the US government should have better anticipated the generals' fears and done more to ensure that Diem and Nhu would not be harmed. The American government may not have ordered the deaths, nor even desired them, but it did not do enough to prevent them either.

Whatever responsibility the United States had for the murders, the South Vietnamese generals leading the coup bore the ultimate blame. The 1963 coup should have been considered a national revolution to save South Vietnam. It should not have been treated like a personal vendetta against the Ngo brothers, no matter how deep the grievances. Secretly killing Diem and Nhu for personal reasons did not represent a clean break from the past; it was a continuation of it. The move signaled that the government would continue to operate deviously and for personal ends, so nothing would truly change even with the hated regime gone. Diem and Nhu, although guilty of many things, did not deserve their fate. For their crimes against the nation, they should have been tried fairly and publicly to establish a precedent of justice. By secretly murdering Diem and Nhu, Big Minh and his accomplices in the military junta demonstrated not only their lack of statesmanship but also their unmitigated duplicity in the conduct of state affairs. Intrigue and backstabbing, unsurprisingly, continued unabated after Diem's overthrow. Consequently, the coup and assassinations only unleashed a whole series of further coups and countercoups that destabilized and completely delegitimized the South Vietnamese government. At least with Ngo Dinh Diem as President there had been some respect for national sovereignty, but the succession of coups put an end to that.

I spent the gloomy days of November 1963, between the assassinations of President Diem on November 2 and President Kennedy on November 22, in Columbia. The news was bad enough by itself, but I was even more sickened by how Mrs. Nhu continued to vehemently curse President Kennedy even after his death. Although both men certainly made their share of mistakes, I thought, both cases were tragedies of wasted potential. It made me sorrowful to think about the early days of Diem's administration, when his future and South Vietnam's seemed to hold such tremendous possibility. Then, he had had a sterling reputation, unquestionable dedication to his country, and the help of many bright and powerful Americans. After consolidating his power, however, Diem began to take his American friends and Vietnamese supporters for granted and increasingly came to mistrust them. Relying on his brother Nhu, Diem became distracted by the problems of his family's corruption and neglected to take care of his true responsibilities to the nation. Instead of frankly cooperating with his American ally to defend Vietnam against Communism, Diem used American aid to defend the illegitimate interests of his family. Inevitably, this subversion of American aid helped the Communist subversion of the country, which was why the army finally overthrew Diem in 1963.

Diem and Nhu thought that they could buy loyalty with carefully parceled-out promotions and rewards, but that policy proved to be a fiasco. By rewarding sycophants for their voluble but empty praise and promises of loyalty, Diem only alienated his most able supporters. In his hour of need he was abandoned by those flatterers who had sworn him absolute fidelity so often before. The ARVN commanders entrusted to key positions because of their supposedly unflinching loyalty, the Can Lao party members, the paramilitary regime-protectors like the Republican Youth: all proved they were too cowardly to stand up in Diem's defense, too inept to do anything significant, or too susceptible to bribery. The capable generals whom Diem had not trusted and had shut out of power, like Generals Don and Kim, ended up being those the United States entrusted to organize the coup. Meanwhile, the ARVN generals Diem had promoted for their loyalty to his family were the ones who put the final nails in the regime's coffin with their betrayals. If Diem had created an army — and a government, for that matter — led by the most capable and courageous, and dedicated himself only to service of the nation rather than his own family, perhaps the 1963 coup might not have happened at all.

More than fifty years after President Ngo Dinh Diem's death, I have often wondered whether I should just forget about him and let him "rest in peace" or if I should share what I witnessed of that tragic period. I have chosen the latter because I think that the truth, however painful or sad, will ultimately help us to understand. Diem's legacy is one that has been too often oversimplified in a way that erases his true significance. His critics see him as nothing more than a petty dictator, bereft of redeeming qualities or good intentions. His defenders overlook far too much that was unjustifiable, shifting blame as if everything good was Diem's doing while everything bad was somehow not his responsibility. To me, though, the tragedy of Diem was that he was indeed a great man and leader — although far from perfect, of course — who was the right man at the right time, and yet he still failed.

President Diem had a unique and golden opportunity to change the history of Vietnam for the better and he missed it. Had he not given in to his family's corruption, he could have focused on the common interests of all Vietnamese. Vietnam was unfortunately divided by the circumstances of the Cold War, but that did not mean that confrontation was the only way to effect positive change. If Diem had adopted a policy of reconciliation with North Vietnam, he would have saved all of Vietnam from years of vicious conflict while securing his own place in history as a great statesman and a true patriot. As one who knew Diem intimately during those times, I saw how his leadership should have turned out so much better for Vietnam. Diem fell short of his own potential, short of his best intentions, and short of the hopes that I — and many like me — had for him. The disappointment I felt because of Diem's failure was perhaps the most bitter in all my life.

Chapter 9

AFTER DIEM

A few days after the coup, I received a cable from Nguyen Ngoc Tho, Diem's former Vice President. The junta had appointed him Prime Minister of the newly formed government and he was requesting that I return to Saigon as soon as possible to assist the new leadership. I had to cable back that it was impossible for me to leave immediately because I was committed to teach at the University of Missouri Journalism School until the end of the semester in January 1964. After a flurry of cables back and forth, however, I agreed to make special arrangements so that I could depart hastily. Everyone at the school was cooperative. I was able to complete my seminar and grade my students early so that I could leave for Vietnam on December 15. I went by myself, leaving my family in Arizona where my wife's sister was. I knew the situation in Saigon was still unstable and dangerous, so it seemed wiser to wait until things settled down before bringing them home.

When I arrived back in Saigon, the government put me up at the Caravelle Hotel, the best in town, while I waited for an assignment and permanent government housing. It was great to be back in South Vietnam after two years away, but I quickly began to sense a severe malaise hanging over the country despite the widely cheered coup. People were initially exhilarated at the prospects and promises of a post-Diem era, but only a month later that sense of enthusiasm was rapidly fading. The consensus emerging was that the new military leaders were not going to be any better than the regime they had overthrown, and that they could very well be even worse.

After a few days, I went to see Prime Minister Tho. Tho was someone I liked because he was one of the more decent and upstanding members of Diem's government. The feeling was mutual, too. Tho knew that I had been one of the few who had dared to tell Diem when he was wrong. I sympathized with Tho when he was Diem's Vice President because he was a patriot who had tried to cooperate with Diem for the greater good of South Vietnam. He had, however, been consistently abused by Diem and was mostly relegated to duties not commensurate with his position. When I came to meet him, Tho was very frank and leveled with me immediately. He said that he was worried that things were not going well with the new government. The generals had the real power, he complained, and they did not really trust him or any other civilian. They clearly preferred to deal with other military officers and to handle matters in a soldierly fashion, whether it was the appropriate approach or not.

During my conversation with Tho, he asked me what I thought of my new assignment. I had just found out that I would be the Deputy Information Minister under General Do Mau, who was going to be the Information Minister. I told Tho that although Gen. Do Mau was my good friend and I was glad to work with him, I was not at all interested in making propaganda anymore. I told Tho that because of that reluctance I thought that I might sit out for a while before beginning to work in the government again. Before I left, Tho wanted to discuss one other matter with me: my old job at Vietnam Press. The position of Director General was vacant and he wanted my opinion on who should take over. Offhand I could not think of anyone, so I told him I would think it over and give him a recommendation later.

Coincidentally — or perhaps not — a couple of days later a series of articles appeared in the *Hanh Dong* daily newspaper attacking my past leadership of Vietnam Press. The articles contained many distorted half-truths and outright fabrications. They said that I had been given "dictatorial power" over the agency by Diem because I was his "favorite adopted son." The articles accused me of hiring and firing according to my whim, as well as bringing in new employees who were my friends and relatives. They also alleged that I hired several beautiful women who had no talent except looking pretty for me. Now, the articles claimed, I was lobbying to resume my old job and the benefits I had purportedly enjoyed before. I was surprised at first by these personal attacks, although nothing quite confirmed that I had truly returned to Saigon like such underhanded slander.

Upon investigation I learned that the publisher of *Hanh Dong*, Bui Anh Tuan, was actually lobbying to get appointed as the new Director General of Vietnam Press himself. He mistakenly thought I was his chief competitor for the post and was trying to discredit me with the articles. Tuan did not get the job, but the incident reminded me that way back in 1954, my friend Dr. Wes Fishel had once asked me what I knew of the same Bui Anh Tuan. Fishel had said that Tuan approached him for help and a recommendation for the job of Director General of Vietnam Press. At the time, I told Wes that I knew nothing of this Tuan, but I thought he had to be a dope to come to a foreigner to get a position in the South Vietnamese government. I joked with Fishel: "Or are you now Diem's representative, Wes, so fools like Tuan come to you to beg for jobs?" A decade later, it seemed that Tuan had not changed much, nor had Saigon. The city was still as full of selfish schemers and intrigues as it had ever been, much to the detriment of the country.

After meeting the civilian Prime Minister Tho, I went to meet with the head of the military junta, General Duong Van Minh. With him were his two main assistants, General Tran Van Don, who was in charge of military affairs, and General Le Van Kim, who was in charge of foreign relations. The atmosphere of the meeting was rather gloomy, and the generals appeared to me very tired and depressed. After the usual greetings and small talk, I ventured to ask them about their program of action for the new government. I needed to know that I would be working for a government that had a clear idea of how to move forward after Diem. To me, this was the most important issue for the new leaders. They had to have thought it over carefully because it had been the reason for the coup itself. To my surprise and dismay, they had no answer to my question. They just looked at each other, shrugged their shoulders, and began complaining about how they were swamped with so many problems and had no time to think about an overall program for the government.

I was saddened by what I had just heard. How was it possible that a coup d'état could have been made without first having in mind what would be done afterwards to turn the country around? At first, I refused to believe what I had been told and tried to rationalize it. I thought, "There's no program of action for the new government? That's impossible!" The generals must not want to talk freely with someone like me, I told myself. I remembered what Tho had told me about how the generals did not trust anyone outside the military and reasoned that they must have a program of action but they just did not want to share it with a relatively unknown civilian. That troubled me too, however. With that sort of secretive and undemocratic mindset, how could the generals hope to bring the country back together under a truly national government? To catch up on the time wasted by the Diem regime they just overthrew, they needed everyone — civilian and military alike — working together. No matter which way I spun it, the meeting was deeply troubling to me.

NEW GOVERNMENT, OLD PROBLEMS

As I had told Prime Minister Tho, I was in no hurry to start work as the new Deputy Information Minister. As much as I liked journalism, I was in no mood to produce more propaganda. Besides, if my meeting with the junta generals was any indication, there was really nothing worth making propaganda about. There was no national program of action and the government was doing nothing substantial, so how could I be expected to convince people to support it? True, they had performed a few symbolic acts already. Some statues of the Trung Sisters, which had been put up by Mrs. Nhu and looked so much like her, had been destroyed and the dancing halls that Mrs. Nhu had shuttered were reopened. Nothing of national significance or real importance to the people of South Vietnam had been accomplished, however.

There was a war against Communists in the country, but nobody really knew what the new government thought about the crucial issue of war and peace. Every day, young recruits and good field officers were fighting and dying under the direction of ARVN commanders whom Diem had promoted based on supposed loyalty rather than on their competence. How would the junta reform the ARVN to weed out the bad officers while preserving the good? How would they approach the war differently than had the Diem regime? Would they listen to international advice from the likes of French President de Gaulle, who advocated negotiations? Or would they follow the lead of Lyndon Johnson and participate in the escalation of the war, possibly including even bombing North Vietnam? On these fundamental national issues, I heard nothing.

Instead, I saw and heard too much about new, made-up issues like how to deal with "old regime people." There was a special committee created to examine the cases of important "old regime people" and to decide how to handle their wealth. A few influential generals of the junta got themselves on this committee and got rich from arbitrary confiscations or from hefty bribes they extorted from people trying to protect their belongings. I personally knew one senior general who was on the committee. After only a few months, having made his fortune, he abruptly retired from the ARVN and went abroad for good as Ambassador to Tunisia. He was all too typical of many of the Saigon generals in the aftermath of the coup; it seemed all they could think of was quickly capitalizing on their power for their own personal interests. The issue of "old regime people" was one of the more hypocritical and blatant manifestations of the generals' selfishness because, of course, everyone in the new government had been associated with Diem's regime in some fashion.

Diem was overthrown because he put the Ngo family's interests ahead of the country and its people. Unfortunately, however, it seemed that after the coup the same mistakes were repeated, with only slight variation. Most of the same intriguing crooks who had got ahead through flattery under Diem remained in Saigon, and many of them continued to scheme their way to power and prosperity. For the most part, all that changed was that Ngo family interests were replaced with new personal or clique interests that still took precedence over the national good. The factional interests were in a way worse, because now there was competition that meant each group had to spend even greater effort maneuvering against the others. It seemed nothing had really changed in Saigon, at least not for the better.

As depressed as I was by the conduct of my fellow Vietnamese, I was even more alarmed with the attitudes and actions of the Americans. They still had no clear-cut policy about what the new post-Diem government was supposed to do and no program of action. Although the United States had to respect the national sovereignty of the Republic of Vietnam, there was still no excuse for the Americans' lack of an overall plan for the future of South Vietnam. America had been so deeply involved in the planning of the 1963 coup that it logically followed that the United States was now responsible, at least temporarily, for making sure the coup paved the way for a significantly better government. The Saigon government could not survive without American support, both practical and political. However, after encouraging a radical political upheaval, the United States proceeded to sit back and act as if Vietnam's politics were outside its realm of responsibility after all. It seemed to give no direction for the South Vietnamese government in the coup's wake. This absence of political initiative enabled the factionalism of the ARVN generals to flourish and led to the paralysis of the government.

The American government was nearly as deeply divided as was its South Vietnamese counterpart, which was the source of this problem. One year before the coup, in *Is South Vietnam Viable?*, I wrote that of all the options available to the United States, the best would be "a timely reorientation geared to help South Vietnam reach a solution to the present political impasse and survive as a non-communist country."[1] The American-backed coup was a result of US officials who felt similarly, who believed that there was indeed a general political impasse in Vietnam and a specific political crisis created by the Diem regime's unpopularity. Those officials, however, were only one faction and they had barely prevailed to get the coup authorized. In the aftermath of the coup, their rivals, who believed there actually was only a military problem in South Vietnam and that Diem had not had a terminal political crisis, reemerged stronger than ever.

The result was that the coup — which, of course, had been executed hastily without proper planning for its aftermath — was not followed by its logical conclusion, a reorientation of policy that addressed the political quandary. The United States instead chose to essentially ignore the political situation and try to solve the Vietnamese dilemma through progressively intensifying military means. Not only did such actions fail but also they increased the costs and magnitude of America's failure by escalating the situation far beyond proportion. Although it was anathema to most American decision makers, I believe that it would have been far wiser to encourage some form of North-South negotiation that could have led to a political settlement and a cessation of hostilities, followed eventually by internationally supervised reunification. Such a policy would have prevented millions of casualties and billions in military expenditures while possibly avoiding the humiliating defeat of South Vietnam in 1975.

COUP OF JANUARY 30, 1964

On the night of January 29, 1964, while I was staying at the Hotel Caravelle in Saigon and wondering what to do next, an aide to General Nguyen Chanh Thi came to see me to give me a message from his boss. Thi had already returned from his exile in Cambodia. I was glad that I had been able to help him and that he had been returned to command, where he seemed to belong. He was a friend I trusted even if I sometimes questioned his political judgment. Consequently, I heeded the advice of Thi's message but I was concerned by it, too. The message the aide gave me was that I had "better wait and not go to work for Duong Van Minh's government. Tomorrow try to stay home because there will be a coup." That was all the aide would tell me, then he departed. I was left alone in my room, puzzling over the message. I wondered, "Another coup? So soon and what for? Who is behind this coup now?"

The next morning (incidentally, my 34th birthday), I stayed home as instructed until about noon. Then, after hearing that the coup was bloodless, I drove around town to have a look. I saw some tanks and armored vehicles at some locations, but everything else seemed quiet and normal. Late in the afternoon, General Thi showed up at my hotel and briefed me on what had been happening. He informed me that the leader of the coup was General Nguyen Khanh. Thi said that Khanh had asked for his help because, as former commander of the paratroopers, he could mobilize them for the "dirty work" of the coup. Thi told me that last night, with the help of a few paratroopers, he had arrested General Tran Van Don, the Defense Minister, and General Ton That Dinh, the Interior Minister. He said it was a very easy operation because neither of them had taken any precautions. He jokingly added that when he telephoned General Dinh, he had expected trouble. Instead, he heard only a sleepy female voice on the other end of the telephone line, so he ordered her to let him talk with General Dinh, who offered no resistance.

Thi said that there were no casualties from the coup, except for the "suicide" of General Duong Van Minh's aide, Major Nhung. Nhung was the officer who killed Diem and Nhu during the previous coup. The new coup leaders had arrested him and ordered him to confess to the murder of the Ngo brothers. Evidently fearing retaliation and torture by pro-Diem officers, he killed himself. That, at least, was Thi's explanation to me and the official story. The real story, which emerged later, was that Nhung was executed by one of General Khanh's henchmen in revenge for the assassination of Diem. Thi did not belabor the point, however, and at that time I did not inquire further about what had happened to Major Nhung. Thi and I both agreed that the killing of Diem and Nhu had been wrong, and nobody was going to feel very sorry for their murderer.

I was more interested in asking Thi why there was already another coup and why he was participating in it. Thi didn't really have an answer to those basic questions. He said that General Khanh had personally come to ask for his help. Khanh had explained to him that this second coup was needed because the "Duong Van Minh crowd was going neutralist and the Americans did not like that." Thi told me that Khanh's American adviser (Colonel Jasper Wilson, as he recalled) knew what Khanh was doing and had supported his move. I had two more questions for Thi: "Are you sure that Khanh and his crowd are going to be better than Big Minh and his crowd? Second, what is Khanh going to do now and did he let you know it before he asked you to join his coup?" Once again, Thi had no answers. Thi, of course, did not tell me the real reason he had joined the coup. Khanh most likely promised to give Thi another general's star and the command of the I Corps in return for his participation. Not long after the successful operation, the promotion did in fact happen.

After hearing Thi's inability to give a reasonable explanation for this new coup, I told him that I was deeply shocked. I said that, as a civilian, I was troubled at how his military friends were staging coups like they were trivial affairs, as simple as changing their shirts. I added that I did not trust Khanh, knowing what kind of person he was and how he had opportunistically leaped to Diem's rescue during the failed 1960 coup. Thi, in an enigmatic way, just shrugged his shoulders at my remarks and said that he also "did not like politics in Saigon." He said that he had to fly back to Hue to take care of his duties there. After he left, I thought to myself about how Thi had once again opened a Pandora's box and gotten himself deep into a political mess that he was unable to control. Just as in 1960, he was involved in a coup without knowing what he was really doing and what would happen to South Vietnam as a result.

NGUYEN KHANH, THE NEW "STRONGMAN" OF SOUTH VIETNAM

General Nguyen Khanh was favored by the Americans because they considered him the smartest of the Saigon generals. The Americans thought he could be the sort of strongman they were looking for, someone who would provide stability as the fight against the Communists proceeded. With hindsight, that was a very big misconception. Even at the time, however, the Americans probably should have known better. General Khanh's checkered past did not inspire confidence in him among most South Vietnamese, and the United States should have shared that wariness.

Khanh had briefly been part of the Viet Minh in 1945 before changing sides to join the French military during the First Indochina War. He only served in a minor capacity and without distinction, but he had already established a pattern of opportunistically switching sides or positions whenever he thought to gain by it. After the departure of the French, Khanh made his way to Diem's Presidential Military Staff through flattery and intrigue. In the wake of the 1960 coup, he had been quick to claim that he had come to the rescue of President Diem. It was true that he had gone to the Presidential Palace and jumped the wall of the compound to join Diem, but it was not really anything that changed the outcome of that coup — the mistakes of the coup plotters themselves had caused its failure. Still, Khanh sold this story of his unflinching and decisive loyalty to Diem and the regime accepted it. It proclaimed him a "providential savior" and rewarded him accordingly. Diem quickly promoted Khanh to Major General and gave him important Corps commands. Khanh was thus representative of the problem of military promotions under Diem being based on appearances of loyalty to the regime and not on real ability. As such, following the overthrow of Diem, the military junta mistrusted Khanh. They stationed him as far from Saigon as possible, sending him north to command the I Corps from Da Nang. It was not far enough, however, as it was from there that Khanh plotted his successful 1964 coup.

Many Vietnamese are believers in horoscopes and, based on the look of his facial expressions, they did not trust Khanh. Khanh's signature goatee gave him a rather comical look, which in the eyes of most Vietnamese was a bad omen for a leader. When Khanh surfaced as the new leader in Saigon, people began to talk about how he had a face typical of an unprincipled intriguer. Furthermore, rumors circulated that he was the illegitimate son of an opera actress, which in traditional Vietnamese views was not at all a respectable background.

The omens, in this case, proved all too accurate. Khanh's misguided rule contributed greatly to the political disintegration of the country. He did not really trust anybody, probably because of how untrustworthy he was himself. Intrigue was his forte, and he thought he could constantly outsmart everyone else. His leadership, therefore, was defined by divide-and-rule schemes designed to bolster himself while undermining virtually everyone else. At a time when South Vietnam needed someone to help bind its wounds and bring it back together, it instead got further division. This dangerous policy, unsurprisingly, resulted only in deepening the confusion and chaos of the country.

The prime example of Khanh's divide-and-rule strategy was how he tried to manipulate Buddhists and Catholics into conflict with each other. In 1963, the Diem government had instigated this religious issue through its own mistakes. Vietnamese are normally religiously tolerant, but the Catholic Ngo family's discrimination against the majority Buddhists was bound to cause problems. The regime's reaction to those problems, arrogant and insensitive as it was, set off the Buddhist crisis, paving the way for Diem's downfall. In 1964, the effects of that crisis were still being felt. The Buddhists had emerged as an organized political force in the country, and a significant amount of religious animosity still simmered. Rather than putting out the fires of that animosity, Khanh stoked them. After he took over, almost every other day there were Buddhist demonstrations against Catholics or Catholic ones against Buddhists. Hordes of people, some armed with crude weapons, roamed the streets of Saigon on a regular basis. There were constantly rumors of yet further and more extreme protests. One day one would hear that Buddhist demonstrators were going to burn down the Saigon Cathedral, the next that Catholic refugees from the Ho Nai area were coming to the city to destroy the Buddhist Institute. Saigon was rocked repeatedly by lawlessness and disorder.

By chance, at that time I knew a student leader from the Cao Thang Technical School in Saigon. Students there were known as tough guys who had access to tools to make weapons. Consequently, crooked Saigon politicians often turned to them to help stage intimidating, "spontaneous" political demonstrations. One day, this student came to see me, looking very disturbed. He told me that he had just met a Major who worked in the secret agency attached to Prime Minister Khanh's office. The Major had given him three hundred thousand piasters (equivalent to almost ten thousand dollars), telling him that it was for his students to stage a Buddhist demonstration against Catholics. He had come to me because he didn't know what to do, whether he should accept the money or not. That was a lot of money for a poor student, but I advised him to return it immediately. He should tell the Major he could not get involved in political demonstrations, I said, because he needed to focus on finishing school. I explained that not only was the scheme morally wrong but it could also be very dangerous for him to get involved in such political machinations.

Thankfully, this student took my advice and returned the money. What he told me still disturbed me greatly, however. He had confirmed to me that General Khanh was indeed secretly instigating the hostility between Buddhists and Catholics. The strategy was playing with fire; there was a big risk that it could get out of control and engulf the whole country in chaos. Furthermore, the hostility Khanh was creating could easily be exploited by Communist agents intent on destabilizing South Vietnam. I decided to try to find a way to stop Khanh's dangerous scheme. I thought the best thing was to help some of the top representatives of the Buddhists and Catholics talk things out with each other.

I already knew two influential men in each camp who I thought might be open to working cooperatively to reduce religious tensions. They were Venerable Thich Tam Chau, the leader of the moderate faction within the Buddhist Institute, and Father Hoang Quynh, who was an adviser of Catholic militants. I had a businessman I knew make the arrangements for both of them to meet at his house. Before the meeting, I contacted a friend at the US Embassy who I knew was a CIA operative. I told him all I knew about Khanh's devious machinations and what I had in mind to stop them. I asked him to give me two radio transmitter sets capable of communicating within 30 miles of each other. I thought that one radio could be put in the Buddhist Institute and the other at a Catholic Church in the Ho Nai refugee area near Bien Hoa. That way the two groups could have instant contact whenever necessary. My CIA friend immediately approved of my idea and readily gave me the two radio units.

When we had the meeting, I told Thich Tam Chau and Father Hoang Quynh what I had learned about Khanh's reckless strategy of instigating religious conflict to divide and rule. They were very interested in working together to stop Khanh's scheme, saying that they already distrusted Khanh. Thich Tam Chau said that he thought Khanh pretended to favor Buddhists in public but that he secretly favored Diem's old Can Lao Party members who were anti-Buddhist Catholic extremists. Both sides welcomed my suggestion of having the radios installed. A Buddhist monk and a Catholic priest would be assigned to man the radios constantly for each group. That way, any time there were rumors of "Buddhist demonstrations coming to destroy the Saigon cathedral" or "Catholic refugees marching to burn the Buddhist Institute," they could talk and instantly dispel the false rumors. Thich Tam Chau and Father Hoang Quynh sincerely thanked me for giving them the technical tools to communicate and avoid more confrontations, and I was quite pleased when there were no more religious demonstrations after the meeting.

At first, I thought that was the end of the story. I had helped restore religious harmony to Saigon and had managed to remain anonymous; I would be unrecognized, but also safe. Shortly thereafter, though, a close friend of mine who was the number two man in the Foreign Affairs Ministry came to see me. He was usually well informed about what was happening behind the scenes in the government and he wanted to warn me that my life was in danger. He had read some top secret orders from General Khanh that said that my yellow Ford Falcon was "targeted for explosion" because "I had sabotaged secret government operations." My friend asked me if I did own the Falcon and what I could have done to be targeted like that. I told him that I did own the car, which I had brought back from America, and then told him of my role in reestablishing religious calm. I told him I was a "fatalist" and was not afraid to die for doing the right thing. To be on the safe side, however, I promised to take his advice and not to use the car anymore. Another well-connected friend also warned me of Gen. Khanh's intention to get rid of me and gave me a Colt pistol for protection. Fortunately, though, Khanh's time in power did not last long so I never had to use the pistol and I was able to resume driving my car after a few months.

ADVISER TO GENERAL DO MAU, DEPUTY PRIME MINISTER FOR CULTURAL AND SOCIAL AFFAIRS

Ironically, even as I was being targeted for assassination by Khanh, I was working for his government. Previously, I had declined to take the position of Deputy Minister of Information for the military junta because I did not want to work in propaganda again. After the 1964 coup, though, I was offered a different, more acceptable government job. General Do Mau had been appointed the Deputy Prime Minister for Cultural and Social Affairs by Khanh, and he asked me to be his adviser. That position involved less of the distasteful work of spinning and distorting information and more upright action within the broader fields of society and culture. I thought it would be better and that I might be able to do some good there, so I accepted.

It was symptomatic of the confusion and instability of the Khanh government that General Do Mau and the two other Deputy Prime Ministers (Nguyen Ton Hoan and Nguyen Xuan Oanh) were not at all in sync with Khanh. After I began working for him, Do Mau confided in me that he did not think much of Khanh and had serious reservations about him. He said that he had accepted a position in the government anyway in order to serve his country as best he could. That was exactly my view as well. Our hope to do something positive despite the poor leadership of Khanh, however, turned out to be overly optimistic.

The Office of the Deputy Prime Minister for Cultural and Social Affairs was supposed to supervise and coordinate the work of the Ministries of Education, Information, Social Welfare, and Labor. Normally, the idea of coordinating the work of several departments like that probably makes sense. In practice under Khanh, however, there was so much political instability that we could not coordinate almost anything. Khanh's style of government created chaos that simply made organization impossible. This was not only because of his own wild gyrations between extremes in policy and rhetoric but also because of his practice of fomenting conflict even within his own government to keep enemies off balance. The case of Khanh's three Deputy Prime Ministers was emblematic of his willingness to undermine even his closest subordinates. At one point in my time working for Do Mau, the conflict between him and Khanh reached such a climax that Do Mau shaved his head in protest and threatened to resign. He told me then that his life was probably in danger and he was not sure what Khanh would do to him.

When he wasn't directly clashing with his Deputy Prime Ministers or setting the Ministries beneath them at cross purposes, Khanh was busy giving contradictory speeches and swinging the country from one excess to another. One day he would sound like a democratic populist, the next day like an autocratic dictator. When he spoke to a Buddhist crowd, he portrayed himself as pro-Buddhist. His next speech, to a Catholic group, would then be anti-Buddhist. He even ventured to have the Constitution of South Vietnam rewritten to suit himself. He secluded himself for a few days in the seaside resort of Vung Tau (about two hours' drive from Saigon) and drafted a new Constitution for the country. With great fanfare, he announced it, proclaiming that he would rule as the "strong man of South Vietnam." He was quickly confronted by a series of authentic student demonstrations protesting the new dictatorial powers he had given himself in this Vung Tau Constitution. Naturally, he suddenly reversed himself and abolished the new Constitution. Nobody ever knew what Khanh had in mind or where he stood.

After a couple of months of seeing both Khanh's misrule and the futility of my own position, I was ready to resign as well. Several times I tried to quit, but Do Mau insisted I stay on with him. I did so, but in my heart I had great doubts about the future of South Vietnam and the usefulness of working for its government. Khanh was clearly a major obstacle to progress in South Vietnam, but I was not at all hopeful that even new leadership could turn things around. I had learned that bitter lesson from the aftermath of the coup against Diem already. I could see that yet another undemocratic coup was unlikely to pave the way for democracy or significantly to alter the underlying problems in Saigon. Consequently, I began mentally to withdraw from the politics of Saigon, aware that there was little I could hope to accomplish. I decided to leave the scheme-filled world to the schemers and try to find something else positive to do with myself.

Chapter 10

HONDA BUSINESS

As I contemplated resigning my government job, my boss Deputy Prime Minister Do Mau was selected to head a state visit to Korea. The South Korean government had invited Nguyen Khanh for the visit, but Khanh feared there would be a coup against him if he went abroad. Consequently, he sent Do Mau in his place. Do Mau had never been to Korea and did not speak English, so he asked me to delay resigning so that I could travel with his delegation and help him in Seoul. I had visited South Korea in the 1950s and welcomed the chance to see the country again, especially because my friend and former schoolmate at Cornell, Dr. Ngo Ton Dat, was then South Vietnam's Ambassador in Seoul.

Our delegation was received by South Korean President Park Chung Hee at the Blue House presidential palace. President Park was an impressive man, seeming quiet and determined. At the time, he had only been in power for a few years and had not really shown his dictatorial character yet. From our visit and my conversations with Dr. Dat, I had the impression that South Korea was making significant progress under Park. In addition to our reception by the President, General Do Mau and I were the guests of several parties given by the top South Korean generals. They were remarkable men who worked hard and played just as hard. Unlike Vietnamese generals, who usually tended to pose as reserved and distant, the South Korean generals were relaxed and straightforward. General Do Mau was impressed with their easy bearing, saying that if

Vietnamese generals behaved more like the South Koreans they would be more united and better able to work together instead of scheming against each other.

Throughout our trip, I was very interested in comparing the situation of the two Koreas with that of divided Vietnam. I had an opportunity to do just that when our group visited Panmunjom to see the 38th parallel separating North and South Korea. What I saw at the Korean Demilitarized Zone was that South Koreans had one major advantage compared with South Vietnam, which was that there was a joint command of American and South Korean forces. That setup not only yielded more efficient military operations but also instilled more trust in the stability of United States support for South Korea. In contrast, the separate American and South Vietnamese chains of command in Vietnam created many operational problems and decreased the confidence of the South Vietnamese public in the United States. I left Korea firmly believing a joint command in Vietnam should be adopted, although it never was.

Following our state visit to Seoul, the government of Japan invited our delegation to visit Tokyo. Prior to our arrival, the Japanese Embassy in Saigon gave us a long list of companies they invited us to tour in order to showcase their growing industries. We were going to be in Japan for only four days, so General Do Mau told me to study the list and pick just one company to visit. He had never been to Japan and wanted to save time for sightseeing. After looking at the list, I decided there were two outstanding firms that would be interesting to check out: Sony and Honda. Because I had already visited Sony during the mid 1950s, I recommended to Do Mau that we tour Honda. He quickly agreed, setting in motion what would become an enormous business opportunity for myself.

When we arrived at Honda Motor Co., Mr. Soichiro Honda himself was there to greet us, along with his top people. Mr. Honda was clearly an extraordinary man, although he was modest and had a good sense of humor. He had an enormous dedication to his work and was proud when he told us of how he had built his company up from an investment of just a few hundred dollars after World War II. He had begun by attaching small, military surplus engines to bicycles and had grown to become one of the world's largest motorcycle and automobile manufacturers. Mr. Honda's passion always remained developing and making technical improvements to the company's products, however. At the time we visited him in 1965, he was still directly involved in testing new engines with the Research &

Development Division's bright young engineers. He confessed to us that, despite being the President of the company, he did not even know how many shares of the Honda Motor Co. stock he owned because he spent all his time at the racetrack testing engines.

Mr. Honda showed us samples of his motorcycles, from the smallest 50cc-engine scooters up to the big 750cc bikes. I was impressed by the quality of the motorcycles and their low prices compared to what was being sold in Saigon. There was an especially big difference in the prices between the smallest 50cc Hondas and the equivalent French motorcycles available in Vietnam at the time. I immediately began thinking that something had to be done to get these Honda motorcycles imported to South Vietnam for the benefit of the public. I requested that Honda give me a complete set of catalogs and price lists to bring back home and see what I could do. When I got back to Vietnam, I gave all the information to a friend of mine who was an assistant to the Economy Minister, telling him that something should be done to introduce Honda to Vietnam for the sake of the consumers.

After returning from Korea and Japan, I still had intended to resign from the government, but then I got involved in helping with flood relief for Central Vietnam. The trips to Hue and Da Nang got me wrapped up in politics again. General Thi, then the Commander of Central Vietnam's I Corps, asked me to see him while I was in the area. At that time, Thi was popular among the "Young Turk" group of generals. Not only was he a Corps Commander but he also retained good connections with the elite paratroopers as well as the Buddhists of Central Vietnam, making him perhaps the most politically influential of the generals. He told me he was being surrounded by an increasing number of sycophants, so he needed my help as a friend who would tell him the truth. I said that I was glad to see him whenever I could and would be especially happy if I could be useful to him as a friend and adviser. During my repeated trips to Da Nang to see General Thi, I shared with him my feelings about Khanh and my intention to quit working for the government. Thi sympathized and said that he was also fed up with Khanh. He confided to me that other generals among the rising Young Turks were thinking of getting rid of Khanh.

Thi was truly a paratrooper at heart. He was always willing to jump into any danger, and as a result he was always in demand when action was called for. Sophisticated planning and complex intrigue were not his strong suits, however. When crises passed, people tended to desert or betray him.

Knowing this, I advised Thi to be extremely cautious when dealing with other generals and politicians. They were likely just to use him for their own purposes. If he helped them without considering the consequences, he would likely accomplish nothing positive for himself while contributing to the political instability of South Vietnam.

Although I told Thi about my plans to leave the government and get into private business, I said that my first priority was still to do what I could to preserve South Vietnam from Communism. We both agreed that probably required that a stable government replace Khanh's. Given South Vietnam's disappointing and disastrous experiences with military interference in politics, however, I said that clearly the solution would not come from generals who resorted to coups so easily. The generals — Thi included — were amateurs at politics who overestimated their ability to simply command away problems. I told Thi that I was ready to volunteer my time to aid him in becoming a stabilizing influence on South Vietnamese politics to pave the way for a decent government. I would even enlist as a private first class in his I Corps so that I could work with him twenty-four hours a day toward our goals, if necessary. The Honda opportunity could wait, I said, because turning around the country's politics was more important.

The main goal I had for Thi was for him to transform the dangerously negative image that American policymakers had of him. Without their trust of him, Thi could never wield his considerable political influence in South Vietnam freely or constructively. Naturally, this goal necessitated that Thi avoid participating in more coups, but there were other changes required as well. Thi had to avoid association with some of the more suspicious politicos and radical Buddhists already in his circle; he had to refrain from making controversial or inflammatory speeches; and he had to work actively on improving his relationship with the US establishment. If he really meant business and would do those things, I would dedicate myself to helping him. I told Thi to think over my offer for a few days before giving me an answer. In the end, he turned it down, saying that the Honda business was a unique and lucrative opportunity that I had better take. I understood his reluctance to accept my offer because it would have been a big commitment. His end of the bargain was a difficult one with significant risks.

GETTING INTO BUSINESS WITH HONDA

After visiting Thi in Da Nang and getting his answer, I flew back to Saigon to finally hand in my resignation from the government. I then called my friend at the Economy Ministry to see what he had done with my Honda file. He said that nothing had been done yet. The file was still locked up, but he thought the Minister might have intended to give the project to a relative eventually. I told my friend to forget about the file and do nothing with it because I was going to take on the project myself. I said that I would go to Tokyo very soon to work something out with Honda. After talking with him, I immediately went to create a limited company to handle the venture, which I called International Business Associates (IBA Ltd.). Although I was the main shareholder and promoter, I invited Le Si Ngac to become the company's first president. Ngac was a respectable elderly engineer I had known for years. Together, we then flew to Tokyo to negotiate a contract with Honda.

At that time, Honda couldn't import anything into Vietnam. Honda already had a Japanese trade agent in Saigon, Nomura Trading Company, but a French company still maintained a tight monopoly on all scooters and motorcycles imported into the country. The company, Lucia, had close connections with the South Vietnamese Economy Ministry, which granted the import licenses. The Economy Ministry made it impossible for Nomura Trading even to bring in sample motorcycles, let alone large numbers for consumer sales.

In Tokyo, I explained the French monopoly situation to the Honda executives and told them that if I were going to represent Honda and help them break the monopoly, I wanted an exclusive agency contract for IBA Ltd. It was a take-it-or-leave-it proposition: they gave me either exclusive agency or nothing at all. The Honda executives protested that their company had never granted such an arrangement before, but I told them that they had nothing to lose. Up to that point, Honda had accomplished absolutely nothing in Vietnam despite the efforts of Nomura Trading. I said that they could give me the exclusive agency contract or they would continue to get shut out of the Vietnamese market.

The Honda executives were in no hurry to make a deal, and they took their time to wine and dine Ngac and myself. We also had marathon negotiating sessions to discuss the same issues over and over, day after day. They would grill us with the same questions asked in slightly different ways. Every time there would be a different executive present, providing the pretext for quizzing us again. The purpose of the whole exercise was to expose any slight discrepancy in our answers and probe our weaknesses. It was typical of Japanese business practices and I expected it, but I also thought that it seemed disturbingly similar to Communist-style interrogation tactics. Ngac, who was not used to this kind of intense negotiation, was very impatient and anxious because of it. He wanted to give up and go home, but I urged him to be patient. I was confident that Honda would realize that working with me was their only chance to do business in South Vietnam.

My confidence and patience were rewarded after a few days of this process, and Honda signed their first-ever exclusive agency contract with me. Having secured it, we returned to Saigon and started working to fulfill our end of the deal by opening the way for Honda imports. I began by looking for a prime location to establish a showroom for our motorcycles. I chose a first-floor annex of the famous Caravelle Hotel in the heart of Saigon. Because the Caravelle was owned by the Catholic Archdiocese of Saigon, I had to negotiate with their business representative, Father Thanh. I explained to Father Thanh how potentially lucrative the Honda business was, and he was so interested that he decided to become a shareholder of IBA Ltd. himself. Not only that, but he also allowed me to use the Caravelle annex for free as a showroom.

Word spread quickly around town that I was the new exclusive agent for Honda. Naturally, Lucia knew what I was trying to do and began snooping on my business. The director general of Lucia happened to know me well and his assistant was a former schoolmate of mine, so they found all kinds of pretexts to stop by my office to monitor my progress. Their spying confirmed my gut feeling that applying for an import license with the Economy Ministry would be pointless. Lucia would know all about it and make sure that their friends in the Economy Ministry blocked it. As a result, my challenge was to find some way to bring Hondas legally into the country without going through the normal import license system.

My initial thought was to use the US military's Post Exchange (PX) system. At that time, the PX system was growing rapidly to keep up with the increasing number of American troops arriving every day. All kinds of different merchandise could be found at the PX in Saigon already, so it wasn't far-fetched that motorcycles might be included. Most important, because the goods were for American servicemen rather than the

Vietnamese public, the PX system had the right to bring foreign goods into the county through the US "offshore system" without depending on a normal Economy Ministry import license. Knowing all this, I made an appointment with the PX director, Peter Mason, who happened to be a friend of mine. I invited Mason to lunch at the Caravelle so that he could stop by my office and see our showroom.

The day of our meeting, there was a headline-making incident in which an American soldier was killed in Saigon. The American had been standing on a street corner, waiting for a bus, when a VC terrorist threw a grenade at him. At our lunch, I used this incident as an introduction to why Hondas would be useful for American soldiers. I said that this soldier's death could have been avoided if he had his own personal transportation instead of standing around waiting for a bus that never came. My Honda motorcycles, I explained, would be a reliable means of transportation for the American troops, ensuring that they did not have to expose themselves to attack while waiting for buses or taxis anymore. They could buy the motorcycles at competitive prices through the PX and then they could ship them back to the United States for free and without taxes at the end of their tours, making it a very good deal for the soldiers. I concluded that everyone involved would benefit if my proposal were accepted and the PX imported Hondas from IBA Ltd. The American servicemen would have new motorcycles at good prices and, more crucial, it would cut down their risk of being victims of VC attacks, thus improving American security. Mason immediately agreed with me that the Hondas should be brought in as soon as possible.

American soldiers quickly ordered many of the Hondas. They bought motorcycles in all shapes, sizes, and colors. It wasn't long before the Vietnamese public took notice, admiring these shiny new Hondas roaring through the streets of Saigon. Vietnamese people were very impressed with the high quality and low prices of the Hondas. The motorcycles we sold to Americans were, in essence, the best advertisements we could have possibly exhibited in the country. The French monopoly on motorcycles still existed, however, and the Vietnamese public could not yet purchase the Hondas they were coveting. I still had to think of what our next step would be to get Honda motorcycles legally into the hands of millions of South Vietnamese.

By that time, Khanh was gone and Air Force Marshal Nguyen Cao Ky was acting as Prime Minister. Ky was eager to do something to show that he cared for the welfare of ordinary South Vietnamese soldiers and their families. I saw that situation as my opening to get Hondas into the South Vietnamese market. I contacted all four ARVN Corps Commanders, including my friend General Thi, to get their help. I asked them to publicize the catalogs of the most economical 50cc motorcycles to their soldiers and get the names and addresses of soldiers who wished to order one of those Hondas. The result was a list of more than 25,000 ARVN soldiers who said they wanted to buy one of our motorcycles.

With that list, I had a friend of mine contact Nguyen Cao Ky and explain to Ky that he would be very popular if he made it possible for all these soldiers to buy the motorcycles they wanted. Ky was looking for something concrete to prove he was really a revolutionary prime minister who cared for average soldiers. This was a perfect opportunity to do just that, enabling all these soldiers to buy economical and convenient motorcycles to transport their families. As a result of that argument and the tangible proof of it that the list provided, Ky approved my proposal to allow soldiers to buy Hondas. Not only that, but he even set up a ceremony in which he symbolically handed over the first of the Honda motorcycles to ARVN soldiers. The order for 25,000 bikes was the largest single order of 50cc motorcycles Honda had ever shipped from Japan. It significantly helped Honda Motor, which was dealing with a serious slump in American sales at the time. The order was so big, in fact, that Honda had to stop all pending outgoing shipments of the 50cc models to other countries to fill our request in a timely manner.

We had gotten Hondas into Vietnam in large numbers and there was no longer any way that Lucia could continue quietly to block importation. This was a big success, breaking the French motorcycle monopoly in a completely aboveboard and legal way. At least that's what I believed at the time. Honda headquarters in Japan had previously asked me, through the intermediary of their shipping agent Nomura Trading, whether any bribe should be given to Nguyen Cao Ky. I told them it was unnecessary because my plan to bring Hondas into Vietnam served the national interest and could be accomplished in a completely legitimate manner. Instead of a bribe, I requested that Honda donate four big 750cc motorcycles to the government to be used for escorting VIPs. Honda did that and at the time I thought that they had also accepted my suggestion against offering a bribe. Years later, though, I learned that Honda did in fact have their Nomura Trading representative give a secret cash bribe of three million dollars to Ky and his aides. This was done behind my back and against my wishes. It was illegal and a gross violation of my exclusive agency contract with Honda. It was also completely unneeded; allowing the motorcycles had been a logical move by Ky and it had just taken a little maneuvering on my part to get him to see that.

With the French monopoly broken, the gates for importation of Japanese motorcycles were wide open. Very soon, Suzuki and Yamaha motorcycles, which both had politically influential local representatives, also made their first appearance in South Vietnam. Where there once had been a monopoly, now there was cutthroat competition. In an attempt to get an advantage in this competitive market, the Suzuki and Yamaha agents resorted to devious schemes to undermine the reputation of Honda. On several occasions, I saw people conspicuously pushing Hondas at busy intersections in Saigon, as if the motorcycles had broken down. Upon investigation, I discovered that Suzuki and Yamaha agents in Saigon were hiring people to push the "broken" Hondas — which were actually fine — in an effort to make people think that Hondas were technically inferior.

These incidents focused my attention on the importance of maintaining high technical quality control to keep the good name of Honda in Vietnam. I therefore asked Honda to send their most qualified engineer to Saigon to train local mechanics to repair Honda motorcycles according to their high standards and to set up a network of repair stations around the country. They sent a close aide of Mr. Honda himself, who quickly set to work on the matter. He suggested to me that IBA Ltd. should order a large quantity of genuine Honda spare parts to be readily available throughout South Vietnam. We did this; then he began training the mechanics. With the help of the Vietnamese General Confederation of Labor, we organized the network of repair stations and dispersed the mechanics countrywide. Thanks to these efforts, we were able to firmly establish Honda's reputation for reliability and quality, despite our competitors' efforts to undermine us. Honda became the biggest motorcycle brand in Vietnam as a result.

The Honda business was so successful that rumors started to circulate that I had a secret partner backing me and pulling strings for me. At first, the rumor was that General Thi was the mystery partner responsible for my success. When his political fortunes eventually waned, the story became that Prime Minister Ky was behind the Honda business. Later, when Ky lost out to Nguyen Van Thieu in their struggle for power, rumors spread that the CIA was my shadow boss. Of course, none of it was true. There was no one else directly benefiting from the project, telling me what to do, or making it happen behind the scenes. Although I certainly made good use of my connections, I was still working alone with just my own ingenuity and persuasion to help.

Despite the collapse of their monopoly, the French businessmen who had previously dominated the motorcycle market did not give up entirely. Whereas my Japanese competitors focused on attacking the Honda brand, the French attempted to attack me personally to stop Honda from taking their business. One day, just after I returned from a trip abroad, Customs agents came to my house and searched it. At that time, there was a draconian law on the books forbidding citizens of South Vietnam from possessing any foreign currency whatsoever. It was unreasonable and never enforced, but the penalties for violation could be as severe as execution. Of course, when they searched me I had a small amount of American dollars from my recent trip that I had not bothered to convert back into local currency. It wasn't really worth the hassle to convert a few dollars. As far as I could tell, most people normally did the same thing I did, just holding onto the cash. The Customs agents discovered the money in one of my jackets and confiscated it as proof of my crime. They were polite about it, though, and apologized for the inconvenience before leaving. Still, I was flabbergasted by the unprecedented search. I had made many international trips over the years and never before had the government searched me, let alone my house, for a few stray dollars.

It seemed suspicious to me that something like that would occur out of the blue. I immediately called IBA Ltd.'s lawyer, who was very well informed about what happened behind the scenes in Saigon, and asked him to find out who was behind the incident. A couple of hours later he called me back and told me that "my good French friends," with whom I often played tennis, had done it. They wanted to get even with me for spoiling their lucrative motorcycle monopoly, so they had their connections in the Economy and Finance Ministries arrange the search. My lawyer told me he didn't expect much legal punishment for my violation, and I certainly would not be "facing the firing squad." He did expect some "juicy articles" related to the incident to appear in the papers, though.

As expected, the next day most of the local newspapers had prominent articles about me, the main shareholder of IBA Ltd., having my house searched on suspicion of "hoarding" foreign currency. I was annoyed with this bad publicity, but I didn't worry too much because I knew who was behind it. Lucia was playing hardball with me, but I figured that even a threat of retaliating in kind would scare them into stopping. I asked my lawyer to get in touch with the French company and let them know that they would suffer a lot more damage than they had inflicted on me if they continued, seeing as how they were actually corrupt and were unlikely to receive the benefit of the doubt from the public because they were French. The rumors that I was secretly partnered with General Thi probably worked to my advantage then, by giving more credibility to my threats. Lucia got the message and ceased their attacks against me. In the end, I didn't even receive a fine for breaking the law against having foreign currency.

After that, I thought the situation was well under control. Two of my associates in IBA Ltd., however, were very disturbed by the newspaper articles. First Le Si Ngac, the honorary president of the company, told me that he wanted to sell his shares and get out of the business. Then, Father Thanh of the Catholic Archdiocese decided to sell his shares too. I tried to explain to them that the newspaper articles and the Customs agents' search were both just the dirty work of the French competitors. I said they needed to take that kind of retaliation in stride, especially because it ultimately did almost no real harm. They were scared, however, and were determined to withdraw. I had no choice but to buy their shares back from them and let them go. The loss of Father Thanh was particularly bad because it threw our arrangement for the Caravelle Hotel showroom into question. On the other hand, I already needed a larger showroom with more storage space, so I was probably going to need to find a new location in the near future regardless of Father Thanh's situation. Luckily, I quickly found a suitable location on Tran Hung Dao Boulevard, the main axis linking Saigon to its Chinese satellite-city of Cholon. It was formerly a large theater and had plenty of space for expansion, so it served nicely.

After two years in business, IBA Ltd. had imported about one million 50cc Hondas into South Vietnam. Hondas became synonymous with motorcycles in the country, so much so that *The Washington Post* dubbed Saigon "Honda heaven" in 1966.[1] They became a status symbol and a marker of social standing, particularly for young people who relished the independence that they provided. More significantly, though, they were a necessity for many people. In a country where mass transportation was not readily available and taxis were expensive, the 50cc Hondas became the basic means of transportation for millions of families. I was glad to see that my business was such a big success and that it contributed positively to the lives of so many Vietnamese.

This experiment in private business was very exciting to me and I devoted more and more time to it as it got more involved and complex. I enjoyed the initial challenge and found it refreshing after the frustrations of working in government. The results far exceeded my expectations. Many of my friends who had been in business their whole lives marveled at my accomplishment and said that I had "struck a gold mine." They all advised me to devote myself completely to capitalizing on my good fortune. In fact, however, I started to lose interest in the business quickly once it was established. The moneymaking part of the Honda venture just didn't engage me in the same way as launching the business had. It was routine, whereas the founding of the company had been an exciting challenge. Getting into private business was in many ways a desperation move that I turned to after my more natural desires to work in government or journalism were frustrated. I had wanted to try my hand at it, but I didn't have much passion for it after the original hurdles were successfully passed.

I also avoided investing too much of myself into the business after it became an established success because I was keenly aware of the fragility of my "gold mine." Many things largely outside my powers could bring it down. First and foremost, if South Vietnam did not survive politically, neither would my business. I also thought it was likely that some corrupt general in Saigon would try to force me into giving him part or most of my business because it was so lucrative. I was surprised that nobody ever did. Additionally, I feared that my exclusive agency contract might be taken away eventually because Honda obviously preferred not to have such arrangements. In fact, Honda did consistently try to subvert our agreement. They tried to hold up IBA Ltd.'s commissions at times and continued to try to sell through their shipping agent Nomura Trading. These actions did hurt, perhaps costing me millions over the years, but they didn't end my business or stop it from being quite profitable.

A final reason I worried was because the importation of Honda motorcycles was being financed by the Commodity Import Program of USAID. Normally, they had a requirement to "buy American" whenever possible, which could have posed problems for our Japanese motorcycle business.

Due to this, I suggested to Honda that there should be a tripartite partnership formed among Honda, IBA Ltd., and an American company like Harley Davidson. They rejected the idea, although thankfully nothing was ever done to restrict our importation. The purchase of so many motorcycles helped prevent extreme inflation in the South Vietnamese economy, which the government and US Embassy were very worried about, so they never did anything to limit us.

ALIENATION AND POKER

With all the easy money I was making in the Honda business, the temptation to totally ignore the war and its miseries was very strong. Frustrated and depressed with the situation of the country, and without very engaging work to sustain me, I increasingly sought distraction and relief from reality. As a diversion and sedative I turned to high-stakes poker, which was popular in Saigon in the late 1960s. In truth, I was almost an addict to poker in those days. In many ways that made me typical of the Saigon elite, who were turning more and more to living the high life and avoiding participation in efforts to solve the nation's problems. Many of them reasoned that the American government knew what it was doing and would solve everything for South Vietnam, so why bother with the effort of staying involved? Instead, it seemed better just to enjoy life and the various opportunities for self-advancement the war offered while forgetting about the war itself. In retrospect, this alienation and disengagement of Saigon's elite seems to me to be one of the main causes for the failure and defeat of the United States and South Vietnam.

I played poker partly to forget, but I played for public relations reasons too. At that time, anybody who was anybody had to be playing. These high-stakes games, which were played for thousands of dollars and that sometimes lasted from Friday night to Monday morning, were social fixtures for important people in Saigon. Playing poker was not only a means to connect with powerful people but also an important way to prove to everyone that I was not involved in opposition politics. Government spies in those days speculated that anybody significant who didn't play cards or otherwise live it up must instead be busy plotting against the government. As a result, if you were not playing poker and living lavishly you would be under a cloud of suspicion and continually watched by the many spies of Saigon. I wanted to be left alone, so I followed the crowd to the card tables.

I did really enjoy the poker, though. I especially liked it for its suspense and because of what it revealed about the personalities of my opponents. It was interesting to see how those colonels, generals, and other "big shots" reacted to my bluffs or how some lost their cool under pressure. Sometimes my observations of people at the table gave me insights into how I could handle them in real-life situations. We only ever played five-card stud, so it could be a quite brutal game where you had to be prepared to risk everything you had on the table at any moment. Everyone started out with an equal amount of money, but losing players could put in more money to keep going after their initial stake was gone. All winnings stayed on the table, so after a few hours of play the stakes got very high, sometimes tens of thousands of dollars. Thanks to all my Honda money it didn't really matter to me whether I won or lost, which meant that I could afford to be more daring than most players. That made the games more fun to me and also earned me a reputation as being a dangerous player. I would hang in on hands even when I had weak cards like a small pair, hoping for a lucky draw on the last cards. When I was successful, I would use the lucky example to bluff my way to more winnings.

Saigon being Saigon, the games were sometimes caught up in the endemic political corruption. I think it was a common occurrence, but it was usually hard to tell if someone was deliberately losing or changing how they played for political reasons. There was one instance, though, where I knew for certain that political machinations were part of the gambling action. A friend of mine had me over for a game one evening that included three colonels, one of whom was an important aide to Prime Minister Nguyen Cao Ky. After the game was over and the other guests had left, my friend confided to me that he was annoyed because he had won big that night. He explained that he had actually wanted to lose and direct the winnings to Ky's aide as a way to give a sizeable bribe disguised as poker winnings. At one point in the evening, the aide had gotten a pair of aces while my friend had only a small pair, so my friend bet big hoping the aide would win. My friend drew a second pair, however, and ended up having to take the pot that was supposed to be a gift. He cursed his untimely luck that ironically caused him to win and thereby fail at his effort to deliberately lose.

We played poker nearly every weekend and often for the whole weekend. People did pretty much whatever they pleased, whenever they pleased at these festivities. Around the clock, hosts provided food, drinks, ginseng, and sometimes "masseuses" for those who wanted them. It was a fun diversion but not an appropriate one in a war-torn country that desperately needed its best talents. We always played in comfortable, air-conditioned rooms and it was difficult to hear anything outside, which was in keeping with how we were all closing ourselves off from the problems that existed out in the real world. I felt powerless to accomplish anything positive at the time, however, so for years I tried to shut out my frustration and depression over South Vietnam's deterioration at those poker tables.

Chapter 11

WAKE-UP CALL

I felt so alienated by the situation in South Vietnam that I avoided dealing with it at all costs. I wanted to forget about the whole thing despite being in the midst of it all. I could not accept what was going on, but I couldn't openly oppose it either because that was tantamount to joining the enemy. I just tried to ignore the war and hope that somehow eventually the United States would change its unwise policy. It seemed inconceivable to me that American policymakers could not recognize how obviously flawed their approach was, so I reasoned that eventually the situation might improve and I could contribute to my nation again. Yet time passed and nothing changed, at least not for the better. As frustrated and disgusted as I was, I often wondered how other South Vietnamese, who had not been educated in the United States and did not understand Americans like I did, must have felt.

I wanted nothing to do with South Vietnam's politics or problems. During that period, some people encouraged me to get involved again, but I flatly refused. My good friend Barry Zorthian, who was the Director of the Joint US Public Affairs Office (JUSPAO, which had grown out of USIS after the American war effort expanded), frequently urged me to get active in some kind of journalistic project to "help the war effort." Every time we met at social functions, he would tell me how my experiences as a Nieman Fellow and as Director General of Vietnam Press made me perfect to contribute positively to national conversations. I told Zorthian that I wanted to do nothing of the kind, however, because I believed the war effort was doomed to failure. My aversion to everything was so strong that I even avoided some people to escape the issues. That was the case with Bernard Fall, who had been a close friend of mine while I was at Cornell and he was at nearby Syracuse. In 1967, he sent word that he wanted to meet with me again while he was in Saigon, but I was in such a mood of denial that I refused to see him because he would want to talk about the war. Much to my regret, I learned a few days later that he had been killed by a mine explosion while on patrol with Marines along what he had named the "Street Without Joy," northwest of Hue.

Despite my intense desire to stay out of politics, I was involuntarily dragged back into them by my friendship with General Nguyen Chanh Thi. Although Thi had refused my offer to become his full-time adviser in order to remake his image and reform his politics, he continued regularly to solicit my guidance. As Thi maneuvered against his rivals for power and influence, he turned to me as someone he could trust to be honest with him. It never occurred to me to avoid helping him because I was his friend and he needed me. The experience, however, only brought me grief and further bitterness toward South Vietnam's situation. That bitterness culminated in the realization, after the wake-up call of a near-death experience, that South Vietnam was indeed doomed and that I had to prepare accordingly. Those preparations included not only withdrawing my family to safety in the United States but also trying to help with negotiations to end the war.

NGUYEN CHANH THI'S MANEUVERS AND OUSTER

One day back in 1965, while I was still busy setting up my business venture, Gen. Thi unexpectedly showed up at my house to ask for my help. It wasn't often Thi left the northern provinces of his I Corps command, so I asked him what had brought him to Saigon. He said that the other generals had asked him to fly to Saigon immediately for an important meeting of the ARVN General Staff. Apparently, the US Embassy and Ambassador Taylor had put out the word that "Khanh had to go," so the generals were going to decide Prime Minister Nguyen Khanh's fate.

It seemed like almost everyone in South Vietnam wanted General Khanh to be removed from power, so I wasn't surprised by what Thi said. It still didn't explain what he was doing at my home and what he wanted, however. I asked Thi, "Why did you come to me here then?" Thi's reply surprised me, but it also gave me an idea of where things stood among the Saigon generals. He said, "I was invited by the Marine Corps Commander to set up my headquarters at his place, but I don't trust anybody these days." Thi wanted me to help him "find a place to spend the night where nobody knows where we are." I asked him whether the situation was really that dangerous. He told me, "I think this is needed," explaining that Khanh's people were everywhere in Saigon and that he had to be cautious with the other generals as well. I told Thi that of course I was ready to help him as his friend, but I thought it was a very bad sign that he could not trust any of his military comrades. Accordingly, we went to spend the night at the home of one of my distant relatives in the suburbs of Saigon.

The next day I called up Dr. Ted Britton, who was back in Saigon and knew Thi well, and told him that we were coming to his house to wait things out. Colonel Sam Wilson of the US Embassy joined us later also. Together, we stayed there all night while General Khanh was being ousted from power. The other Saigon generals elected Thi to lead them and decide what to do about Khanh. He was given the fancy, Communist-sounding title of "Commander-in-Chief of the Forces for the Liberation of the Capital." Thi was picked mostly because the other generals preferred to let him test the waters for them. They were being cautious, preferring not to stick out their necks, whereas Thi was his usual reckless self and accepted the job without much reflection.

At first, Khanh appeared to give up. He announced that he was resigning as the Prime Minister and as the Head of the Military Council. He did not say, however, that he was giving up his position as ARVN Commander-in-Chief, the job that mattered the most under the circumstances. He began flying around the country, appealing to various Corps and Division commanders to side with him against the Young Turks who were attempting to replace him. Meanwhile, the Young Turks and Khanh were all negotiating, but without any decisive conclusion. Khanh was not yet able to rally much support to his rescue, but the Young Turks could not seem to find a way to get Khanh to resign as ARVN Commander-in-Chief.

That night, after the long day of maneuvers and negotiations, I stumbled upon the solution for Thi and the Young Turks by accident. Thi, Sam Wilson, Ted Britton, and I were unwinding from the day's tense drama over a bottle of scotch. Out of curiosity, I asked Thi if Khanh still had the legal right to give orders to Thi and the other generals if he was still Commander-in-Chief. Thi casually responded that in principle Khanh still could. Because Khanh would not resign his position voluntarily, I thought something had to be done to strip him of his legal authority. Although Khanh's practical authority was disappearing as we spoke, I worried that he might get ARVN officers to follow him again if the situation dragged out and he continued to retain that official power. Suddenly, a thought came to me. The civilian Chief of State Phan Khac Suu was normally a mere figurehead, but perhaps his authority could be used to legally sidestep Khanh and strip Khanh of his position. I suggested to Thi that we draft a statement for Suu to sign appointing a new ARVN Commander-in-Chief to replace Khanh, effective immediately. I asked Thi if he knew of anyone who had seniority but would be a non-controversial and non-threatening pick to the rest of the generals. Thi said that everyone would probably find General Tran Van Minh ("Small Minh") suitable because he was considered apolitical. I agreed that Small Minh was the right choice for a temporary Commander-in-Chief, so we wrote up the statement for Suu to sign. I also advised that Radio Saigon should broadcast the statement as soon as Suu signed it to make it clear to everyone that Khanh was done.

One of Thi's aides rushed to get the statement signed and put on the radio. Within a few hours, Khanh signaled that he would leave the country. He was allowed to become an "Ambassador-at-Large" as a face-saving gesture, but it was a small price to pay to be rid of him. Ever the charlatan, before his departure flight he made a dramatic show for photographers of picking up some dirt and putting it in his pocket as if he were suddenly some great patriot who was passionately attached to his fatherland. His leadership, however, had been perhaps the most detrimental of anyone's (aside from Diem's) to South Vietnam's survival. Khanh's legacy was the destruction of the people's confidence in their government.

With the bloodless coup against Khanh over, Thi was the man of the hour. He emerged as the most prominent of the Young Turk generals now in control, with General Nguyen Cao Ky beneath him. As usual though, Thi had not planned his moves in advance and he had not consulted any Americans, who were happy to see Khanh gone but still distrusted Thi. I feared Thi would be outmaneuvered in short order. With the crisis over, though, I told Thi that I had to get back to my business rather than spending my time counseling him. That didn't stop Thi from continuing to solicit my advice, but I wanted to avoid the politics and intrigues as much as I possibly could. Before we parted, I cautioned him against the advice of self-interested schemers and against making any more hasty decisions.

Thi's first decision was whether to stay in Saigon to replace Khanh as Prime Minister himself, or to return to his I Corps Command up north and let General Ky become Prime Minister. He decided to go back to I Corps thanks to the advice of his "friend" Colonel Pham Van Lieu. Col. Lieu convinced Thi that he would "handle Ky" in Saigon while Thi could hold on to his strong political base in I Corps. Lieu, who had become the new Director General of National Police, planned to strengthen and militarize the police in the style of Thailand. That method, he claimed, would give him the ability to control Saigon and, therefore, Ky. Ky, however, had plenty of power himself and would be difficult to "control."

Thi's lack of American support also played a role in his decision. Before he decided to leave the Prime Minister job to Ky, Thi was summoned to see the American MACV (Military Assistance Command, Vietnam) commander General William Westmoreland at the ARVN Marine headquarters. Thi asked me to go with him to the meeting. I wasn't expecting it to go well, but I was still surprised by Westmoreland's message. He was condescendingly blunt, and it was clear that someone had been working to give him a bad impression of Thi. Westmoreland lectured Thi about his past coup participation and essentially said that he thought Thi was a troublemaker. Westmoreland strongly urged Thi to get out of Saigon and go back to I Corps. It seemed to me a good indication that Ky was already working to marginalize Thi.

Before Thi left for Da Nang, I told him he was in a precarious position and he had to be cautious. First, I explained, Thi could not really trust Col. Lieu to help him. Lieu clearly had a lot of political ambitions and had given advice that primarily served his own interests. Lieu was also originally from northern Vietnam, like Ky, and was friends with many of the same northern Vietnamese politicians as was Ky. I also pointed out to Thi that he clearly had very little American support or even sympathy, as the meeting with Westmoreland made painfully obvious. Finally and most significantly, I told Thi that I believed that he was underestimating Ky in a dangerous fashion. Ky was a skilled intriguer and he had the Americans' attention. Thi was acting out of the mistaken assumption that power came only from the muzzle of a gun and that his continued command of troops would keep him on top. In South Vietnam, however, American influence was the trump card in any competition for power. Ky, as it turned out, knew how to play it.

In short order, Ky cleverly convinced the US establishment that the four ARVN Corps Commanders had to be removed because they were acting as "warlords." They exercised too much autonomy in their territories and were supposedly challenging the authority of the central government. They had to go to ensure that the ARVN remained under the unified control of the government. Ky's true desire and intention was just to remove his rivals and consolidate his rule, but Americans found the reasoning persuasive because of their desire for stability in Saigon. Because Thi was the most powerful of the Corps commanders, Ky left him as the last to be removed. Many officers serving under Thi strongly supported him, as did the Buddhists of Central Vietnam. They all vehemently protested his potential removal. Some Americans who worked closely with Thi even backed him, especially Marine General Lewis Walt who commanded American forces in I Corps. It was a messy affair for Ky to get rid of Thi, but he had the backing of the American establishment in Saigon, which was key.

Before he was sacked officially, Thi invited me to come to Da Nang to consult with him. When I arrived, he told me that he was afraid he would lose his job at an upcoming meeting of the General Staff in Saigon, which he had been ordered to attend. Col. Lieu had assured him that the rumors were false, though, telling him that Ky was still a good friend. I said that I believed the rumors and thought it might be too late for him to mend fences with Ky. Thi had indeed been challenging Ky's authority and essentially running I Corps as if he were the supreme authority there. Thi had also been making inflammatory and disrespectful statements against Ky while stirring his followers against Ky's government in Saigon. I told Thi it was his decision to make though, and left Da Nang to return to my business.

During the afternoon a few days later, one of Thi's aides came to my office and asked me to go see Thi at his house in Saigon. When I arrived, Thi looked very depressed. He had followed Col. Lieu's advice to attend the generals' meeting and had been removed from command. Lieu had been following Ky's orders to give Thi false assurances, of course. Lieu didn't defend or help Thi because he hoped Ky would keep him as Director General of National Police. Naturally, Ky did no such thing and replaced Lieu a short while later with his own loyal man, Colonel Nguyen Ngoc Loan. Thi said that all the other generals supported Ky's move, so he guessed that the Americans had demanded it. Despite anticipating it, he was still in shock. He said he couldn't understand why the Americans didn't support him when all he had ever tried to do was his best as I Corps

Commander. He then handed me a letter from General Westmoreland that had been delivered to his place after the meeting. The letter, typed on stationery with the four-star general's flag on top, read:

> Dear General Thi:
>
> I understand that you are interested in securing medical attention in the United States. It occurs to me, therefore, that you might welcome an invitation from me, on behalf of the United States Department of Defense, offering you the use of our medical facilities for a complete physical examination and checkup, as well as the administration of whatever treatment is found necessary.
>
> If this offer appeals to you, I wish you to let me know and I will immediately make all the necessary arrangements.
>
> With every good wish,
>
> Very sincerely yours,
> (Signed) W.C. Westmoreland
> General, United States Army

Clearly, the United States wanted Thi out of Vietnam, one way or another. Westmoreland was giving Thi an extremely flimsy pretext to leave, without any attempt to soften the blow or preserve Thi's dignity. Nevertheless, I advised Thi that he should accept the offer and his inevitable exile for the good of the country. I reminded him that the situation was one of his own making, stemming from his overconfident belief that he could control Ky. Thi was furious about the situation, though, and about the letter in particular. He said that he had never discussed any health problems with Westmoreland and he only had a mild sinus problem anyway. He was tempted, he told me, to leak Westmoreland's letter to the Vietnamese press and "blast it out" against the letter. He was going to tell the public of Ky's intrigues and the American interference in South Vietnam's politics, which "smelled so bad" that his sinus problem had worsened enough that maybe he actually did need treatment. He also threatened that he would cancel sending his children to school in Virginia, which Colonel Sam Wilson had generously arranged before. Thi was a single father and he struggled to take care of his kids because of his many official duties, so the arrangement was a great opportunity for them. I urged him to reconsider it all. At best, attacking Westmoreland would amount to a meaningless Pyrrhic victory. I especially implored him not to jeopardize his children's future with such spiteful gestures made in a fit of pique.

While Thi was fuming with anger over the letter, Ky's right-hand man Colonel Loan showed up at his place. Thi was virtually under house arrest at this point and Loan seemed to be there as a warden of sorts, checking in to monitor Thi's behavior. Loan had gone to school with me at Khai Dinh Lyceum, but two decades later his presence did not inspire warm and friendly feelings. He was widely feared around Saigon as Ky's executioner and somebody capable of killing at will. Later, during the 1968 Tet Offensive, Loan became notorious worldwide when he was captured on camera personally executing a Viet Cong agent. When Loan showed up, I was afraid that he would think I was advising Thi *not* to leave Vietnam. I decided, though, that I would not explain to Loan what I had been telling Thi because that was between my friend Thi and myself. It was an awkward and tense moment for me, but fortunately Loan wasn't there to ask questions. Instead, his visit appeared to be a menacing reminder from Ky that Thi needed to leave the country soon. After Loan departed, I explained how Loan's visit had been conveying the same message as Westmoreland's letter: get out of Vietnam, Thi! He had lost out in the contest for power and it was time to accept the outcome and make the best out of a bad situation. Although no threats had been explicitly made yet, continuing to resist would surely lead to harmful consequences for him.

Because the Americans' attitude toward Thi was the most frustrating aspect of the whole situation to him, I attempted to explain to him why they were in favor of Ky. In the Americans' eyes, Ky had the position of official authority already, the winning argument of central government versus warlords, and the better overall image. At this point, I told Thi, the United States and President Lyndon Johnson valued stability in South Vietnamese politics above all else. Johnson could not justify the need for increasing American assistance to the South Vietnamese government if that government kept changing and was in constant crisis. That meant no more coups or sudden shifts in leadership. Philip Habib, the US Embassy Political Affairs Officer, had related the point to me personally. Habib had stressed to me the need for a solid central government in Saigon. He said that if Thi, like a regional warlord, continued to challenge Ky's authority as the leader of the central government, he would have to go.

The Americans were predisposed to listen to Ky because Ky had essentially let them know that he would do anything they asked of him. On the other hand, they considered Thi too erratic and too independent to be trusted. He had jumped into coups in the past without American approval and sometimes gave speeches that seemed anti-American, although really they were mostly just nationalist. He had also surrounded himself with associates whom Americans distrusted or disliked. Many of his followers were extremist Buddhists and a few were suspected of being Communist spies. There was one particularly suspicious individual, a man cryptically known as "Ong Sau" (Mister Number Six), who had been part of Thi's household since his return from Cambodia. I had previously urged Thi to have the CIA check on the man, but Thi never bothered. After the war my friend, the master Communist spy Pham Xuan An, confirmed to me that this Ong Sau had indeed been a Communist mole. As a friend speaking frankly, I concluded, there was quite a long list of valid reasons for the United States to distrust Thi.

Thi did not immediately accept my advice, but after a few weeks he did back down and accept the cover story that he was leaving for medical treatment in America. Really, he was being sent into exile. He ended up remaining in the United States for the rest of his life. On several occasions I tried to intervene so that he could return to Vietnam, but we never succeeded. The closest I came to getting Thi back to Vietnam was around Christmas in 1971. I organized a press conference at the National Press Club in Washington, DC, for Thi to explain publicly his desire to return to live in his country as an ordinary citizen. After this trial balloon, we received conflicting reports on whether Thi would be allowed back. I got word that President Nguyen Van Thieu (who had replaced Ky by then) wanted me to guarantee Thi's behavior if he was going to return because he was still considered a "troublemaker." I replied that there was no way I could make such a guarantee, but allowing Thi back was the right thing to do and would show that the government was willing to be more open than it had been in the past.

Thi decided to make the attempt at returning despite the warnings that he might not be permitted. A couple of months later, he boarded a Pan Am plane filled with American soldiers bound for South Vietnam. When the plane landed at Tan Son Nhut airport outside Saigon, it was cordoned off and all of the passengers disembarked except Thi. ARVN soldiers guarded the plane as it was refueled and Thi waited inside. The plane was then sent back to the United States empty, but for Thi. We had expected he might not be allowed to stay, but it was still surprising that President Thieu and the American establishment were so anxious to not have Thi in Vietnam that they didn't even wait for the next regular flight. The US government footed the bill for Thi's personal flight back to America, which had to be one of the stranger and more wasteful uses of American tax dollars during the war.

After the war, I maintained some contact with Thi, but eventually I had to disavow our friendship. As a member of the Vietnamese exile community in America, Thi allowed himself to be tricked — once again by his "friend" Lieu — into being one of the founding members of the "National United Front for the Liberation of Vietnam." This Front, led by Hoang Co Minh, was supposedly going to rally all patriotic Vietnamese to liberate Vietnam from Communism. In reality, it was mostly a racket to raise money for Minh and others by exploiting Vietnamese Americans' desperate hope to freely return to their homeland. Thi was not really a leader in the organization and had been enlisted mostly because his name leant credibility to the Front.

Eventually, Thi realized the organization's fraudulent nature and lamented his mistake to me. I had had enough of such blunders from Thi, however, particularly because I found the continued fanatical anti-Communism of the Front distasteful and obsolete by the 1980s and Thi did not disavow that. He had once bragged about how the Front "torched a Vietnamese restaurant" because the owner had visited his family in Communist Vietnam. I was planning such a return to Vietnam myself at the time, so I thought such behavior was nihilistic. Vietnam needed reconciliation, not to hold onto such hatred. As a consequence of Thi's involvement with this Front group, I told him that we had to part ways. I had tried to help Thi numerous times over the years, but he had mostly ignored my advice and listened to the wrong people, as he himself admitted.

MY WAKE-UP CALL

Despite my attempts to ignore the carnage in my country, the war caught up with me because of the deteriorating military situation in I Corps that followed Thi's ouster from command there. In May 1967, my grandmother passed away and I had to return home to Hue for the funeral. For most South Vietnamese, it would have been impossible to get to Hue from Saigon at the time. Viet Cong attacks and sabotage had heavily damaged Hue's airport, so civilian flights had been suspended indefinitely. General Tran Van Trung, the Director of ARVN Psychological Warfare, was attending the funeral, though, so he arranged for a military plane to transport us. Nguyen Cao Thang, an influential and wealthy pharmacist, also joined us because his wife was related to my grandmother.

The Buddhist ceremonies preceding my grandmother's funeral were supposed to take place in my aunt's house. Her house was in a VC-infested suburb of Hue, making it far too dangerous for General Trung, Thang, and myself to stay there overnight. We had to find somewhere secure in town to stay, so Gen. Trung invited Thang and me to join him at the Government Delegate's Mansion, which was heavily guarded. I told Gen. Trung that as a civilian I felt more at ease at a hotel. Thang decided to join me and we went to the best hotel in town, the Huong Giang Hotel on the right bank of the Perfume River.

The hotel was fairly full of guests, many of them Americans and other foreigners. Because of this, Thang and I had rooms located far apart instead of having adjoining rooms. It didn't seem like a big deal, though, and we were quite comfortable. We had no problems the first two nights in Hue. We attended the religious ceremonies at my aunt's during the day and returned to the hotel at night. On the third day, which was supposed to be our last in Hue, we did similarly. After dinner and a few drinks, Thang and I retired to our rooms to sleep. That's when I started to have strange feelings of premonition that something unusual was going to happen. It was hard to pinpoint what I sensed, but I was very nervous and on edge. I stayed up reading to calm down and finally went to sleep sometime around one in the morning.

Suddenly, I was awakened by gunfire and explosions. It was probably about 2 a.m. I thought for a second perhaps it was only firecrackers like those used during Tet, the Vietnamese New Year. Tet was in February, however, and it was already May. The sounds were also clearly coming from within the hotel itself. It was nothing other than a VC attack on the hotel. My first reaction was to go down the hall and knock on Thang's room so we could get together for some protection. I went and knocked a few times, but Thang didn't answer. Later, he told me he had been too scared to open the door. In his panic he hadn't recognized my voice and thought I might have been a VC commando coming to get him. It seemed too dangerous to stay out in the hallway, so I went back to my room to hide when he didn't answer the door.

I thought that my best strategy was to stay alert and watch out for VC coming and searching the rooms. I hid in the closet next to my room's entry, which enabled me to listen and hear what was going on in the hallway. I imagined a plan that if they were coming toward my room I would have to run and jump into the Perfume River on the opposite side of the hallway. I heard a steady patter of gunfire punctuated with some very loud explosions, each of which made the ceiling plaster clatter down on my head. I decided to get up and pull the bed mattress over my head, which I hoped would protect me by absorbing the worst from any of those explosions.

At the exact moment that I stood up, I heard a thunderous explosion in my own room and immediately felt a burning sensation in my left leg. Reaching down to touch it, I realized that my tibia bone was shattered and my leg was nearly severed by a projectile and explosion. I was bleeding profusely and my left foot quickly began to feel cold. I tried to stop the bleeding by making a tourniquet out of some pajamas. I stayed alert, mostly because I felt raging mad that I was being killed like a dog by some VC terrorist despite being a civilian. That intense anger kept me awake despite the heavy blood loss. The attack continued around me and I heard a large explosion that made the whole building shake, but the VC never came into my room.

As I lay there, the shooting finally ceased and I eventually heard footsteps in the hall. Someone speaking English with a heavy Indian accent called to me, "Are you wounded? Where are you?" I responded, "Yes. I am in here." The man came into my room and I saw he was an Indian medic from the International Control Commission, which had also been staying at the hotel. He lit a candle for me but then left quickly, saying that he was going to get help. I waited a long time but he didn't return. I had to put out the candle because it was threatening to burn the mattress next to me. I thought my situation was pretty desperate then and I worried I would bleed out before any help came. I could hear a lot of moaning and groaning around me, so I guessed there were many others in the same predicament.

I waited a while longer, then I heard Thang's voice calling my name and trying to find where I was. I told him that my left leg was shattered and that he had better get me to the hospital. I knew it would have to be amputated and that the sooner, the better. He said he had to go get help because he could not carry me by himself. He came back after a little while with two other people. One was a Vietnamese USIS employee I knew and the other was a tall American. Thang later told me that the American had been standing by a Jeep outside the hotel and must have been a CIA operative checking the scene. No one else would have dared to hang around the hotel like that after such an attack. The three of them carried me on a chair through all kinds of debris and broken glass. They then put me in the American's Jeep and drove me to a nearby hospital.

At the hospital, I saw many people with serious injuries like mine, all casualties from the hotel attack. I was put on an operating table immediately, but then nothing happened for a long time. My leg felt very cold and I was really afraid of gangrene setting in. I asked a Catholic nun who was a nurse if the doctor could quickly come to amputate my leg. She said that there were many people more seriously injured than me, so I would have to be patient. In the meantime, Thang came back and told me some good news. He had found a friend of his and had managed to get the hospital's last bottles of blood for my surgery. He then stopped a doctor who was passing by and pleaded for him to take care of me. Thang looked like a lowly hospital janitor in his bloodstained clothes, so he had to explain who he was. He told the doctor about how he was the wealthiest pharmacist in Vietnam and about all of the influential friends he had. Thang also tried to persuade the doctor that I was a very important person in Saigon, telling him how I was a successful businessman and how I was so well connected. The doctor was apparently convinced and he quickly did the amputation.

I passed out from the sedatives they gave me before the operation. When I woke up, I felt a strange, painful sensation in my leg. When I tried to touch it, the leg was no longer there. It was the typical phantom limb feeling. Unfortunately, the Hue hospital was just a poorly equipped provincial one and that night it was quite overwhelmed. The doctor who performed the procedure was probably no expert in orthopedic surgery and had not done a good job. Only my tibia, below the knee, was shattered, but he had amputated above the knee. I suppose he was acting on the safe side and doing so to simplify the procedure, but a more skilled surgeon could have saved the knee. Even with the simpler approach, the doctor still managed to mess up the amputation somewhat and I soon developed a bad infection.

My parents came to see me in the hospital the next morning. The hospital was lacking in pretty much everything and was extremely uncomfortable. I was lying there on a steel bed with only a simple straw mat for cushioning. The sun was shining through the windows and it was stifling hot. There was no air conditioning, not even a fan. Seeing me in these miserable conditions with my serious injury, my parents were appalled. They were clearly much more saddened by the loss of my leg than I was. They had a typical Vietnamese perception of the situation, viewing the loss of the leg as a personal catastrophe that made me a worthless invalid. I, on the other hand, was glad to have lost only my leg and not my life.

I was indeed very lucky to be alive. A number of people had been killed in the attack, including guests in the room next to mine. The VC had systematically fired B40 anti-tank rockets into each hotel room from an adjacent building. They aimed very low to the floor so that anyone seeking cover by lying flat would be directly hit. I happened to be doing the wrong thing — standing up — when the rocket was fired, so I was only hit in the leg and survived. The day after the attack, General Trung sent one of his aides back to my room to pick up my belongings, but he returned with nothing but a charred fountain pen. He said my briefcase had been reduced to ashes. It appeared that the rocket that hit me had entered the opposite side of the building, gone through three walls, hit the briefcase, and then exploded. Among the rockets, bombs planted by VC sappers, and fires the VC set, the hotel was nearly destroyed and there were many casualties. Although I was one of them, I felt fortunate to have not suffered a worse fate.

After my amputation, General Trung and Thang both decided that I had to be moved out of that underequipped Hue hospital and taken to Saigon for proper care. They quickly got me moved to the Grall Hospital in Saigon, where my wound was reopened by a French surgeon to clean up the infection I had developed. I stayed in the hospital for a couple of weeks in order for the wound to heal and to get ready to go to the United States for treatment and a prosthesis.

In Saigon, the news about the VC attack was completely blacked out. It did not appear anywhere; it was missing from the local papers, Vietnam Press bulletins, and Saigon Radio. The government was afraid of the psychological impact if the people knew that the VC could strike with impunity in the country's second largest city. People often tuned into the BBC or Voice of America (VOA) to get accurate news about their country, however. Apparently, some of my friends had been listening to VOA while playing poker on the night of the attack. The broadcast not only described the attack but also specifically mentioned that I had been injured in it. My friends were puzzled, though, and wondered if it was really me or someone with the same name who had been hurt. They could not imagine what I was doing in Hue because they knew there was no civilian air travel there and they had played poker with me only a few nights before. It wasn't until they came to see me in the hospital that they knew for sure that I had in fact been wounded in the attack.

General Edward Lansdale came to see me in the hospital in Saigon a couple of times. We had been friends since 1954 when he had first come to Vietnam to help Ngo Dinh Diem, and by 1967 he had returned to Saigon as an aide to Ambassador Lodge. Lansdale brought me comic books to read and joked with me to keep my spirits up. He told me he was surprised that I had taken my serious injury and amputation so well. I replied that I was a fatalist at heart, but actually the injury was a blessing in disguise. It had been a wake-up call for me. It made me realize that I could not continue to ignore the war as I had been doing. I decided that I needed to try as much as I could to help find a way to end the war, no matter how futile a task that seemed. More personally, however, I also came to the determination that I had to remove my family and myself from the growing turmoil in Vietnam and from the potential chaos of the South Vietnamese government's collapse. In hindsight, I feel lucky to have gotten that sudden wake-up call even if it cost me a leg. Without it, I shudder to think of what might have happened to my family and me in 1975 when Saigon fell.

Talking with Lansdale, I was struck by the contrast of the hopelessness I felt then against the optimism we had shared during the early days of Diem's government. Then, I had been an idealistic young aide who was helping Diem pave the way for a prosperous and democratic future for South Vietnam. Lansdale had been a brilliant man of legendary renown who was subtly steering Diem in the same direction. Now, however, I was sitting broken in a hospital bed, with a broken country surrounding me. I shared my sense of powerlessness with Lansdale: how it seemed that there was nothing I could do to positively affect my country amidst such a destructive war. Lansdale, in his typical way, didn't say much but indicated he felt the same. He looked very tired and did not appear at all to be the dynamic man I had known in the 1950s. He had returned to Vietnam not as a leader as before but as a relatively unimportant assistant to someone else. To me, that scene of a worn-down Lansdale by my sickbed in that Saigon hospital spoke volumes. It represented to me the hopelessness of the war and what it had done to many of the people who had attempted to create a better future for South Vietnam.

RETURN TO THE UNITED STATES

As soon as my stump was healed, I left for America. I arrived in Los Angeles on July 17. My good friend Dr. Omar Fareed came to the airport to greet me. Dr. Fareed was an impressive person. I first met him when he came to Saigon to make contacts for his medical foundation, which was promoting preventative medicine throughout underdeveloped countries. After picking me up, he immediately drove me to see his friend, who was one of the top orthopedic surgeons at the UCLA School of Medicine. His friend examined my stump and the work that had been done. He said it was a shame that they had not tried to save the knee. I had to get fitted with a prosthesis as soon as possible, he said, and start to practice walking to build up the muscles in that left leg. Dr. Fareed, in his usual efficient way, drove me to a shop in Santa Monica right away to get a temporary prosthesis. As we left the shop, he threw away my crutches and insisted that I start walking as if nothing had ever happened. We then went to his home in the Westwood area of LA, where I was going to stay with him.

The American way of looking at amputees and the Vietnamese way were quite different. In Vietnam, people generally saw amputees as hopeless and helpless, but Americans tended to believe amputees were capable of living full lives still. Dr. Fareed said I had to keep in mind that I could still do anything and that I could not let the amputation hold me back. To drive this point home, Dr. Fareed told me, "Thai, starting tomorrow and for as long as you are my guest, you are going to swim and play tennis with me." His house had a tennis court and swimming pool, but I was surprised because I didn't really think I was capable of those things yet. I was even more surprised when he told me we would play doubles tennis against the likes of Jack Kramer, Pancho Segura, Tony Trabert, and Pancho Gonzales. They were all world-famous tennis champions, so I had a hard time convincing myself I could do it, but Dr. Fareed insisted, saying, "You are perfectly normal, Thai!" I greatly appreciated his positive attitude and tried to show up on the tennis court to please him. My orthopedic surgeon advised me that I had to regularly practice walking with my new prosthesis under the supervision of a physical therapist, but I couldn't find the time to do so. I really should have, but I felt like I had so much to do after my wake-up call and needed to get working. As soon as I got fitted with my regular artificial leg, I was off.

My first task was to find an American home for my family, safe from the dangers of the Vietnam War. I selected Newport Beach because Ed Lansdale recommended it. His brother Phil already lived there and sponsored my application to the homeowners' association. I was very happy because the house was in a nice area and was only a few blocks from my kids' school. As a parent, I felt that I had been neglectful of my children's upbringing in the past. I regretted that I had not always spent more time with them in Saigon, busy as I was with politics and business. I saw the move to America as a chance to redeem myself somewhat with a fresh beginning. War-torn Vietnam was, of course, a dangerous place to grow up in and, as I increasingly saw it, a country without a future. I felt an obligation to make sure my children would be safe and would have the opportunity to develop to their fullest potential. In America, they would get a good education and be free of the war's fears and sacrifices. I was extremely grateful that I had the opportunity to move my family to California before the war ended, unlike so many others.

EFFORTS TO AVERT THE INEVITABLE

With my family's future seen to, I turned once again to the politics and diplomacy of the war. After my near-death experience and wake-up, I was desperate to do something to try to save South Vietnam from the destruction it was facing. In retrospect, it seems to me that the tragedy was inevitable, but at the time I thought I had a duty to try everything possible. I told Nguyen Cao Thang, to whom I grew quite close after he saved my life in Hue, that we had to make an effort at "finding a solution for the South Vietnamese problem" even if nobody else seemed willing to try.

I had a feeling after losing my leg that the May 1967 VC terrorist attack in Hue was only a small precursor for something much larger. I feared there would be an attack significant enough that it might fundamentally shake American confidence in the war effort. As it turned out, the 1968 Tet Offensive did just that less than a year later. I had already abandoned my physical rehabilitation in favor of my personal fact-finding mission by then and was in Paris when the offensive began. It, and the American public's reaction to it, confirmed my fears by crystallizing the American notion that Vietnam was a lost cause.

From my conversations with knowledgeable Americans at that time, I saw that they had realized there was no possibility for a successful conclusion to the war, not as long as thc leadership of South Vietnam remained so weak and blindly self-interested. They saw no way of fixing that fundamental weakness of the Saigon government and, consequently, decided it was time to minimize America's losses. The word *abandonment* was never used, but that was the drift of American policy after the Tet Offensive.

After comparing notes with my trusted American friends, I came back to Saigon in 1969 to convince key figures in the Saigon establishment of the urgent need to change their ways and govern responsibly. I explained to any who would listen that although the United States would try its best to sugarcoat its new policy, as it did with euphemisms like "Vietnamization," the heart of the matter was that the United States was fed up with the war and the poor performance of the corrupt South Vietnamese government. There was no reason for America to continue spending blood and treasure while the Saigon elite stuffed its pockets. There was still perhaps time for Saigon's leadership to reform itself and make South Vietnam worthy of the tremendous sacrifices Americans were making, but they had to act now. If they did not, the American withdrawal would continue, eventually leading to the end of South Vietnam. More important to the Saigon establishment, this would also mean the loss of their power and prestige.

I shared my thinking with a number of my influential friends upon returning to Saigon, but of course I had to be somewhat secretive and careful not to give President Thieu the impression that I was plotting against him. My friend, Senator Pham Nam Truong, arranged the most significant opportunity I had to preach my sermon of reform. He set up a meeting that included him, another Senator who was a publisher of a major paper, the politically active leader of the Vietnamese Confederation of Labor, and the well-connected Deputy Minister of Foreign Affairs. Additionally, a cousin and aide of President Thieu was supposed to attend but couldn't make it, so he got my message later. Everyone listened politely to what I had to say, but when I was finished they told me I was being too pessimistic. They said to relax because the United States was firmly behind Thieu and there was nothing that the Americans couldn't do if they wanted. At one point, they even reasoned to me that because the United States had "just succeeded in landing a man on the moon," it was obvious Americans would be able to do something as trivial as winning the war in Vietnam. "Relax," they told me, "the CIA has contingency plans for everything" so we had "nothing to worry about."

There was simply no sense of urgency amongst the Saigon elite. Everyone was all too willing to bury their heads in the sand about the impending disaster awaiting the country and instead try to milk American generosity for all it was worth while they still could. After failing to convert any group of Saigon's leaders to my thinking, I focused my effort on convincing my friend Nguyen Cao Thang. Thang was an adviser to Thieu and had significant influence because he had been the financial backer of Thieu's 1967 election campaign. I told Thang he had the ability to "steer Thieu in the right direction" just as he had steered the election, if only he would "go for broke" pushing for change. I freely admitted that "swimming against the current" was not going to be easy and involved some serious risks. We both had thriving businesses with a lot of money that could be jeopardized by rocking the boat. On the other hand, if we sat and did nothing as South Vietnam collapsed — which it was going to do — we would lose everything anyway. With his influence over President Thieu, I said, we had a shot at preventing that. It was worth a try, I concluded.

Thang told me that what I had said was very convincing, but he wanted to consult his wife about it. When I saw him a few days later he said that although he agreed with my assessment of the situation, he could not personally commit himself to "get involved politically" as I asked. The main reason he could not, Thang explained, was because he was terminally ill with throat cancer and had very little time left. My reply was that was yet another reason to "go for broke." I told him that he had nothing to lose and would know in the end that he had done a brave thing to save his country. He had nothing to say to that except that he was "very tired."

I understood Thang's desire to stay the course and focus on his health, so I didn't press the matter further. Soon after our conversation, Thang left Saigon to get treatment in the best hospitals in the world, first in Paris and then at the Mayo Clinic in America. His cancer got to the point, however, that nothing could be done. I went and visited him around Thanksgiving in 1969 to say goodbye. I also helped at that time to arrange everything for his second wife, who was my cousin, to inherit his fortune. Thang passed away shortly thereafter in December. I was deeply saddened by his passing and disappointed that he did not have the opportunity to help his country because of his cancer. I was glad, though, that I was able to help him towards the end with the important matter of his estate.

One of the specific issues I had been pressing for after returning to Saigon was the need for the government to shift its focus to economic development. Making real strides in economic development would have accomplished a number of important objectives for the South Vietnamese government. It would have improved the common people's lives and therefore shored up the government's sagging popularity, which was ultimately a root cause of the war. Diplomatically, economic progress was perhaps the clearest way for the South Vietnamese government to prove itself in the eyes of the United States. That was particularly true if the development could be done in cooperation with major American companies, which would increase American business interest in Vietnam.

Realizing the urgent need for Vietnam to step up economic development, I had made a couple of important contacts on the subject back when I was rehabilitating in America. With Thang's support I had been able to get a briefing from Pentagon officials on the possible conversion of American military equipment and bases in South Vietnam to civilian economic use. The ARVN would not need all of the American assets so it was a great opportunity for South Vietnam to acquire many useful facilities to jump-start new industries. The second contact I made was with the Stanford Research Institute (SRI), which had previously started successful large-scale economic development plans for the Republic of Korea and Taiwan. I convinced Thang to become an SRI member and attend one of their conferences to have him meet American business leaders who might get involved with Vietnam. Thang was impressed and agreed with me that the combination of the American military assets along with SRI's expert planning could help South Vietnam make rapid economic progress.

Unfortunately, by the time I had returned to Saigon Thang had lost interest in the two projects. He even started complaining about the high annual dues for SRI membership and said he wouldn't renew it. The membership was a few hundred dollars, which was nothing for a multimillionaire like Thang, but obviously his health problems had eclipsed such long-range concerns. I did get Thang to inform President Thieu of these economic development opportunities. Thieu was no more far-sighted than Thang, though. Thieu sent word to me through one of his aides that he wanted to have lunch to discuss only the Pentagon program.

The aide told me Thieu found the program I described to be "far too ambitious," but Thieu was still interested in obtaining a list of American equipment that could be sold locally. I saw right away that Thieu wanted to make a few quick dollars selling the equipment on the black market, nothing more. I had no interest in getting involved in such foolishness, so I told the aide that I wouldn't be able to have lunch because I was busy with some family matters. Not only would meeting with Thieu have been pointless, but also I was worried that if I did so it would have been misinterpreted around town that I was lobbying for a job in Thieu's government.

THIEU JOB OFFERS AND PARIS PEACE NEGOTIATIONS

I did not want to work for Thieu, and I didn't want anyone to think that I wanted to work for him. In fact, however, both Thang and Thieu were trying to get me into a government position. Bui Diem was the Ambassador to the United States, but he had been appointed before by Nguyen Cao Ky. Thieu was apparently worried Bui Diem might still be loyal to Ky and was considering replacing him. Thang, who rarely missed an opportunity to get friends and relatives into important government positions, was already trying to get me to join Thieu's government in some capacity. With my American connections and profile, Thang thought I was perfect to become the new Ambassador in America, so he went about lobbying both Thieu and me to make it happen.

I didn't want the job, but I did see the offer as another opportunity to nudge Thieu toward change. I told Thang that it didn't really matter who represented the country in America. What mattered was what was actually being done in Saigon. Compared to the massive US establishment in Saigon, the South Vietnamese Embassy in Washington was tiny. The flow of information from American officials in Saigon to Washington was so immense that there was no way the South Vietnamese Embassy could persuade anyone that the Saigon government was anything other than what it was. Only if there was a real change for the better on the home front could the Ambassador really accomplish anything more in Washington. I also said to Thang that, in any case, from everything I had heard Bui Diem was doing a good job in Washington considering the circumstances. He was well connected with the Nixon administration, so replacing him risked antagonizing the United States.

Thieu apparently was also concerned about the risk of angering the White House by replacing Bui Diem, so I wasn't appointed. I'm sure Thieu was also not thrilled by my contention that real improvements were necessary rather than just changing messengers. Thang, however, still wanted to circumvent Bui Diem in Washington. He proposed that I act as a direct conduit between Thieu and Henry Kissinger, Nixon's influential National Security Adviser. Thang would send "top secret" communications from Thieu to me personally in California, and then I was supposed to forward them confidentially to Kissinger. Thang also wanted to have me appointed as Saigon's new Ambassador in Mexico City. I rejected that position and objected to the whole scheme as being unnecessarily convoluted and meaningless compared to the urgent need for improvement of the government in Saigon.

Thang started sending me the "top secret" communications anyway, so I reluctantly forwarded them to Kissinger. What Thang sent were reports on the progress of the pacification and land reform programs in South Vietnam. The documents had simplistic colored charts and looked more like elementary school homework than state secrets. I was surprised when I got a fairly enthusiastic reply from Kissinger. He told me he was pleased to get back in touch with someone from Harvard (we met while I was a Nieman Fellow there) and he was glad to know that I was assisting Thieu's government. I really had no desire to serve as a secret intermediary like that, however, especially when I was just relaying worthless documents. Thankfully, Thang eventually accepted my lack of interest and stopped asking for my help in the scheme.

Thang's surrender on that matter did not mean I was done with efforts to conscript me back to government service, however. My former boss Tran Chanh Thanh, who had been Diem's Minister of Information and was now the Foreign Affairs Minister for Thieu, asked me to go to Paris as his representative for the peace negotiations there. He told me "to have a good look" around and report back to him how I saw the situation. I was also supposed to make recommendations for a public relations campaign to enhance South Vietnam's international image. I also declined this offer at first, using my ongoing business work and heavy travel as excuses. Eventually, though, Thanh persuaded me. I convinced myself that it would be a good opportunity to observe firsthand what was going on at these negotiations. I seriously doubted I would be able to accomplish anything, but I figured that even a slight chance to help bring peace to Free South Vietnam was worth the effort.

As soon as I arrived in Paris I met with the South Vietnamese Ambassador there, then I met with a CIA contact who had been introduced to me by friends in Washington. I planned on making extensive contacts with the Communist side in Paris, so I wanted to make clear where I stood and that I was only gathering information. My goal was to get a sense of the attitudes and dynamics of everyone involved in Paris, including the Hanoi and National Liberation Front (NLF) delegations as well as Communist sympathizers in the community. The main thing I discovered with the Communist delegations was that they were concentrating on proselytizing for their cause with their public representatives. The real negotiations in Paris were being done secretly, behind closed doors between Kissinger and Hanoi's Le Duc Tho, so the public negotiations were just a façade. That left the official, Communist representatives free to focus their energy on public relations. In particular, they worked to win over the Vietnamese expatriates in France and the young French students who were joining anti-war organizations. Unusually, they also had the support of the Vietnamese Catholics in Paris. This was largely thanks to the Vatican policy favoring an immediate end to the Vietnam War and because of Father Nguyen Dinh Thi, who operated a publishing company in Paris and worked behind the scenes on behalf of the Communists.

I managed to meet unofficially with most of the leading Communist representatives to size them up. The "superstar revolutionary" NLF Foreign Minister, Mrs. Nguyen Thi Binh, was among those I was able to assess up close. She was someone Hanoi was building up in the public's eye. They always pretended to defer to her as the head of the NLF delegation when, in reality, she was firmly under the direction of Le Duc Tho and Hanoi. I got Father Thi to arrange for us to talk at a casual cocktail party. She was extremely stiff and formal, confirming to me that her public image as a revolutionary diplomat was more pretense than substance. Still, it was an effective one. Her role as a female leader did much to generate international sympathy, especially among the French, whose gallantry was proverbial. I found her deputy, Ambassador Dinh Ba Thi, to be more engaging and astute. We had been classmates back in Hue and quickly fell into a nostalgic chat about our student days. Our conversation was soon interrupted, however, by a comrade trying to steer him away from me before he was contaminated by talking with an anti-Communist of the "puppet regime" in Saigon.

In contrast to the discipline and drive on the Communist side, I found the South Vietnamese delegation to be hopelessly drifting without any purpose. Most of the delegates were well-connected lawyers, doctors, or bureaucrats who managed to get appointed in order to enjoy free trips to Paris at the expense of the government. Even then, these delegates wasted months arguing with the government over their per diem payments and over who should foot the bill when they found it necessary to return to their private practices in Saigon.

Leading this pathetic delegation was Nguyen Cao Ky, the former Prime Minister and now Vice President. President Thieu had dispatched his rival-cum-Vice President to Paris ostensibly "to supervise the peace negotiations," but of course Kissinger was handling the real negotiations secretly. It was mostly an excuse for Thieu to get Ky out of Saigon. Thieu also understood that many South Vietnamese would see the peace negotiations as selling out to Communists, so putting Ky in charge was a great way to undermine Ky's political prestige. Making matters worse, Ky had previously made many anti-French declarations when he was in power. As a result, he was persecuted routinely in the French press. Thieu delighted in Ky's bad publicity and used the government-controlled press in Saigon to repeat it endlessly.

After a few months in Paris, I reported back to Foreign Affairs Minister Tran Chanh Thanh. I told him that the South Vietnamese delegation was ineffectual and consumed with competition between factions representing President Thieu, Vice President Ky, and Thanh himself. I said that implementing a successful public relations campaign under such circumstances, especially considering the rottenness of the Saigon government itself, was "mission impossible." I considered my time in Paris to have been a waste. Because President Thieu himself didn't care about the negotiations, there was nothing to be accomplished there. I ended up spending a great deal of my own personal money to be there, unlike the many pleasure-seeking delegates. I also had my application for permanent residency in America disrupted because of my long absence from the states.

The only thing I really got out of my involvement with the Paris negotiation was to realize that Thieu could not be trusted with the peace process. I strongly believed that he was posturing and trying to leverage the situation merely to preserve his own personal power, not to accomplish honest goals like bringing peace or continuing the struggle to keep South Vietnam free. The United States had already decided to quit South Vietnam, but

Thieu mostly hid that brutal fact from the people. Nixon and Kissinger were focused on withdrawing the United States from Vietnam at all costs and their so-called "peace with honor" dictum was a charade built upon a policy of deception. They disguised their true intentions through the policy of "Vietnamization" and through Thieu's business-as-usual act. As long as South Vietnam survived for a blame-deflecting "decent interval" after American withdrawal, Nixon and Kissinger were not concerned that it would fall eventually.

Thieu and his subordinates knew all about this but cooperated and did not raise the alarm to the South Vietnamese public. As I saw it, they were primarily concerned with staying in power and continuing to reap the benefits of their corruption for as long as possible. They understood that the fall of South Vietnam would not hurt them personally because the CIA would protect them and ensure their safe escape. The collapse of South Vietnam would actually nicely cover up their corruption too. Thus, although they could see a national disaster coming they had no personal interest in changing course to save the country or even warning the people. Thieu, in fact, did his best to lull everyone in South Vietnam into a false sense of security.

Thieu acted out against the American plan for abandonment through the Paris peace negotiations only once, in 1972. For a time, he put up some protestations against the agreement Kissinger signed both to bolster his nationalist image and to get one aspect of the agreement removed. Thieu primarily objected to the provision creating a "Council for National Reconciliation and Concord." This tripartite Council was supposed to be a centerpiece of the peace process. It would be composed of anti-Communists from the current Saigon government, Communists of the Provisional Revolutionary Government, and neutralist independent nationalists. It was supposed to be a "government structure" that would ensure the orderly transition toward peace, not an actual coalition government. I sincerely believed that it was a necessary component of any peace agreement because it would have helped create an atmosphere of reconciliation among the bitterly divided Vietnamese. That was necessary to change the status quo of animosity and refocus the country on moving ahead with the best interests of everyone in mind.

For Thieu, such a Council was unacceptable. The last thing he wanted to see was a group of Vietnamese genuinely interested in reconciliation and moving the country forward. It would end his profitable position in the status quo and risk exposing his corruption. In the end, Thieu got his way and got the Council practically deleted from the final language of the Paris Peace Accords. As my last political act, I tried my best to keep the Council in the agreement. I helped form a Movement of National Reconciliation in 1972 and tried to promote the Council. The Communists would accept such a Council only if Thieu were removed from the Saigon government first, however. That was a decision entirely up to the United States at that point, and the Americans had no interest in anything that might disrupt their smooth exit from Vietnam. I did what I could to try to change that, including writing a letter to the editor for the *Los Angeles Times* and personally writing to Henry Kissinger. Kissinger wrote back with a vague reply thanking me for my views and the "useful input." To me, that was confirmation that the United States was determined to abandon South Vietnam and did not care about the fate of the people. After returning from Paris that last time in 1972, I reapplied for permanent residence in America and turned in my South Vietnamese passport. It was only valid for a short while longer, but so was the country.

SOUTH VIETNAM'S END

I was one of the few South Vietnamese who saw the handwriting on the wall, but that did not make the last few years any easier for me psychologically. Although I had physically moved my family and myself to the United States, I could not truly make a clean break from Vietnam. It was like tending to a terminally ill relative: I knew that death was imminent, but somehow I kept wishing for a miracle so that I wouldn't have to let go. It was taxing and painful wrestling with what I knew to be true and that persistent, hopeful denial.

When Saigon finally did collapse in April 1975, the years I had spent anticipating it did not really reduce the trauma I felt. For over a decade afterwards, I was in a prolonged daze because I could not accept the enormity of the loss. I even neglected my Honda business interests because of the disgust I felt. The fall of South Vietnam had given Honda the excuse to end my exclusive agency contract without any compensation or settlement. Rather than fight aggressively against that or rally my friends within Honda's management, I did nothing and lost the business. I didn't want to even think about Vietnam anymore. It was just too painful for me and so I did my best to avoid speaking or hearing about it.

I felt a certain shame that what had happened was at least partly my fault. I had been in relatively important positions but had grown frustrated trying to figure out how best to be of service. In writing *Is South Vietnam Viable?*, though, I had attempted to change the course of events for the better. I tried my best to do what was right. I could also honestly say that I never compromised my sense of honor or honesty during a period when many did, even if I could have done better at times. I was simply powerless to swim against the much stronger currents of history that led South Vietnam to disaster. Certainly, others suffered worse misfortunes from the war than I did, but in the end I was just another victim to an immense historical tragedy that could be neither rewritten nor redressed. The only thing that could be done was to move forward.

After South Vietnam

EPILOGUE

When I first met Ngo Dinh Diem as a political refugee in 1952, he told me how much he admired the wisdom of the great democratic leader George Washington. Washington, he explained, had known to refuse the flattering proposals to call him "Your Highness" and had gracefully left power at the right time, earning the respect of generations. Diem contrasted Washington with Napoleon Bonaparte. Bonaparte was a military genius, but he did not know the limits of his power and ambition. Because he refused to give up his power at any appropriate time, he ended in disaster. Diem, at that time, had clearly understood that even the greatest leaders must eventually step aside for their own good and for their people's.

Later, when Diem became the President of the Republic of Vietnam in 1955, he had stressed the importance of morality and Confucian ethics in his leadership. For his presidential symbol, he adopted a bamboo shoot, which represented how moral straightforwardness and integrity would be the foundations of his government. When Diem came to power with his reputation as an honest and patriotic nationalist leader, South Vietnam was in a good position to compete against Hanoi for the hearts and minds of the Vietnamese people.

During the 1960 coup, however, Diem demonstrated that his "integrity" was nothing but a façade. The bamboo he had chosen to represent himself had grown deformed and crooked. In November of 1960, Diem revealed his true personality. He was no Confucian gentleman, he was just a poor leader who ignored the lessons of history. Somehow, in the space of only eight years he had forgotten or set aside that example of Washington. By refusing to reform or relinquish any powers whatsoever, Diem proved that he was a weak and unwise leader. He was a prisoner to his corrupt family and had decided to hold onto power at any cost, no matter the will of his people or the lies he might need to tell. His failure left a tragic legacy.

Unlike Hanoi's Communist dictatorship, the South Vietnamese dictatorships that emerged under Diem and continued with his successors were not bound to a motivating ideology or a system of rule shared by collegial leaders. Instead, the Saigon dictatorships were ineffective and inconsistent because they were based loosely on the divergent interests of corrupt individuals competing for spoils. Most of Saigon's key leaders never had a national policy other than trying to make money for themselves. Hanoi, on the other hand, claimed they had a sacred mission of defending the county from foreign aggressors and their local "puppets." That driving mission was reinforced by ideological indoctrination and tight organization that was never matched in South Vietnam. America's generous aid was intended to shore up these obvious weaknesses in Saigon, but in reality this would-be strength for South Vietnam only amplified the weaknesses. The aid became a prize for the Saigon elite to fight over, fueling the corruption rather than counteracting it. The aid and American assistance also meant that Saigon's leaders never had to be held accountable for mistakes; the United States could always be called upon to bail them out or to be a scapegoat for the blame. I often heard excuses from other Vietnamese that I should "relax" because "the CIA has lots of money and tricks up their sleeves. They'll fix things for us."

The combination of this decadent corruption and submissive inaction drove many honest, patriotic Vietnamese away from the Saigon government. Some just turned their backs on the matter and gave up trying to contribute to their country. Others, driven by the injustices created by corruption or the desire to participate actively in solving the nation's problems, defected to the other side. Typically, they did so in spite of Communism and not because of it. This dynamic greatly undermined South Vietnam from within and enabled Hanoi to win the war of intelligence. After their victory in 1975, Hanoi revealed only a limited number of their moles in South Vietnam, but it was still frightening to realize the massive scope of the Communist spy network. For highly trusted and important people like my friend Pham Xuan An to have been hiding in our midst, spying or manipulating decisions, was disastrous. Making intelligence matters worse, many of Saigon's leaders had defeatist attitudes so they too were secretly dealing with the Communists to protect themselves in the event of South Vietnam's fall.

Ineffective and selfish leaders who did not believe in their own cause. A population that did not believe in its cause or government because of rampant corruption and political ineptitude. A government riddled with traitors and spies exposing its most sensitive information to the enemy. With such poor leadership and handicaps, it was little surprise that South Vietnam was ultimately defeated, although it was far from inevitable.

REFUGEES AND RETURN TO VIETNAM

I was lucky to have already been in the United States before 1975. Although the collapse of Saigon was emotionally painful and drove me into a prolonged depression, at least my family was safe. We did not have to flee during those chaotic last moments of the Republic of Vietnam, unlike so many others. After April 1975, many of the newly arriving South Vietnamese refugees sought me out and asked for my help. I was already established in America and my Newport Beach house was only a few miles from the temporary resettlement camps at Camp Pendleton. As a result, I received appeals for help from many relatives, friends, and even mere acquaintances.

The refugees presented me with a dilemma. Helping them was a constant reminder of the disaster of South Vietnam, which I just wanted to forget about. The worst thing was being asked for help by my friends and acquaintances from Saigon's elite. That was an awkward situation because I had no real sympathy for them, knowing how they had exploited South Vietnam to the very end without bothering to try to save it. On the other hand, I could not bring myself to refuse helping them in their moments of need. Some told me they wished they had listened to my warnings and that they felt embarrassed to need aid now. Others, however, showed little remorse. Helping relatives was less of a moral dilemma but brought other more practical frustrations. I ended up moving to Fresno to help my in-laws start some businesses for themselves, only to have them give up their projects after a short while. After that I moved to Oakland because I liked the area and it was close to my children's colleges. I started working for California's unemployment service, which I liked very much. It was interesting and rewarding to help people. The inconspicuous, apolitical nature of the bureaucratic work also suited me fine after decades of worrying about South Vietnam's politics.

By the late 1980s, my melancholy over everything related to Vietnam started to subside. I felt ready to forget about the past and move forward with a clean slate. At the same time, Hanoi's leaders realized that they were losing the peace despite having won the war because their strict Soviet-modeled economy was not bringing prosperity. They started to reopen the country to both foreign business and visitors. The United States still had an embargo on Vietnam, but the Vietnamese government began granting visas to people who fled Communism before. In 1990, I decided to take advantage of the reopening to make my first return visit. I told myself that, even if it was Communist, it was still Vietnam and my home country. I was curious what the new Communist Vietnam would look like and I wanted to explore the country as a tourist, especially in northern Vietnam where I had not been since before the country was split in 1954. Mostly, however, I went to see my relatives and old friends who had stayed behind.

When I arrived, I was told by Hanoi officials that I was the first high-ranking official from the "puppet" South Vietnamese government to return. I told them that I was visiting strictly for personal reasons and did not represent any organization or government. I added that my returning to Vietnam did not imply any approval or disapproval of the existing Communist government. The Hanoi officials were surprised that I would return without any preconditions or political agenda. They told me that other former Saigon officials had been making propositions for return visits, but all the others demanded to be invited by the government and have certain protocol requirements fulfilled. Hearing that, I could only shrug my shoulders at such continuing inanity.

The Communist officials I met on that first return to Vietnam in 1990 were surprised and impressed that I held no grudge against my "Communist enemies" for having blown off my left leg. They expected me to harbor a personal grudge over that, especially because they presumed all high-ranking members of the Saigon government had a deep hatred of Communism. I, however, had adopted a forgiving attitude regarding my leg since almost the day it happened. When I arrived in Los Angeles back then, Dr. Fareed had asked me if I hated Communists for taking my leg. I told him, "Certainly not, because it was only part of the war and the Communist soldier who fired his rocket just did his job." By 1990, I felt even more strongly that way because I was trying to be open-minded about the whole war period and put it behind me. That was not something the Communists I met expected of their former adversaries.

I made four visits between 1990 and 1994. During that time, as a Vietnamese American in Communist Vietnam, I definitely felt discriminated against. Returning overseas Vietnamese — referred to as "Viet Kieu" — were the victims of many slights when they came back to Vietnam and I was no different. Very often, overseas Vietnamese like myself would be charged two or three times the normal rate for things like plane tickets. People in Vietnam regarded us oversees Vietnamese as being unfairly wealthy, so many people considered ripping off Viet Kieu to be like Robin Hood stealing from the bad rich folks to feed the good poor people. Considering that some of the overseas Vietnamese coming to Vietnam at the time were flaky opportunists who were trying to exploit Vietnam, I found the economic discrimination to be somewhat understandable even if it was unfair and obnoxious. Even worse than the economic discrimination, however, was the psychological discrimination against overseas Vietnamese. We were very much seen as second-class people who no longer belonged in our home country. That was very disheartening, especially because there were many intelligent and well-educated overseas Vietnamese who really wanted to help contribute to Vietnam's recovery and development. Instead of being welcomed for their valuable assistance, they were scorned in a humiliating way.

CIA RUMORS AND ACCUSATIONS

I was not only discriminated against when I returned to Vietnam, I was also watched over as if I were an enemy of the state. Given my background, I could understand the special scrutiny. Although being tailed by Hanoi's secret security agents all the time was annoying, it didn't bother me too much. There were reasons for them to keep an eye on me, and I recognized they were just doing their job. I had nothing to hide during my visits to Vietnam, so I had nothing to fear. I was just there as a tourist and to visit my friends and relatives, so I didn't worry too much about the surveillance.

In the early 1990s, before the United States lifted its embargo on Vietnam, Hanoi's security services were still paranoid about possible CIA anti-Communist activities in the country. Repeated visits by a former high-ranking Saigon official were bound to raise suspicions in such an environment. Making matters worse, the motives of my trips were not readily apparent or understandable to the security officials. They must have wondered what I was really up to coming back to Vietnam so often. Why wasn't I making any business investments or seeking other economic opportunities or advantages? Ironically, they suspected that I had to be up to something like stirring up political trouble because I wasn't obviously up to anything improper. The plain truth that I had returned to Vietnam for personal reasons was too simple for them to accept at face value.

Naturally, my background and my well-known connections to important CIA figures contributed immensely to these suspicions against me. The most famous CIA operative of the entire Vietnam War, Ed Lansdale, was a close friend of mine and his brother Phil had helped me when I settled in America. That was not a secret and was enough to put me on Hanoi's watch lists. Furthermore, I was also well acquainted with Bill Colby, who had been the CIA station chief in Vietnam and later became the Director of the CIA. After the Vietnam War, I had also became somewhat involved with Allison Thomas and Charles Fenn, who had been operatives in the World War II predecessor of the CIA, the OSS. They had been part of the OSS efforts to rescue downed Allied pilots from the Japanese in Indochina and southern China. Both had worked closely with Ho Chi Minh and the Viet Minh to accomplish their mission. When I met them, Thomas and Fenn were interested in making sure the world knew of this time when America and Vietnam's Communists had been friendly partners. As part of that goal of sharing their story, they wanted to meet with some of Ho Chi Minh's close associates, including General Vo Nguyen Giap and former Prime Minister Pham Van Dong. I helped Thomas and Fenn arrange these meetings, which the Communist government did not want to happen, so that was another red flag for Hanoi's intelligence services.

In fact, the rumors that I was a CIA agent went all the way back to the early 1960s. To many people who didn't know me very well, I seemed to be someone who knew too much, and my tendency to operate behind the scenes was suspect to them. On several occasions, people wondered how I had anticipated important events in advance. The answer was typically a combination of intuition, listening to my many connections, and dumb luck, but that wasn't a satisfying explanation and didn't fit with the conspiratorial mindset of Saigon. In particular, some people questioned how I had so prophetically anticipated Diem's downfall when I left Vietnam in 1961 if I had not been somehow involved or in the know. They also couldn't understand why I returned to the dangers and political turbulences of Saigon after the 1963 coup unless I had some secret, direct connection.

Such gossip was ridiculous but typical of the mistrustful atmosphere of the time. Similar stories had followed me throughout the Vietnam War era. When I sustained my injury in Hue in 1967, some whispered that I must have been there on CIA business. According to the theory, ordinary civilians had no reason or way to go to the city from Saigon, so I must have been there on some secret mission. Later, when I was involved with the Paris Peace Conference, some did not believe that I could be staying at the expensive Hilton Hotel for months at my own expense. They reasoned that I had to be on the CIA payroll to be "spending that kind of money." The CIA rumors didn't bother me much and, in fact, they probably benefited me in some ways. I suspect that the possibility of my CIA connection shielded me at times from punishment for my political heresies against the likes of Nguyen Khanh and President Thieu. Consequently, when I was once again suspected of being a CIA agent by the Communists in the 1990s, it didn't surprise me.

Just before my first visit in 1990, the hearsay and rumors of my being a CIA agent developed into an outright accusation in the *People's Army* newspaper (*Quan Doi Nhan Dan*). Colonel Bui Tin (who deserted Vietnam over dissatisfaction with the Communist regime shortly thereafter), did an interview for that paper with my old friend Pham Xuan An. An was among Hanoi's best spies during the war and was decorated as a "hero of the people" afterwards. In the interview, An related how he had infiltrated South Vietnam's highest political circles. As background, Bui Tin explained how An got his first job from me at Vietnam Press after returning from his journalism training in America. Bui Tin then added that I "was a close aide of Ngo Dinh Diem, a CIA *agent*, and a friend of CIA officials like Bill Colby and Ed Lansdale."

When I arrived in Hanoi, security officials confronted me with the article, seemingly to intimidate me into telling the truth. They demanded to know if I was a CIA agent or not. I was annoyed by this, but I patiently explained that the accusation was not true. I pointed out that while it was a fact that I was a close aide to Diem and that I had friendly relations with several CIA officials, that did not mean that I had ever worked for the CIA. After explaining myself, I seized the opportunity to ask the security officials for permission to see An. I had not talked to him since 1975 and wanted to see him regardless of the interview. I wasn't sure I would be able to do so, however. An, despite being a "hero of the people," had been put in a reeducation camp after the war for being too close to Americans and was still viewed suspiciously by Communist leaders. I told the officials, "He knows that I have never been a CIA agent, so I am surprised about what he said in the interview. If I can see Mr. An and ask about the interview, we'll know the truth." To my surprise, the security officials had no objection to my meeting An.

As soon as I got to Ho Chi Minh City, I went to see An. When I showed him the interview, An said, "This guy Bui Tin is giving me headaches! I never saw him and we never had any interview." The entire interview was fake and the quotes were made up. An told me, "I knew you were not a CIA agent and I have never said that you were to Bui Tin or anybody else. I tried to protest against this fake interview, but Bui Tin has clout in Hanoi and nothing was done about it." I asked An if he would be willing to write a report so I could clarify the record with the government, which he was happy to do. I then sent the report to the Security Minister to put this CIA agent matter to rest. It was mostly a nuisance, but at least it helped me to reconnect with An. During that first trip and my subsequent visits I spent a great deal of time talking with An, delving into his encyclopedic memory of what had happened behind the scenes of the Vietnam War.

The purpose behind Bui Tin's article, I later found out, was to scare me into cancelling my first trip to Hanoi. With Vietnam under embargo by the United States, anti-American feelings still ran strong. There were some in Vietnam at that time who did not want to welcome Vietnamese Americans. My visit as the first high-ranking official of the anti-Communist government to return signified another step forward for reconciliation. Some in Hanoi wanted to prevent that kind of progress, just as some Vietnamese Americans did. That unwillingness to let go was something I understood, although I opposed it vehemently.

Even after Pham Xuan An had cleared things up for me, I was still closely watched in Communist Vietnam. The surveillance I experienced as a result of the suspicions surrounding me varied widely in terms of its disruptiveness. In Hanoi, where I stayed with a cousin who was well connected, the surveillance was usually discreet and relatively unobtrusive. In Ho Chi Minh City, however, it was clumsy and bothersome to me. One time there, the owner of the apartment I was renting told me he had a dilemma regarding me and he didn't know what to do. He revealed that an agent of the secret service had approached him and told him to open my locked suitcase. The landlord told me he felt very awkward breaking into my suitcase like a thief, but if he didn't comply he could lose his government job. I told him that he should have the secret service agent contact me directly and I would have no problem having the suitcase examined. I had nothing illegal, so it wasn't a problem for the agent to have a look if he really wanted. The agent never did call me, though. Instead, the landlord invited me out for lunch the next afternoon and when I returned to my room I found that my suitcase had obviously been tampered with. I told the landlord I was deeply disappointed with the amateurish and dishonest way it was all handled. He apologized for it but said that it was beyond his control, which I'm sure was true. To me, the incident illustrated the inability of some die-hard elements in Communist Vietnam to let go of mistrust and give up these old, conniving habits.

RECALLING MY EXPERIENCES

After going back to Vietnam a number of times, I still struggled to make sense of what had happened to my country. Rather than avoid thinking about South Vietnam's tragedy, as I did for a decade after 1975, I began to explore it and try to understand it better. This led me to begin writing, to try to make sense of it all. At first, I mostly just took notes of my own experiences and my thoughts for my own peace of mind. I had read too many self-serving memoirs by other Vietnamese after the war, so I was apprehensive that I would only be joining their boastful ranks if I shared my story.

As I wrote, however, I became more convinced that I had something valuable to add. I saw more and more how Diem's rule and collapse were central to explaining South Vietnam's tragedy. Just as Kennedy had lacked authoritative Vietnamese voices when trying to decide what to do about Diem in 1963, the historical writing of this period was over-dominated by American evaluations of Diem. Having been inside the regime and close to Diem, I had a perspective that needed to be represented. Like before Diem's collapse, I decided to tell my story in as objective and critical a way as possible. I would do so not just to tell about what I did but to help everyone, Vietnamese and Americans, understand how people *like me* felt and thought under Diem. So many good, patriotic Vietnamese from the Diem era, like Diem's personal secretary Vo Van Hai, were unable to tell that story. I felt a duty to speak for them, just as I had in 1962 with *Is South Vietnam Viable?*

One realization I made as I recorded my thoughts was that although I had often felt helpless as an individual in the face of what seemed unavoidable, South Vietnam's tragedy was not inevitable. Looking back on my own personal experience, I saw several missed opportunities when Vietnam's destiny could have been diverted from the destruction that came. Throughout the 1950s while Diem was in power, more could have been done by both Americans and Vietnamese like myself to make Diem live up to his reputation as a selfless patriot. Reexamining the 1955 Bandung Conference, in particular, showed me an alternative vision of what Diem could have done instead of taking the road of belligerent anti-Communism. Instead of speaking out and encouraging Diem to follow a more magnanimous course, however, I and others like me largely sat and watched while the Ngo family used reflexive anti-Communism to abet their corruption.

The failed 1960 coup against Diem stood out as a potentially pivotal moment to me, as well. It was an alarming incident that should have jolted the United States into seriously reexamining its unconditional support for Diem. We Vietnamese who understood the problems with Diem's regime should have spoken up to make sure that reexamination took place. Fearing reprisals for even being suspected of disloyalty, however, most dissatisfied Vietnamese like myself remained silent at that instant when our voices could have had an impact.

There were numerous other moments in history that might have shifted the course of events in Vietnam for the better, of course. France could have had a more enlightened colonial policy that would have precluded the need for violent revolution or radical politics. The United States, after World War II, could have followed through with President Franklin Roosevelt's idea of an international trusteeship to prepare Vietnam for independence. America might have pursued a compromise political solution before the Vietnam War broke out, or shortly thereafter, rather than vainly escalating the conflict. As I saw myself, the United States could have sincerely negotiated at Paris, prioritizing reconciliation and a true resolution to the conflict instead of aiming only to save face while making its withdrawal.

By examining these missed opportunities of the Vietnam War, I hope we can avoid similar mistakes in decisions of war and peace around the world today and in the future. For the United States, the Vietnam War experience has taught an important lesson of the limitations of power and has helped make America a more humane superpower. The Iraq War shows that the lesson has not been complete or always heeded, however, which is why the past's mistakes must be reconsidered continually if they are not to be repeated.

For Vietnam and other small nations like it, I believe the war showed above all the need to unite as a country and solve one's own problems. As a Vietnamese saying wisely advises, when "buffaloes and elephants" are fighting, the "flies and mosquitoes" better get out of the way. By relying on the two superpowers of the Cold War, Vietnam's competing factions added immensely to the destructiveness of their own conflict while making it so much more difficult to solve. Not only that, but the solutions brought from the outside to Vietnam were never really suited for the local conditions of Vietnam. Although the Communist system of North Vietnam helped it win the war, slavish adherence to that same system after the war kept the nation impoverished and prevented real recovery from the war. In South Vietnam, dependence on the United States to solve everything was a defining weakness of the Republic of Vietnam. It produced the fatalism and resignation of South Vietnam's leaders that led many to act in selfish, shortsighted fashion.

Although there are many mistakes in Vietnam made by many people, including myself, reviewing my experiences led me to the unmistakable conclusion that no individual deserves more criticism than Ngo Dinh Diem. I deeply wish that that were not the case, because he was a friend of my father and I had regarded him essentially as a beloved uncle. I originally had such great respect for his reputation for integrity as an honest nationalist leader. Diem, unfortunately, did not fulfill those expectations I had of him. He wasted the greatest opportunity for the Vietnamese people to achieve peace and prosperity along with democracy. His corruption and ineffectual repressiveness set the disastrous pattern that was continually repeated until South Vietnam's collapse.

Had the bamboo stalk of Diem's rule grown straight and true from the shoot of his reputation, South Vietnam could have flourished. Instead, Diem's leadership developed twists and flaws that left South Vietnam crooked, unable to thrive. Diem had the opportunity to accomplish so much, but he put South Vietnam on the path to tragedy. I had high hopes for Diem and have no bigger disappointment in my life than his failure to meet them.

ENDNOTES

Introduction

1. Nguyen Thai, *Is South Vietnam Viable?* (Manila, Philippines: Carmelo & Bauermann, Inc., 1962), 225.
2. Letter from Wesley R. Fishel of the MSUG in Vietnam to President John A. Hannah of MSU, February 17, 1962, *Foreign Relations of the United States, 1961–1963,* 2: 259.
3. Ibid.
4. Rufus Phillips, e-mail message to the author, May 10, 2016.

Chapter 2

1. Edward Geary Lansdale, *In the Midst of Wars: An American's Mission to Southeast Asia* (New York: Harper & Row, 1972), 308–9.

Chapter 3

1. Russell Baker, "Eisenhower Greets Vietnam President, Extols Patriotism," *New York Times*, May 9, 1957, 1.
2. O.K. Armstrong, "Biggest Little Man in Asia," *Reader's Digest*, February 1956, 144–148.
3. Thai, *Is South Vietnam Viable?*, 225.

Chapter 4

1. Nguyen Chanh Thi, *Viet Nam: Mot Troi Tam Su* (Los Alamitos, CA: Xuan Thu Publishing, 1989).

2. For my wife's account of the election "test," see: Nguyen Tuyet Mai, "Electioneering: Vietnamese Style," *Asian Survey*, vol. 2, no. 9 (November, 1962), 11–18.

Chapter 5

1. Vuong Van Dong, *Binh Bien 11-11-1960: Khoi Diem Mot Hanh Trinh (Coup of 11-11-1960: Beginning of a Journey)* (Westminster, CA: Van Nghe Publisher, 2000), 73.
2. Thi, *Viet Nam: Mot Troi Tam Su*, 116.
3. Dong, *Binh Bien 11-11-1960*, 127.
4. Stanley Karnow, *Vietnam: A History*, revised ed. (New York: Penguin Books, 1997), 253.
5. Dong, *Binh Bien 11-11-1960*, 143.

Chapter 7

1. John D. Montgomery and the NIA Case Development Seminar, *Cases in Vietnamese Administration* (Washington, DC: Agency for International Development, 1963). See also: Letter from Wesley R. Fishel of the MSUG in Vietnam to President John A. Hannah of MSU, February 17, 1962, 2: 259.
2. David Brooks, "The Art of Intelligence," *New York Times*, April 2, 2005.
3. Thai, *Is South Vietnam Viable?*, 143.
4. Nguyen Thai, "A Vietnamese Speaks Out," *The New Republic*, June 8, 1963, 14–17.

Chapter 8

1. For example, see: "From the Vietnamese Press: Now and Then," *The Times of Vietnam*, April 25, 1963, 4.
2. See: Nguyen Thai, "Diem and Religion," *The Christian Science Monitor*, June 20, 1963, 16.
3. "Mme. Nhu Flies to US, Denies Lust for Power," *Los Angeles Times*, October 8, 1963, 2.

Chapter 9

1. Thai, *Is South Vietnam Viable?*, 18–19.

Chapter 10

1. Eric Wentworth, "Saigon's Scooters versus the Taxis," *The Washington Post*, October 15, 1966, A12.

INDEX

ABOUT THE AUTHOR

Author **Nguyen Thai** served Ngo Dinh Diem as a personal aide and as Director General of Vietnam Press. He also founded *The Times of Vietnam*. After being awarded an Associate Nieman Fellowship in Journalism at Harvard, he left Diem's service and went on to publish *Is South Vietnam Viable?* to speak out against the Diem regime.

Editor **Justin Simundson** earned his PhD in History from Texas Tech University, where he works in the Office of International Affairs and teaches for the History Department.